P9-CKO-858

306.7663
SL15

The Lesbian Family Life Cycle

WITHDRAWI

Suzanne Slater

University of Illinois Press
Urbana and Chicago

LIBRARY ST. MARY'S COLLEGE

*To Judy, whose love and irrepressible spirit
enliven me constantly*

Illini Books edition, 1999
© 1995 by Suzanne Slater
Reprinted by arrangement with The Free Press,
a division of Simon & Schuster, Inc.
Manufactured in the United States of America
P 5 4 3 2 1
This book is printed on acid-free paper.

Library of Congress Cataloging-in-Publication Data
Slater, Suzanne, 1955–
The lesbian family life cycle / Suzanne Slater. — Illini Books ed.
p. cm.
Originally published: New York : Free Press, c1995.
Includes bibliographical references and index.
ISBN 0-252-06783-5 (pbk.)
1. Lesbian couples. 2. Lesbian mothers. 3. Life cycle, Human.
4. Lesbians—Family relationships. I. Title.
HQ75.5.S65   1999
306.85'086'643—dc21   98-29598
CIP

Contents

PART ONE

Enduring Realities of Lesbian Family Life

1

Lesbian Families

It's May 12th, and I'm up early to be ready for two noteworthy events. I drive to the office to meet with Caroline, a forty-five-year-old professor who has prepared for a year to make tonight's disclosure to her parents.* She is uncharacteristically anxious and in need of our connection today. Her eyes meet mine intently and frequently — a connection she seldom allows herself. I ask if she feels ready for tonight, and we begin to discuss how she'll get herself to break into the small talk and begin. Her focus drifts to her desire to take care of her parents, and we begin to sound like paramedics planning triage at the scene of a disaster. I remind her she doesn't need to take care of all three of them, and that they will all survive. I tell her, too, of what a gift her honesty is to her parents, and we acknowledge they may not agree. When I ask her to rehearse by telling me how she came to this decision, she talks about living a lie, about it being impossible to share anything meaningful with her parents without this disclosure. She tells me of her joy with her lover, quickly adding that maybe she'll go easy on the word joy.

Later that day, I dress for the wedding of my lover's niece. She, too, has spent a year planning for this day. We arrive at the house to find the

---

*All vignettes presented in this book are composite stories borrowing from disguised client material, personal experience, and the experiences of friends and family members. In many cases, they are wholly fictitious. None come purely from the experience of one specific couple or individual in the author's psychotherapy practice.

bridesmaids already dressed, the wine opened early, and the jumpy, anxious bride. Her working-class parents have poured their life savings into their only daughter's wedding, and they can be heard telling guests that it was all worth it to make Nicole's special day perfect. From the horse-drawn carriage to the six hundred dollars wedding cake, they have used this ritual to convey their love and their welcome to the new life she begins today. At the reception, we stand and applaud the entrance of the new Mr. and Mrs. Robert Jennings, and the bride unself-consciously proclaims her joy.

A week later, Nicole visits us to show us pictures of her special day. She lets slip the amount of money she received and asks if we can use any of the couple's duplicate appliances. She tells us she is relieved that the wedding is over; now her life can get back to normal.

The day after that I see Caroline again. She tells me she hadn't been able to do it; the visit came and went without any disclosure. Instead, amid great self-blame, she had sent a coming-out letter to her parents the day before this appointment. We struggle to retrieve her self-esteem, and we talk of what a huge moment passed in silence at that lonely mailbox. Contrasting the exuberance of Nicole's wedding with the utter void in which my client acknowledged whom she loved, I cannot keep myself from intervening. At my urging, Caroline agrees to gather her friends to celebrate the passage she has finally negotiated. Three long weeks of complete silence from her parents follow her letter; her agony and fear are palpable. So much for her life getting back to normal.

Lesbians are creating families, often broadening and reworking the very concept of family to include their own special—if stigmatized—relationships. Lesbian couples are claiming their status as complete and valid families. One- and two-parent lesbian families with children defy the notion that their families are incomplete or illegitimate groupings.[1] Unpartnered lesbians are claiming their closest friends and their own ex-lovers as their adult families and are developing ways of life that respect and nurture these precious kinship bonds. Because of this rich diversity, a book such as this one (which focuses specifically on lesbian couple relationships) addresses but one of many lesbian family forms and, while nontraditional by heterosexual standards, leaves far more unique constellations to be discussed by other authors.

Lesbian couplings have in all likelihood existed for generations.[2] Because every previous generation of lesbians faced tremendous dangers for revealing their sexual identity, however, many of these relationships remained invisible to most or all outsiders. Cut off from their hidden predecessors, each new generation of lesbians must therefore start from scratch, discovering for themselves the joys and stresses of lesbian family life.

Social Support Versus Social Exclusion

Society's support of family life is so constant and pervasive that it is scarcely even noticed by many of the families who receive it. Heterosexual couples from identical racial backgrounds who have children are held up as prototypical American families and go through life with the culture's assistance and congratulations. The social rituals devised to affirm key moments in family development—from weddings and baby showers to anniversary celebrations—guide heterosexual families through the key passages of family life. Member families are able to anticipate the moments designated by the culture as major milestones and are invited into oft-repeated traditions of family responses to these events.[3] These social messages are conveyed through virtually every aspect of social interaction and the mass media. Television continually depicts images of "normal" heterosexual family life, as do books, theater, dance, art, music, and children's games. Even greeting cards predominantly feature the experiences of heterosexual families confronting the socially prescribed transitions of family life.[4]

> *Joan left extra time for browsing in the card store, knowing she would have to search for an anniversary card that would be at all appropriate. Twenty minutes into the task, she had located only cards with men and women pictured prominently on the cards, or pictures of men's and women's hands displaying their wedding rings. Inside, the words* husband *and* wife *disqualified even more of the cards; there was nothing she could buy for Eileen. All she wanted was a card expressing a couple's love that didn't exclude her by announcing the heterosexual identity of the couple. It seemed so simple. Discouraged, she left the store, wondering where she thought she was going: The store down the street would not be any different.*

The supportive relationship between society and its member families hinges on two essential points of agreement. First, society at large must agree that a particular group of assembled individuals in fact constitutes a family unit. Second, the family and society must agree about how family life will proceed. When this shared vision exists, society invites families to participate in a vast array of rituals and supports.

As surely as heterosexual families receive social validation and support, lesbian families are powerfully excluded from this sense of membership and approval. Formal rejection of lesbian families includes laws against homosexuality in general, or specifically against lesbians getting married; rescinding of custody rights to known lesbian mothers; and legally sanctioned discrimination against gay people in housing, employment, and other fundamental aspects of daily life. Lesbians (and other non-heterosexually identified people) also encounter a myriad of everyday examples of deliberate exclusion. The concept of "family membership" in everything from rates and privileges offered by HMOs, to family memberships and family events offered through recreational and social clubs, to workplace-provided benefit plans conforms to socially prescribed views of what constitutes a family. Lesbians are deliberately excluded from the vast majority of these opportunities because of the shared social assumption that all-female groupings are not and cannot be families.

> *Anne and Claudia got their daughter, Mary, settled into her cabin at camp and helped her learn the schedule of events for the week ahead. They heard one of the other parents teasingly draw their own daughter's attention to a large sign hanging in the back of the cabin: "Sunday is 'Dear Mom and Dad' day. Rest hour will be extended thirty minutes to write your postcards home." Anne said nothing, as she wearily thought about how the struggles never end. She didn't want to go remind the camp directors that not all kids live with their mothers and fathers. Once again, though, her child had been made to feel uncomfortably different. Camp had hardly begun, yet Mary was already just a bit left out.*

Lesbian families are inundated with social rejection as others ignore these families' existence by pretending all families are heterosexual and through specific and forcible refusal to grant basic rights to all lesbian families. The resulting contrast between the experiences of heterosexual and lesbian families is usually profound. Heterosexual families enjoy a well-mapped-out pathway for their life together, complete with reinforcements in moments of accomplishment and support in predictable times of family stress. Lesbian families struggle to survive without these fundamental supports, lacking both the social reinforcers in managing challenges or periods of transition and sufficient access to other lesbians' accumulated wisdom on how to chart a family's life paths.

Life Cycle Models for Heterosexual Families

Because social images of the stages of heterosexual family life are presented so pervasively, few people need formal instruction in how families look and function over time. The average school child could articulate the ordering of the major events in heterosexual family life: a wedding, childbirth, the children reaching school age, and so on. Nonetheless, these general understandings have been formally encoded by anthropologists and sociologists, as well as more recently by family therapists in the form of family life cycle models.

The importance of mapping out the expectable progression of family life over time hinges on the fact that families can be powerfully encouraged to see themselves as anything from fully healthy and normal to utterly deviant, depending in large part on the responses they receive from the surrounding culture. Generally understood conceptions of family life offer selected families a view of themselves as similar to others and as part of the accepted social fabric. Welcomed families are offered social support during times of inevitable stress and are encouraged to view their difficulties as normal, temporary, and survivable. Further, mainstream families enjoy models of "normal" family life that provide advance information about likely future stresses and moments of accomplishment, easing transitions and powerfully reassuring the family of its membership in good standing among other, similar families. By offering families a window into what they and their neighbors expect, these models forge crucial and supportive social connections.[5]

Like many other minority families, lesbian families are excluded from this network of social support. The stress that results creates many of lesbian families' most difficult problems, and genuine social inclusion could eliminate much of the burden these families carry. In other words, much of the stress that lesbian families experience comes not from unique aspects of their family life but from avoidable problems that social conditions create, and for which there are obvious social alternatives. Some of the most painful manifestations of these problems do not necessarily require unique, lesbian-oriented solutions; instead, they could be alleviated by the same uncomplicated validation routinely provided for heterosexual families.

> *Chris was glad to run into Janet at the pediatrician's office. They hadn't seen each other in the year and a half since they had been in an aerobics class for pregnant women. Janet discussed how hard the first year of parenting had been for her and her husband and commented on the great support they'd received from the "new parents support group" their obstetrician had recommended. "It was great to hear from other couples going through the same struggles," Janet said. Chris felt envy and anger. The first year had been just as hard for her and Susan, but no one had suggested the group to them.*

Benefits of Developing a Lesbian Family Life Cycle Map

No comprehensive family life cycle model has yet been articulated for lesbian families. While some writers have usefully proposed particular stages common to lesbian relationships, these models are not sequential and do not extend throughout the course of the entire family life cycle.[6]

Because so few positive images of lesbian family life exist within the mainstream culture, these families may actually need life cycle models far more than their heterosexual counterparts do. Charting lesbian family life can communicate to lesbian partners that their relationships—like other couplings—change and grow over time. Family life cycle models can provide this recognition of the family's momentum, interrupting the damaging impression that relationships stagnate during periods of stress and transition.[7]

If lesbians do not chart their own generalizable progressions through family life, then heterosexual life cycle models will continue to be the only ones we have. Far from accurately describing family life for all heterosexual people, existing models have been criticized for holding white, male-dominated middle-class experience up as an example for all families. Feminist family therapists have powerfully exposed the sexist underpinnings of mainstream perceptions of "normal" family life, and they have particularly targeted their own profession in their critique.[8] Laird, for example, charges family therapy with sexism, observing that "women's stories, like women's rituals, have been confined, for the most part, to a private rather than a public world, as have women themselves."[9] In the process, women's essential and varied contributions to family life become obscured, and their roles continue to be portrayed as supportive or ancillary within patriarchal, male-centered family groupings.[10]

Families of color have also been largely excluded from the construction of models of normal family life, despite an increasing body of work on racial and ethnic variations among families.[11] By reducing these families to the status of a "variation" of family life, central, normative kinship ties are relegated to secondary status because they do not mirror traditional white notions. Varying family constellations, intergenerational ties, patterns of autonomy and interdependence, involvements in chosen social communities, and other differences are lost when white heterosexual family life is elevated to the position of the universal standard.[12]

Even progressive evaluations of current conceptions of supposedly generic family life fall short of dismantling the underlying heterosexism of these theories. Carter and McGoldrick's revised work on "the changing reality of the family life cycle"[13] barely addresses lesbians. Similarly, the Women's Project in Family Therapy specifically describes family life as inherently functioning to provide a structure for the relationship between the male and female partners presumed to head the family as they approach their assumed task of raising children. While these authors call on therapists to consider "multiple contexts" in evaluating the functioning of any given family unit, they do not name sexual orientation as one of the contexts to be considered.[14]

The failure of these otherwise progressive clinicians to recognize the exclusion of lesbians from their definitions of family reflects the effectiveness of our culture's efforts to teach heterosexism. Despite their honest attempts to analyze the political and oppressive foundations of social conceptions of family life, heterosexist underpinnings remain unchallenged even by the authors most receptive to more expansive views of normal family constellations. While some of these authors are beginning to include information on lesbians in their work,[15] these particularities still are not yet integrated into their primary theses concerning family life.

Insufficiently challenged, conventional social and professional images of family life present lesbian families—like other families from nondominant social groups—as if they are inherently and fundamentally deviant. If lesbians describe their family lives for themselves instead of depending on inappropriate models, however, a very different perspective can emerge. As lesbian couples identify their own transitions and moments of particular success in family life, the points of intersection between similar families will become clear. Demonstrating that the lives of these families also evolve over time, new life cycle models can foster lesbians' confidence in their own family's strengths and capacities (and free them from inevitably pathologizing comparisons to heterosexual family life cycle models). In addition, lesbian families can use their newfound common knowledge of lesbian family life to validate their own relationship's momentum, to select future directions, and to recognize their relational evolution.

Family life cycle models can also offer an effective rebuttal to the social message that lesbian couples cannot form families. (This invalidating image results from many people's insistence that the two women are simply friends, not partners, and therefore are not moving along any family life cycle at all.) As oppression serves to cut lesbians off from predecessors, peers, and role models, lesbian individuals and families are especially vulnerable to overpersonalizing any apparent deficit and attributing it to their lesbian identity itself.[16] In this vacuum of information and connection to other lesbians, couples experience elevated levels of ongoing stress. Society encourages the partners to attribute this duress to the inherent failings of lesbian couple relationships themselves,[17] and to downplay the impact of the homophobia they encounter on a daily basis. Lesbian family life cycle models can positively reframe efforts to thrive in the midst of this socially imposed isolation and finally credit couples for their creative—rather than pathological—responses to externally imposed obstacles.

Even lesbian families that are particularly hidden socially can benefit greatly from the charting of normal lesbian family life. Such models can provide these couples with coveted information about how other lesbians are constructing their lives, allowing the couples to recognize their own experience in the gathered descriptions. This simple act can powerfully support isolated lesbian families and help them positively connote their own experience of family life.

Rita and Stacy stood outside the café for twenty minutes before getting up the nerve to walk down the street and into the lesbian bookstore. Someone could see them go in, or they could run into someone inside the store that they didn't expect to see. They hated this nervousness, but couldn't give up the only chance they allowed themselves to be around other lesbians and books about lesbian life. They bought a few books each time, since they couldn't risk coming very often. At home, they would pore over the books, discussing and comparing their lives to the depictions they had read.

For all of the compelling benefits of articulating common lesbian family experience, a note of caution is also needed. In the absence of ready-made models, lesbians have turned to themselves, creating rich and varied family lives outside of the constrictions of typical heterosexual patterns. The very act of generalizing about lesbians' lives excludes some women's experience from the discussion, creating new (albeit wider) parameters of "normal" versus "abnormal" ways of being. The last thing lesbian families need is yet another source—this time perhaps from within their own community— telling them that their lives are atypical or off-course.

In addition, unlike many other minority groups, lesbians do not all share common racial, ethnic, religious, or class backgrounds. No single model can accurately generalize about a subgroup of lesbians that contains such profound areas of diversity. A variety of authors from diverse backgrounds must contribute to this task. My own identity as a WASP, middle-class, coupled lesbian therapist in her late thirties, living in a well-established lesbian community, necessarily both informs and deforms the material that follows.

Moreover, where lesbian couples satisfied with their relational patterns find that a life cycle model contrasts with their own experience, it is crucial that they continue to validate the family life they have created. In this way, our models can expand as we encounter additional successful adaptations by particular families.

The Inapplicability of Heterosexual Life Cycle Models to Lesbian Families

Heterosexual family life cycle models have very little to say about couple relationships.[18] The authors of these models assume a rather speedy arrival of children after the wedding, and frame every subsequent nodal event occurring for the couple almost purely in terms of their roles as parents. Families without children will simply not find their experience highlighted in any further stage of the model. Parenting families move through the stage of "becoming parents" and on to "transformation of the family system in adolescence." For example, Carter and McGoldrick describe this transition as the family moves from "a unit that protects and nurtures young children" to "a preparation center" for the adolescent's approaching adulthood. Next the family moves into the "launching children and moving on" stage, where the authors suggest that the children's adulthood forces a renewed focus on the couple relationship—a task assumed to be challenging after years of diminished attention to this dyad. Finally the authors describe the partners' old age, in which the couple's return to a focus on their own relationship is mitigated by their presumed access to both children and grandchildren.[19]

Are we to believe that couples' roles as lovers and partners apart from parenting quickly become irrelevant as the family life cycle progresses? Must parenting partners de-emphasize the further development of their romantic connection in the service of supporting their children's growth? Many lesbians resist diminishing their focus on their couple relationships over time. Both because they are women (and hence tend to be relationally oriented) and because their couple relationships cost them so much on a daily basis, lesbians tend to maintain high expectations of these relationships. Frequently deprived of full connection to their extended families, lesbians may particularly look to their lovers for most or all of their family connection. Also, because many lesbian couples do not parent children, the couple relationship retains its central place in the lesbian family life cycle.

As a result, lesbian couples may provide an illuminating example of the dynamics of ongoing couple relationships. Their typically vigilant attention to their relationships allows them both to inform models of lesbian family life and to contribute to this neglected focus within heterosexual family life cycle perspectives. This and other differences between lesbian and heterosexual family life, however, require that specifically lesbian family life cycle models be developed. While all couples share some basic motivations and general hoped-for connections, lesbian family life differs from heterosexual norms in several defining ways.

First, existing life cycle frameworks assume the existence of a heterosexual couple at the apex of the family, without examination of this bias. This couple is presumed to be part of a multigenerational family network whose mutual and dependable support flexibly shifts its focus and form to fit various stages across the family life cycle.[20] Carter and McGoldrick make this explicit: "Our aim is to provide a view of the life cycle in terms of the intergenerational connectedness in the family. We believe this to be one of our greatest human resources."[21] They base their view on the assumption that the couple will both be linked to older generations of the family and create future generations through parenting.

This premise cannot be central to a model of lesbian family life; many lesbians' families of origin severely limit or cut off those relationships upon learning of their daughter's sexual identity, and many lesbian couples do not parent children. In addition, the model's assumption of intergenerational family involvement presumes that partners receive guidance in ways of family life from their parents and consider using those parents as models for their own adult roles. Few lesbians, however, receive such usable guidance. "The family of origin rarely views it as their task to train the young lesbian adult in the ways of establishing a [lesbian] family life."[22]

Second, the heterosexual family life cycle map is based on the assumption that family ties are created through either blood or marriage. Such a model has no application to a group that is legally barred from marriage. Lesbians form families based purely on personal (and socially unsanctioned) selection of family members and mutual agreement by the couple that from this point forward they will constitute a family. Lesbians use broader criteria for family formation than do heterosexuals, and they often may consider friends and ex-lovers to be genuine family members.[23]

Michelle and Sarah knew clearly who would be standing next to them during their commitment ceremony. Under the sacred Jewish canopy (or Choopa) *would be the rabbi, the couple's closest loved ones, and the couple themselves. They had chosen Michelle's former lover, Sarah's sister, and Nina and Joy, two of the couple's oldest friends. This was their family, chosen long ago and made up of the women they trusted most in the world.*

Existing family life cycle models also assume that family-of-origin members will share a common group identity. Families within particular ethnic, racial, religious, and other groups all share these special identities, although members do at times depart from family tradition in their religious affiliation. Although more than one family member may adopt a homosexual identity, lesbians cannot assume shared group identity with their parents, their siblings, or their own children.[24] This inherent and stigmatized difference between a lesbian and her family of origin frequently has a powerful effect on her adult experience.

Finally, current family life cycle models are child centered. While a substantial (and growing) number of lesbians do have or raise children, lesbian family life does not presume that this will occur. Accurately delineated lesbian family norms must include a description of couples who are parents without *assuming* that the family will necessarily include children. Each of these distinctions between heterosexual and lesbian family norms frames the complex task of clearly—yet loosely—sketching common family life patterns for lesbian couples.

In conclusion, lesbian couples can be greatly supported by an articulation of the paths of their unique family lives. Rather than fitting lesbians into models intended for heterosexuals, we must create new models that reflect both the rich diversity and the points of common experience among lesbian families. Depictions of common lesbian experiences by multiple authors can tip the scales in favor of supportive (rather than pathologizing) understandings of lesbians' unique social position and common relational preferences. While the complexity of this task is enormous, so is the potential benefit this shared knowledge can provide.

2

A Model of the
Lesbian Family Life Cycle

LIKE ALL FAMILIES, LESBIAN COUPLES FACE BOTH ENDURING AND stage-specific influences on their lives together. Unlike heterosexual couples, however, lesbian families' sources of stress, reliable rewards, and areas of strength are all influenced by society's responses to their sexual orientation. While the specific challenges within the couple relationship change over time, some version of these primary stressors is always present, forcing lesbian families to devote precious emotional resources at all times to managing their status as stigmatized families. No action the couple can take can fully alleviate these stressors, as they are caused by homophobia embedded within the culture rather than the dynamics of the particular couple's relationship.[1] Each of these stressors will be described in Chapter 3.

Lesbians have created a series of commonly lesbian coping mechanisms designed to shield the family from the damaging effects of homophobia-related stress. Because the stressors are permanently present, these coping mechanisms are needed through the entire lesbian family life cycle, emerging in different forms during different relational stages. For example, friendships with other lesbians may serve different functions at various points in the lesbian family life cycle. In addition, many lesbian families create stage-specific rituals to highlight particular passages and moments of accomplishment. These creative coping mechanisms are presented in Chapter 4.

15

The Stages

Like all families, lesbian families are influenced by a myriad of factors, only some of which can be generalized to the group as a whole. Moreover, idiosyncratic factors unique to each set of partners color the couple's overall experience of any given period within their relationship. Nonetheless, couple relationships go through discrete time periods marked by particular events, challenges, and accomplishments that are common to most lesbian families. Couples can understand their own past and present experiences differently when they know they are in a particular relationship stage, and this knowledge can help them respond to a given difficulty or moment of success.

The model described in this book consists of five stages, although future adaptations of this map may revise the number or exact nature of the stages presented. The stages are sequential and of limited durations; however, some endure far longer than others. The couple's adaptations to the challenges of previous stages become incorporated into their relationship and strengthen their capacity to confront subsequent obstacles. For example, the middle years of their relationship include pitfalls that could well be fatal if issues remain unresolved from earlier years. Likewise, some of the experiences and feelings associated with the partners' initial bonding cannot be fully reproduced later in the relationship, when the couple must instead depend on the different quality of love, romance, and sexuality that develops over time.

If this linear movement through discrete and nonrepeating stages sound simple, it is not. While all couples juggle competing variables during their time together, lesbian couples face particular complexities that add to their challenge as they progress through the stages of their family's life cycle. (These complications will be fully addressed later in this chapter.)

Without articulated models of the stages of lesbian relationships, many couples recognize that they are in a point of transition only when their relationship comes to feel disrupted. The partners feel pressured to change primarily in response to events that appear to threaten the fundamental stability of the couple relationship—leading the partners to believe that change is inherently linked to danger.

"If you pull away from me one more time, I think I am going to scream," Jess blurted out. "What the hell is going on with you lately, anyway? All you ever want to do is go out, and every time we get a chance to be alone together you run to the phone to invite friends to come over. When are you going to tell me what's happening with you?"

"I'm sick of spending whole weekends alone together," countered Becky. "We say we have friends, but it feels like we never see them. We've spent lots of time alone together in the months we've been together, and now I feel like it's time to get back to the rest of our lives. I'm tired of my friends telling me they don't see me enough. I can't spend the whole weekend at home with you anymore."

This couple easily could interpret their situation as one in which Becky has become withdrawn and ambivalent about her relationship with Jess. Without sources of support, and particularly without sufficient access to other couples who have been together for a similar length of time, these partners could convincingly conclude that they are losing their bond. One partner becomes the spokesperson for more social connection, the other for preserving their privacy. In the process, they may appear to be reconsidering their choice to be together, and this perspective may be reinforced by others around them.

However, the couple instead may have arrived at the transition into the next stage in their relationship—a point at which their earlier norm of preserving much time alone must now give way to the equally valid need to deepen their connections to a surrounding social group. Viewed in this light, the couple has reached this juncture through accomplishment, not failure: They have successfully created the cohesion as a couple needed in the first stage of the family life cycle. As is common, one partner is voicing the need to move on before the other, creating a temporary—but ultimately growth-enhancing—disequilibrium between the partners. Thus it would be a mistake for Becky and Jess to interpret their momentary discord as an indication that their relationship is falling apart.

In the homophobic and socially isolated atmosphere within which many lesbian couples live, though, partners can be easily persuaded that a brief period of conflict reflects a serious relational problem. The resulting fear can lead one or both partners to resist change at exactly the moment when they need to welcome the inevitable upheaval that accompanies growth.

While this resistance to transition actually endangers the relationship, it is little wonder lesbian couples would take this approach. Continually confronted with destabilizing influences created by societal homophobia, lesbians have correctly understood that they must at times strive to be impervious to influences that threaten family stability. Change does not always bring growth, particularly to oppressed families who must learn how to avoid externally created invitations to family upheaval.

As lesbian couples achieve fuller access to each other and create social rituals that celebrate their rites of passage, they may no longer associate their transitions into new life cycle stages with danger to their relationships. For example, ceremonies that commemorate a couple's movement into long-term commitment, celebrate significant anniversaries, or congratulate them on becoming parents may create more positive feelings toward change in general. As couples learn to welcome these relational transitions, they may be better able to maintain their confidence in the face of more challenging or seemingly frightening changes.

Added Complexities of the Lesbian Family Life Cycle

In addition to the ongoing stresses (and related coping mechanisms) typical of lesbian relationships plus the distinctive influence of each of the family life cycle stages, couples are also influenced by other layers of development. For example, the ages of each partner will certainly color their experience of what occurs within the couple relationship. Life looks different to twenty-five-year-old partners than it does to lesbians in their fifties. In addition, all lesbians traverse the stages of the lesbian identity development process. The substantial range of levels of development in this critical arena will heavily influence the couple's approach to the tasks of each relational stage. Finally, for lesbians of color and for others with another primary stigmatized identity, a corresponding process of minority identity development also proceeds as the family life cycle unfolds. Taken together, these layers—the partners' chronological development, lesbian identity development, other minority identity development, and the stages of the lesbian family life cycle—intersect continually, shaping the stresses, challenges, and rewards present for particular lesbian couples.

Individual Development

Heterosexual family life cycle models make life simple. Imbedded in the models are assumptions about what ages the partners will be at each family life cycle stage. Partners will marry in their twenties, have children fairly quickly, reach middle age as the children are ready to be "launched," and become grandparents by their late fifties or sixties. By the time the partners approach the last years of their lives, they will presumably have been married fifty or more years.[2]

While contemporary family theorists do recognize the increasing diversity in family progression,[3] the above assumptions are still used in discussing the interplay of individual and family progression across the life cycle. Partners releasing their children into adulthood just as they reach their own midlife evaluation, though, will have a different experience than will couples close to retirement age. Knowing the ages of the partners therefore allows for a deeper analysis of a particular family's actual experience.

In constructing a lesbian family life cycle model, such generalizations are even more problematic. Many lesbian women do not even begin forming their family relationships until they are well beyond early adulthood. The severe social pressure against creating lesbian families causes many women to not even recognize their own lesbian identity until later in life. Therefore there is a much greater range in the ages for beginning lesbian as compared to heterosexual couples. The lesbian family life cycle may be set in motion by young adults, married or divorced women in their thirties, middle-aged nuns, or retirees in a senior citizen community.[4] Under these circumstances, it is far more difficult to generalize about the reciprocal influence between the partners' stages of individual development and their relationship's progression. Because heterosexual people do not confront obstacles to claiming their sexual identity, they do not go through a stage of identity formation that postpones or obstructs their entry into the family life cycle.

A central challenge in understanding lesbians' family life cycles is that any model must acknowledge the impact of chronological development without relying on assumptions about the partners' ages to predict a couple's experience of a given relational stage.[5] As a result, a mosaic of possible scenarios emerges in the lives of lesbian couples.

Generally speaking, the older the partners are at the time they form their couple relationship, the more pressure they will feel to accelerate their movement into committed partnership. The tentative, experimental nature of a new relationship—and the disruption it implies in one's previously established daily life—is more in sync with the life stage of partners in their twenties than that of women in their fifties. A younger woman may more easily arrange to spend nights or weekends away from home, or relinquish domestic responsibilities to join a potential new partner in some activity. As a result, younger women may feel more comfortable during this early period and may cultivate it more fully before moving on. Older women, in contrast, often struggle with the stress of having the well-established rhythms of their individual lives interrupted by their new lover. Wishing to decrease this dissonance, some older women look to move into a more committed relational stage earlier than would younger couples, with varying implications to the couple bond.

When considerable age difference exists between partners, the layers of complexity increase further.[6] Then the couple relationship must manage not one but two stages of individual development concurrently, as well as responding to the couple's progression through their relationship's development.

> "We've been seeing each other for six months now," Greta began in what was by now a familiar argument. "I have no interest in dating forever. That part of my life is long since over, and I want to get on with it if we are going to build a life together. I've had it with packing overnight bags and leaving home to be with you. I'm much older than you are, and this just doesn't cut it for me."
>
> Terry never knew what to say to this lecture. It wasn't a big deal to throw the next day's clothes in a bag and spend the night together; life was just fine the way it was. She was afraid Greta wanted to act like old ladies together, with all this talk about settling down and making a home. She had a feeling they didn't picture the same thing when they imagined moving in together.

While these complexities continue to affect lesbian couples, liberalizing social trends may allow more lesbians to begin their family lives earlier in adulthood. Many lesbians, rather than being intimidated into misguided heterosexual marriages, are reaping the benefits of the gay rights movement by understanding their true sexual identities at a younger age and creating couple relationships with a higher chance of success.[7]

In the chapters that follow, I will borrow the advantage enjoyed by researchers of heterosexual family life cycles and assume that the partners come together in their mid to late twenties. The appeal of this assumption is that it allows the relational stages to span across decades of the partners' adult life cycles, rather than being compressed into a much shorter time period. Particularities common to older new couples will be addressed in the description of each family life cycle stage.

The Lesbian Identity Formation Process

Whether a woman plans or is surprised by her first lesbian sexual encounter, she has reached a major milestone. If she has not already started, this woman now begins an internal process that aims to account for her deviance from purely heterosexual behavior. She will pass through a series of internal stages which she may or may not negotiate well. She will gradually come to one of a limited number of possible conclusions about her sexual identity, and she will construct a relational life that reflects this amended self-concept. Being human, she will more than likely enter into couple relationships long before the process has reached a stable conclusion.

Since Vivian Cass proposed the best-known model of gay and lesbian identity development in 1979, a growing number of theorists have put forth revised paradigms tracking this developmental process. Discussions that focus exclusively on lesbian identity development appear most useful, as they more accurately account for the significant differences between gay men and women.[8] Generally, these models suggest that the identity process begins with an internal awareness that one's sexual orientation might be other than fully heterosexual. The person then proceeds through a period of identity confusion, using denial and rationalization to ward off full recognition of the lesbian nature of her sexual and affectional feelings. Over time, and often based on key social experiences, she becomes willing to acknowledge her true identity.

From this point on, the woman must work to understand what her lesbian identity means. She will need to purge socially constructed stereotypical images of lesbians so that a more positive image can replace these homophobic representations. Finally, according to most of the stage models, she will likely reach a point of identity integration or synthesis, at which her lesbian identity takes its rightful place among the other primary components of her definition of herself.

Virtually all of these models, however, assume that some women will not reach the final stage. The fundamental affects of internalized homophobia are primarily responsible for this unfinished process, as not all women can recover positive self-images from the damaging socialization they received. Cass refers to this phenomenon as "identity foreclosure" and suggests it can occur at even the early stages of lesbian identity development. Others have identified specific rationalizations commonly employed by women needing to block the emergence of a clear homosexual identity. For example, some women involved in lesbian relationships tell themselves that their attraction could only be to this one woman, a belief that allows them to maintain a primarily heterosexual self-concept while explaining this "special case." Others frame their lesbian involvement as a temporary identity, recognizing their lesbianism on a purely present-tense basis while denying its more enduring implications.

Still other women involved in lesbian relationships define themselves as "ambisexual," persuading themselves that they love "the person," regardless of his or her gender. (This situation is quite different from those who adopt a bisexual identity, consciously claiming both men and women as primary potential partners. Self-proclaimed ambisexuals instead deny the significance of gender altogether as a variable in sexual identification.) Finally, some women will adopt a stance referred to as "personal innocence," in which they believe they have been seduced into their lesbian involvement through no particular action of their own.

Partners who cannot fully achieve lesbian identity will face an obstructed path through the tasks of the lesbian family life cycle.

These partners' reliance on denial will significantly impede their capacity to enter into future-oriented relational commitments. To ward off losing either the relationship or their individual defenses, these partners propose what they think is a compromise: the couple relationship will stay exactly where it is—not ending, not moving ahead. Perhaps unwittingly, the partners risk relational stagnation in the service of personal safety.

Over dinner, the two couples got to talking about their mutual friends Jane and Rachel. "Do you think they will ever stop pretending they're still experimenting with being lovers? I mean, come on—how can they really believe this is still some kind of fluke? They've been together for three years!" "I know," Ellen responded, "but you have to remember how blown away they both were when they got together. Underneath, they are still so homophobic, and they really hang on to this 'one day at a time' line. They both swear they're going to make a commitment to each other in the future, you know. They say they just don't want to rush things." "Rush things!" Gail exclaimed. "They're not exactly in any danger of doing that!"

Other partners in the early stages of recognizing their lesbian identities may employ a seemingly opposite coping strategy. These women are most afraid of finding themselves alone during the tumultuous process of developing their sexual identity. They are determined to hold fast to each other for refuge, and they reframe their defensive interdependence as relational certainty. All too eager to make a commitment, these couples profess few substantial doubts about their young pairing, and they pass too quickly through the uncertainty of early couple formation.

Each partner wore a gold wedding band on her left hand. The couple talked freely about their home, their pets, and their plans for the future. They seemed to have been together for years. Rhonda wondered what they were doing in this group for new lesbian couples. Later, when the facilitator asked each couple to tell the group how and when they had come together, Rhonda could hardly believe her ears: They had only been together for eight months! "How could they be so much more established than Julie and me?" Rhonda exclaimed to herself. "God, we don't even live together yet."

For the purposes of this discussion, I will assume that the partners have experienced at least the early stages of internalizing a lesbian identity prior to the beginning of their relationship. Under these conditions, the couple's progress as a family will suffer less interference from basic identity conflicts within the partners. Clearly, though, not all lesbian couples begin in this supportive circumstance.

PATHWAYS TO LESBIAN IDENTITY. Research has repeatedly indicated that there is no uniform personal history which results in women adopting a lesbian identity.[9] Nonetheless, observations concerning this identity process usefully distinguish between two general pathways.[10] One group of lesbians describe feeling in their early years that they were fundamentally different from the other girls around them. Many of these women also knew early on that the difference was related to sexuality; for them, their awareness of homosexual desires preceded any actual involvement in lesbian experiences. Their experience is similar to the process outlined in gay male identity models, characterized by early recognition of homosexual desire, awareness that homophobic stereotypes have at least partial personal relevance, and a perceived need for secrecy associated with their sexual nature. These women typically do not construe their lesbianism to be a matter of their own personal choice.[11]

In contrast, many other lesbian women report no conscious awareness whatsoever of their true sexual identity throughout their formative years.[12] After going well into adulthood with undisturbed heterosexual self-images, these women encounter some sudden and life-altering experience that leads them to adopt a lesbian self-identity. Many of them view their earlier orientation not as a manifestation of denial but as an authentic—but now discarded—sexual identity choice. Their transformative experiences successfully challenge these women's earlier, homophobic views of what it means to be a lesbian.[13] A positive redefinition of lesbianism precedes their own personal identification, possibly reducing their internalized homophobia before they approach the task of adopting a stigmatized identity.[14]

Participation in the women's movement has provided this awakening for a substantial portion of interviewed women.[15] Frequently offering women their first personal experience relating to known lesbians, feminism powerfully challenges mainstream views of universal heterosexual superiority. A number of the architects of previous models of lesbian identity development now point to feminist involvement as specifically relevant to many women's arrival at a lesbian self-concept.[16]

Nevertheless, falling in love with another woman is still the most frequently reported catalyst behind adult women identifying themselves as lesbians.[17] For these women, the early stage of their couple relationship becomes the container for an extraordinary array of powerful emotional experiences. In these cases, one or both partners enter the relationship with virtually no established lesbian identity. Just as this situation can intensify the initial excitement of their coming together, it also distorts their perceptions of what lies ahead. These partners will turn to their relationship to support their individual progression through the lesbian identity development process, which, in turn will complicate their progression through the lesbian family life cycle as well.

LESBIAN IDENTITY DEVELOPMENT AND THE LESBIAN FAMILY LIFE CYCLE. Most all of the lesbian identity development models agree on one point: Couple relationships begin before the partners have reached the final stage of incorporating their sexual identities.[18] Given that many of these partnerships begin even before the bulk of the identity development work has occurred, many couples move through the family life cycle without fully formed lesbian identities. Hence, some level of interplay between lesbian identity development and the lesbian family life cycle is virtually assured.

According to most models, a period of sexual experimentation serves a central function in gay and lesbian identity formation.[19] Referred to as a "lesbian adolescence" (or a "second adolescence" for women with previous heterosexual identities), this experimentation is intended to precede relational commitment, providing a woman with an opportunity to test her still-tentative suspicions about her sexual identity. Especially for women, though, securing a period of sexual experimentation tends to be difficult.

Women frequently are quick to associate sexual contact with emotional intimacy. As women, then, lesbians often view even initial sexual contact as signifying an emerging couple relationship.[20] For women exploring their sexual identity as the result of suddenly falling in love with a particular woman, the momentum toward immediate coupling may be even stronger. This typically female tendency toward understanding sexual desire in terms of enduring relational interest may explain the relative absence of dating rituals within the lesbian community.[21] The resulting pressure to form a couple prematurely can be considerable, frequently leaving potential partners unprepared for the tasks of the couple formation stage.

> *The partners, each of whom was in her early thirties, had been togeth-er for eleven years. They reported to the therapist that they could not recover their mutual trust in each other after each had admitted to affairs. Each believed her behavior proved she was unfit to be a partner, and neither understood why she had felt so compelled to sleep with anoth-er woman.*
>
> *Upon closer examination, the therapist found that this was both part-ners' first lesbian relationship. Neither had experienced a period of uncommitted experimentation prior to their meeting. The relationship quickly progressed, and with it came the assumed promise of sexual monogamy. The therapist's task was to help the couple understand the difficulties inherent in coupling before either had established her own les-bian identity. Their affairs reflected not an inability to partner, but an identity process cut short. Years later, the couple was facing the conflict between their desire to stay together and each partner's delayed desire to venture out on her own.*

Despite the dangers of new lesbians being too quick to form a cou-ple relationship, there are also advantages to coupling early. In partic-ular, many researchers cite the important role of positive contact with other lesbians in the early stages of the identity development process.[22] Because newly lesbian-involved women frequently share their emerging sexual identity with no one but their partners, gratify-ing and healthy experiences within a couple relationship serve to rebut previous homophobic images.

In a kind of reciprocal action, then, lesbian identity development is enhanced as the couple relationship deepens. The growing dissonance between societal views of lesbianism and the women's own positive experience pushes development forward; this, in turn, fosters the couple relationship over time. While no one relationship should serve as the sole argument against internalized homophobia, this mutual influence of individual and couple development may allow even particularly closeted couples to experience tangible growth in their personal and relational identities.[23]

PARTNERS IN DIFFERENT STAGES OF IDENTITY DEVELOPMENT. The interplay between the stages of the couple relationship and emerging lesbian identity is further complicated when the partners are in different stages of the identity formation process. These differences can emerge in any of a myriad of situations, most notably in the partners' attempts to negotiate increasing relational commitment and coming out as a couple. Particularly during transitions between relational life cycle stages, the partners must assess the compatibility not only of what changes each one wants for the relationship, but also of what degree of increased visibility their individual lesbian identities can tolerate. As Roth notes, "Female couples commonly seek therapy in periods of forward movement, when they are mutually deepening their relationship and identity issues are stirred up, or when one partner's demonstration of greater comfort with her lesbian identity is frightening to the other."[24] This observation suggests that the couple may react awkwardly to transitions both in the course of their relationship (which pressure the partners for furthered personal development) and in either partner's development of an individual lesbian identity (which require accompanying relational change). This is especially true if the couple does not understand the interplay of individual and relational tasks they are confronting.

While each couple's experience will be somewhat unique, Roth notes that the partner who is farther along in the identity development process frequently pushes for increased social exposure of the relationship and deepening relational commitment.[25] She is likely to experience her partner's hesitations as a threat to their relationship, interpreting her partner's reluctance as an inability to support them as a couple. The slower partner, in contrast, may experience the demands for forward movement as a threat to her sense of self. She may fear major interpersonal losses or relinquishing of basic safety if she agrees to her partner's requests. She fears, too, that her partner may not safeguard the secrecy on which she depends so completely.

*As soon as she and Jema said their good-byes and got back into their car,
Sheila exploded. "What the hell did you think you were doing, dropping
my hand the minute Sharon came into the room? We've been all through
this, Jema. You swore you would not do this again. I'm sick to death of
being suddenly pushed aside every time you go into a homophobic panic. I
just can't tell you how you hurt my feelings when you do this. I can't take it
anymore—either you're ready to be my partner, or you're not."*

*"That's just so easy for you to say," Jema yelled back. "But you weren't
born being out to the entire world. You had years to work this out and
you've even admitted to me that it took you a long time. How dare you
suggest I should just skip over all that so I can make you more comfortable? Look, you knew when we started that I'd never been involved with
a woman before. I'm worried that my friends won't accept me anymore if
I tell them. Don't tell me you never felt that fear. You know nobody comes
out in a day."*

BISEXUAL WOMEN IN LESBIAN RELATIONSHIPS. Not all women in lesbian
partnerships are lesbians. For these women, their rejection of the label
lesbian does not indicate a failure to embrace their sexual identity, nor
does it mean that their lesbian couple relationships cannot proceed
indefinitely. Rather, these women may have gone through an identity
development process that has much in common with the adoption of
a lesbian identity. They, too, defy the social dictate that all women
consider only a heterosexual identity. In so doing, bisexuals pay some
of the same social costs typically exacted of lesbian women, including
both crucial interpersonal losses and ongoing assaults on their self-
esteem. Their status as members of an unsanctioned sexual minority
will influence their couple relationships as surely, although not in precisely the same way, as does lesbian identity.

Bisexuals have found themselves at the center of some extremely
heated debates. In question is the very definition of bisexuality itself,
as people widely disagree about the social implications of accepting
bisexuality as an authentic sexual orientation. While it is beyond the
scope of the present discussion to explore bisexuality in depth, it is
important to acknowledge that bisexual women working to establish
successful lesbian relationships may be viewed by members of both
the mainstream community and the gay and lesbian communities as
being latent homosexuals who are avoiding the consequences of

acknowledging their "true" gay identity.[26] These women and their partners are likely to be familiar with the charge that self-proclaimed bisexual women are lesbians with either not enough self-esteem to come out or not enough political commitment to relinquish "heterosexual privilege" and join lesbians on the front lines against homophobic oppression.[27] The resentment is increased by the frequent social myth that bisexuality amounts to a desire to "have it both ways"—to be sexually active with both genders at will.[28]

The fact that some percentage of bisexually identified women do later conclude that they are in fact lesbian compounds the difficulties of those who try to wrest social recognition for bisexuality as an enduring and accurate orientation for some people. Instead, bisexuals' stated identity is viewed by some as a halfway measure, to be followed up later when the woman has mastered more of the lesbian identity development process. The message to the couple relationship is that the identity of the bisexual partner(s) should be viewed as evolving and unformed. Such an impression may significantly impede the partners' developing confidence in their relationship, creating another layer of challenge for them.

Bisexuals have argued that labeling sexual identity by present sexual behavior alone precludes a bisexual label for anyone involved in only one relationship at a time.[29] If a bisexual woman's involvement in a lesbian couple relationship signifies that she must now be a lesbian, this partner will feel increasingly misidentified as the relationship progresses. Ironically, then, bisexual women in lesbian relationships may not experience the sense of newfound symmetry between sexual identity and type of couple relationship that many lesbians enjoy. In addition, couples that consist of one bisexual and one lesbian partner have the additional complexity of the partners not sharing the same sexual orientation. The impact of this obvious difference has not yet received sufficient critical attention.

Couples in this situation may particularly have to attend to building confidence in their relationship. These women may experience less support from some factions of the lesbian community; for many, their identification with the feminist movement makes this alienation especially painful.[30] Without reliable access to a supportive community, these couples may have to supply affirmation of their relationship for themselves.

The experience of lesbian couplings in which one or both partners are bisexually identified warrants serious and sympathetic study. These couples' experiences can no doubt shed light on aspects of coupled life for all lesbian partnerships, and their struggles and accomplishments deserve the same articulation that those of entirely lesbian-identified couples do. It is beyond the scope of this book, however, to consider both orientations simultaneously. Therefore this particular model of lesbian family life assumes both partners are lesbian, not bisexual. This distinction is important in order to allow for sufficient detail in examining the interplay of lesbian identity formation and couple relationship development. While much of what follows will be pertinent to bisexual women partners as well, I wholeheartedly support additional specific inquiry into bisexual women's experience.

MINORITY IDENTITY DEVELOPMENT

The experience of having several oppressed identities means being constantly encouraged to pluck out some one aspect of [your]self and present this as the meaningful whole, eclipsing or denying the other parts of self.[31]

In virtually every environment they enter, lesbian couples of color (and other marginalized minorities) must actively protect some crucial aspect of their identities. Facing ongoing assaults to their self-esteem based on racial identity, sexual identity, female identity, and lesbian couple status, these couples navigate four primary tracks of development simultaneously.

As Espin (1987) notes, the stages of lesbian identity development and racial identity development present parallel challenges.[32] First, lesbians and people of color must work to dislodge the negative self-images created by external homophobia and racism. Next, both groups must gradually develop positive images of their disparaged identities; this task usually requires meaningful connections with other lesbians or people of color. The individuals also often need to separate themselves, sometimes dramatically, from the oppressive, dominant culture. This redefinition of self allows lesbians and people of color (and members of other oppressed groups) to reintegrate themselves into the mainstream environment with a clear sense of both avenues for nonoppressive connection and also for enduring areas of distinction between themselves and the majority of the population.

To illustrate the difficulty of pursuing multiple levels of reclaimed minority identity at the same time, consider a woman of color working to externalize the racism she has been taught and substitute an affirmative vision of the meaning of her racial identity. To expedite this task, this woman may surround herself with members of her own racial community, who can support her in embracing especially valued aspects of her heritage. However, if this same woman of color now discovers that she is a lesbian, and that she wishes to pursue a particular lesbian relationship, this immersion within her racial community may be severely threatened. As her emerging lesbian identity will pull her toward contact with other lesbians, she may find she must make extremely difficult choices. Her racial identity receives affirmation within her racial community, but often at the expense of her also-developing lesbian identity. Her lesbian identity can receive validation from the lesbian community, but this usually means she must enter a group dominated by whites. As a result, many lesbians of color spend inordinate amounts of their time feeling marginalized. Crucial aspects of their identity vie for primacy in an impossible competition that further challenges each process of personal identity development.

Lesbian couples of color, then, progress through the stages of lesbian *family* life while the partners move through the process of their personal *chronological* development. They evolve through the stages of adopting an positive *racial* identity while also traveling through the stages of individual *lesbian* identity development. At the same time, these women confront the ongoing sexism present in all three of their primary environments: the mainstream culture, their racial community, and the gay community. These frequently conflicting layers of personal identity make for certain complexity in the lives of lesbian couples of color.

Lesbian Couples' Social Relationships

Life for lesbian couples does not occur within a vacuum. Like anyone else, these partners maintain a series of significant relationships with people and institutions outside the couple relationship. As oppressed and socially endangered families, lesbian families devote particular energy to selecting and managing these external relationships to secure their place within the wider social community. This lifelong concern influences the couple's experience of every family life cycle stage, complicating the normal challenges of couple's relationship.

In the model I will present, the lesbian family itself is referred to as the *family of creation*. While lesbians create a variety of family constellations, the present focus is on families consisting either of the lesbian couple alone or a lesbian couple and their children. Because I propose that lesbian couples constitute complete family units in and of themselves, the terms *couple, family*, and *family of creation* will be used interchangeably.

The mainstream community refers to the wide array of institutions and social relationships that occur within the dominant culture. For most lesbians, their places of employment may constitute their most formal tie to the mainstream community, but practically all lesbian couples create additional ties as well. Other primary institutions relevant to particular couples' lives include the health care system, the school system, and for some families, the welfare system. Social relationships, the mainstream media, and cultural events that reflect the dominant culture are all aspects of the mainstream community, which exerts a central influence on lesbian couples' lives.

The *family of origin* includes the members of a partner's previous immediate and extended family. Younger, nonparenting lesbians may identify their parents, siblings, and extended family relatives as their primary family-of-origin group, while older lesbian parents, for example, may highlight their relationships with their grown children as their most significant "family of origin." For some ethnic and racial groups, family will be defined more broadly and will include members not related by marriage or blood. Regardless of the basis for inclusion of particular members, this family grouping typically holds great emotional significance for lesbians and nonlesbians alike. Families of origin can link the partners to the family's collective past, present, and implied future; when they are willing, they also can offer the couple a set of values, family customs, and a partial blueprint for family living. When families withhold these connections from lesbian members (and their families of creation), the power of those conflictual or disengaged relationships can be even more profound.

The lesbian community serves as another central social sphere for many lesbian couples. Often an ambiguous entity, these communities vary in different geographical areas and change over time as well. Couples' involvement in the events and relationships within a lesbian community may serve as a practice ground for revealing their shared sexual identity in a quasi-public setting which is more likely to be supportive than that of other social groupings. Also, couples who have experienced painful rejections by their families of origin or society at large may rely on the lesbian community for a compensatory feeling of inclusion and affirmation.

Perhaps more than in any other social grouping, there is great variety in how involved particular lesbian couples become in the lesbian community. Some couples are only dimly aware of this community, either because they live in an area where no such gathering exists, because the couple has determined that involvement in lesbian social activities is too dangerous for them, or because they simply are not interested in participating. For other couples, this is an especially primary community, supplying the bulk of their social, political, and even (chosen) familial involvement. (The functions and influence of the lesbian community on lesbian couples is discussed in Chapter 4.)

Finally, lesbians who have an additional primary identity may maintain active membership in another social grouping, referred to as a *community of affiliation*. Lesbians of color, those active in a nondominant religious group, or other ethnically identified lesbians are examples of women who often cherish ties to communities of similarly identified people. For example, African-American lesbian couples may sustain primary ties to the African-American community, just as Jewish couples may devote themselves to the local Jewish community and hearing-impaired lesbians may rely greatly on their connections to the deaf community. For some individuals, these social relationships offer irreplaceable affirmation of central aspects of their particular identity.

Few lesbian families are "out" in all of their dealings with the social communities in their lives. More typically, families decide on a case-by-case basis when to present themselves as a lesbian family. For example, a couple's parents may know of the relationship, while the partners may work hard to keep their bosses from knowing of their true identity. Similarly, a couple may socialize together with a circle of lesbian friends, but they may hide from their daughter's day care providers the fact that she lives in a lesbian family.

As a result, instead of the relative consistency heterosexual families enjoy in their relationships to various social systems, lesbian families continually weigh trade-offs that support one aspect of their lives at the expense of another. Frequently the same behavior that facilitates the couple's relationship within one social grouping threatens their security within another.[33] For example, functioning within the family of creation may be greatly enriched and supported by the partners' expressing affection for each other in front of their children.[34] This action gives the children needed reassurance of family cohesion and positively connotes the meaning of the parents' lesbian identities. In the presence of the family of origin or the mainstream community, however, this same action may draw a homophobic response.[35]

This point is also illustrated by a couple who decides to deepen their involvement in the lesbian community. While the partners themselves may find this involvement deeply nourishing, their families of origin, for example, may react critically to seeing the couple center their social lives around connections with other lesbians. The support the family receives from these new social relationships may be at the expense of their also-important relationships with members of their own families.

The partners' decisions about their social involvements are also influenced by where the couple is in the family life cycle. A new couple in their twenties, for example, may feel relatively independent of many mainstream (heterosexist) involvements, as the partners temporarily experience their new partnership as self-sufficient and impervious to social ridicule. Their temporary hiatus from full involvement in the dominant culture may be bolstered further if they are active in a lesbian community, which can substitute for social dependence on the mainstream community. Years (and life cycle stages) later, however, the couple's situation will have long since changed. Social connections now may feel especially crucial as the partners experience often-unprecedented dependence on mainstream resources and no longer feel comfortable in a youth-oriented lesbian community.

Time not only changes the partners themselves but, with any luck, opens up some of their significant others, as well. Families of origin frequently grow in their acceptance of the lesbian couple over time and may relinquish (or at least soften) their initial dismay or rejection.[36] Many lesbians who come out to coworkers or heterosexual friends discover that they are introducing influential change into their acquaintances' perspectives, even when these individuals had no particular intention to ever examine their internalized homophobia.[37]

"If you had told me right away, I don't think I would have gotten to know you at all," Shelly admitted over lunch. "But I'd worked alongside you for four years before you came out to me, and I couldn't suddenly undo my feelings of trust and affection for you by that point. I admit I was shocked, and I really needed the distance you gave me for a while afterward. I had a lot to sort out, and I was mad to be confronted with your being gay. But now I've really come to see how wrong my stereotypes of lesbians have been. You really shook me up, and in the end it was really good for me."

In conclusion, the task of outlining a lesbian family life cycle is complicated by the numerous simultaneous influences determining a couple's journey through the stages of its relationship. While each couple will experience influences idiosyncratic to their own particular family, most couples are centrally affected by several primary layers of development. Against the backdrop of all of these competing influences—lesbian identity development, typical lesbian stressors and coping mechanisms, chronological development, other minority identity development, and the couple's lifelong voluntary and required social relationships—lesbian couples traverse a family life cycle. Each primary stage of the cycle will be powerfully shaped by these simultaneous influences, just as the progress of a couple's relationship will influence these other developmental layers. Identifying the patterns that emerge has much to offer lesbian couples and reveals more clearly the long unarticulated, particularly contextual nature of lesbians' family lives.

3

Persistent Stressors in Lesbian Couples' Lives

MANY LESBIAN COUPLES DO NOT REALIZE THAT SOME OF THEIR MOST difficult relational challenges are actually quite common for lesbian relationships. These couples may feel further persuaded that they are off course when the same lesbian-specific stressors appear again and again in their relationships. While each family life cycle stage presents couples with unique struggles, lesbian couples also face persistent challenges that extend across the entire cycle. Without knowing that these stressors commonly exert an active and continuing influence, couples may attribute problems to their own personal or relational failings, rather than to socially imposed obstacles they can neither successfully avoid nor permanently overcome.

While lesbian couples frequently turn to psychotherapists for help in responding to these obstacles, many family therapists frame the couples' struggles as reflective of failed development or faulty coping abilities. Trained to view the repeated confrontation of the same stresses as evidence of personal deficit, therapists frequently underestimate the impact of immutable external stressors on lesbian relationships.[1] Lacking an articulated description of the intangible stresses faced by these couples, such therapists may fail to understand that many of the key difficulties for lesbian couples occur repeatedly not because of the couple's failure to respond effectively but because sustained stress is a fact of lesbian family life.[2]

Identifying these difficulties as typical stressors can stabilize a couple relationship and can help the partners to develop confidence in their relationship's viability. While only massive social change can actually eliminate these stressors, understanding their nature and origin can facilitate creative responses by the couple that help to preserve their relationship and guard against overpersonalizing the source of their struggle.

Homophobia

In 1973, Weinberg coined the term *homophobia* to describe the "irrational fear, hatred and intolerance of homosexual men and women" by the surrounding society.[3] No lesbian (or other nonheterosexually identified person) fully escapes the effects of societal homophobia, and no lesbian individual or couple has the capacity to fully transcend its influence. Homophobia is embedded within each of the other central stressors as well, and lesbians must confront it continually throughout their lives.

Homophobia stigmatizes identifiable lesbian couples by bombarding them with the culture's assessment that they are inferior, pathological, and immoral.[4] With homophobia communicated through nearly all major social institutions, including lesbians' families of origin, school systems, community organizations, and most churches and synagogues, lesbians have little respite from challenges to their self-esteem. In response, many lesbians, like members of other oppressed groups, develop a guarded social stance that represents not an exaggerated state of alert but rather a realistic appraisal of potential danger.

Lesbians also experience a similar phenomenon known as *heterosexism*, in which people present heterosexuality as if it were the only valid—or even existing—form of sexual identity and family life.[5] By omitting lesbians and other nonheterosexuals from language, books, and other major vehicles of the mass media, cultural image-makers suggest powerfully that only heterosexuality is normal. Taken together, homophobia and heterosexism create an ongoing challenge to lesbians' self-esteem and sense of social inclusion.

"What do you mean, you didn't tell him you want to bring me?" Lynn said. *"We've been all through this. Everyone else gets to bring their*

spouse. I thought we agreed we were going to go together." "I tried to, I really did," Kara replied, "but he announced to the whole staff that I was welcome to come if I didn't mind being the only single person there. How could I say 'Excuse me, but did I mention that I'll be bringing my lesbian lover?'" Donna stood there furious, not knowing who deserved her anger. "God, this is frustrating," she screamed, and went to the gym to try to work off her rage.

Virtually every lesbian discovers that she has taken in some aspect of society's negative evaluation of homosexuality and finds her self-esteem has been compromised in any of a variety of ways. In the most extreme instances, women report suffering from total self-hatred. Suicide statistics demonstrate a significantly increased incidence of reported suicidal feelings and deaths from suicide attempts among gay people compared to rates for heterosexuals.[6] These reported rates must be assumed to underestimate the actual prevalence of suicidal feelings and acts, since many gay people struggling this desperately from homophobia will keep their identity a secret. Elevated substance abuse rates for lesbians and gay men also reflect the self-destructive ramifications of continual exposure to homophobia.[7]

For lesbians to internalize homophobic attitudes means that they have replaced their personal valuing of lesbian experience with the culture's assertion that heterosexuality is a superior lifestyle. This social campaign largely succeeds both because it is so pervasive and because it is presented so early in life. Young children lack both the capacity and the motivation to resist the teachings of their parents. Although girls who later adopt lesbian identities will reevaluate this early training, it will, to varying degrees, resist later rebuttal. Many lesbians discover that by the time they become aware of their true sexual identity, this homophobic teaching already runs deep.

Ongoing social oppression continually reinforces homophobic messages to lesbians. Direct social reprisals include threats that lesbians may lose their jobs, their homes, their physical safety, and custody of their children. Many lesbians live with the continuing fear that they will lose crucial friendships or other social ties if their sexual identity is disclosed. In addition, as lesbians inevitably internalize homophobia, their confidence in their couple relationships becomes compromised—particularly in times of relational difficulty.

Homophobia further challenges lesbian couples' faith in their mutual bonds by infiltrating the partners' private images of each other. This especially insidious manifestation of homophobia may operate on a primarily unconscious level, planting doubt in one or both partners about the actual health and sanctity of their relationship. These doubts become especially pernicious at moments of trouble, when the partners must generate additional belief in the relationship.

> *Lynn banged on her friend's door, knowing it was too late at night to be coming over. She was shaking badly now, convincing herself that this fight with Karen was sure to be the final blow to their partnership. As Sally made some tea, Lynn dissolved in tears, crying that some part of her had known from the beginning her relationship with Karen wouldn't make it. Tonight's fight had proven it, Lynn asserted, surrendering further into her grief.*
>
> *As Sally listened to Lynn exaggerate the situation, she thought of her own marriage, and how she and John rarely leapt to such dire conclusions in a fight. She knew she needed to bolster Lynn's confidence, but she wondered why her otherwise self-assured friend had such trouble believing she and Karen could work things out.*

Finally, homophobia both creates and maintains the social isolation many lesbian couples suffer. In an effort to avoid homophobic attacks, many lesbian couples remain invisible, thereby doing without the validation other lesbians (and supportive allies) could provide. In the process, lesbians who cannot initiate these meaningful social connections—whether due to actual homophobic dangers or to the silencing effects of internalized homophobia—live without essential group identity. They are caught in a closed circle where homophobia creates shame and social isolation that, in turn, create fertile ground for more homophobia to take root. This stressor repeatedly challenges lesbians' individual and coupled lives.

Withholding of Social Recognition

Likening themselves to the proverbial tree falling in the woods, two women may wonder: If we are lovers and no one knows it, are we really a couple? Lesbian partners live without the simple social consensus that they can in fact form couples.[8] Instead, society denies the

very possibility, and it asks lesbians to believe this homophobic assertion over their own contrasting personal experience.

Many heterosexual people simply refuse to see lesbian couples,
assuming that women without male partners are simply unattached
individuals engaged in superficial social relationships. When forced to
recognize them, many people dismiss lesbian relationships as a brief
stage shared by "roommates," "friends," or "girls" who will go on to
select male partners.[9] Likewise, lesbian couples' attempts to build
clear boundaries around their relationships are met with more social
resistance.

> Clear boundaries around the heterosexual family are encouraged and
> respected by the larger system in many significant and little ways. The
> boundaries around the lesbian family usually are unrecognized, ignored,
> or reacted to with hostility and negative judgement.[10]

Moreover, social pressures force lesbians to collude in their own
invisibility. Many women retreat into silence, concluding that revealing themselves is simply too dangerous; the pain of being treated as if
one is nonexistent is perversely transformed into the protection of
hiding the relationship. Lesbians, in short, are encouraged to produce
the exact silence about their lives that punishes them with isolation in
the first place. Lesbian couples find themselves in a double bind:
Either they suffer the stress of being unrecognized by the world
around them, or they take on the stress of being identifiable to that
same world.

Remaining invisible (or closeted) as a couple creates real stress on
the relationship, leaving it vulnerable to various intrusions by people
who may not respect the women's bond as familial and private.[11]
Gartrell warns that "the cost of this secrecy cannot be underestimated.
The constant need to lie, to be on guard, and to pretend heterosexuality must be understood . . . in terms of the toll of psychic energy and
injury to self-esteem."[12] Crawford adds that

> when the relationship between the . . . [partners] is unrecognized,
> either because they choose to hide it or because others choose to ignore
> it, then no matter how defined the system may be internally, ex-lovers,
> ex-husbands, and members of the couple's families of origin can walk in
> and out at will, as though the family unit does not exist.[13]

Social invisibility creates serious obstacles to forming crucial family boundaries. Since partners are not free to identify who they are coupled with, outsiders do not respect the couple's need for privacy or follow social mores in requesting a partner's time and attention. Closeted lesbians protect themselves from direct public challenge and cope instead with having their couple bond ignored.

> *It was a huge step for Sharon and Tracey to take the swing dance class together. The couple hoped there would be the usual excess of women in the class, so they could get away with "coincidentally" dancing together. When the dance teacher approached and announced that there were men available to dance with, Sharon and Tracey's eyes met in a secret exchange of disappointment. Silently, Sharon followed the teacher across the room.*

At the same time, being socially recognizable (or "out") as a lesbian couple carries inevitable dangers for the relationship. Once identifiable, a couple may be targeted for the various forms of homophobia commonly suffered by lesbians. Not all couples willingly contend with these problems. Lesbian couples who live in progressive communities may enjoy a partial reprieve from the daily effects of these stressors. Yet neither a relatively tolerant community nor a personal support network can fully insulate a couple from the dominant culture's homophobia. Lesbian couples cannot simply request and receive society's recognition whenever they happen to need it. Couples who fully come out, though, frequently conclude that the personal and relational costs of denying their authentic identity are too high to warrant staying in the closet.

> *Cheryl and Debra finally signed up for the swing dance class they had wanted to take for years. At the first class, the teacher attempted to pair the single men with women who came without male partners, but they both had agreed they would never collude with anyone treating them as unattached heterosexuals. When the teacher suggested they separate, Cheryl responded, "We're a couple. Like all the other couples here, we came to dance with each other. Maybe some of the unpartnered women would like to dance with the single men."*

Still other couples combine these two positions, recognizing the fact that social responses can vary widely, as can the consequences of claiming their lesbian identity in various settings. Combining an awareness of the stresses of invisibility and the potential dangers of disclosure, they weigh each situation individually, determining when to stay hidden and when to reveal their coupled status. Yet even this approach does not fully protect the couple from stress. Couples in this position must cope with having different identities in different relationships and situations, and they cannot totally control who will or will not know of their relationship.

> *Abbie and June were nervous before their first dance class. They knew they might be the only lesbians in the class and they'd decided they would only continue if they felt comfortable. Once inside, the couple recognized both acquaintances they were not "out" to and also other clearly lesbian couples. When the teacher suggested they each go dance with unpartnered men, they hesitated a minute, deciding on the spot how to respond. The presence of the other lesbians buoyed their confidence. Knowing they were identifying themselves as a couple, Abbie and June nonetheless told the teacher they preferred to dance with each other.*

Lesbian couples cannot provide themselves with social recognition. Social validation is an inherently interactional process, requiring someone from outside the couple relationship to affirm the partners' bond. Despite lesbians' many creative responses designed to counteract others' disapproval, attaining and maintaining social recognition for their family units remains an ongoing burden.

Public Versus Private Identities

All lesbians must be multicultural. They operate in two different and often directly conflicting worlds—one inside their homes, and the other in the mainstream culture.[14] This tension affects most lesbian couples, particularly those who maintain the sharpest contrast between their public and private lives.

> *Gina and Mariel had spent the day at home, making love and simply being together after the long work week. Tonight they were meeting a mixed group of friends and acquaintances at the theatre. After they got their coats on, they gave each other a now-common final kiss, stealing one last moment of uninhibited affection before pretending to be straight*

in public. They joked that most couples don't kiss good-bye when they are going out together.

The mainstream society forces on lesbians an exaggerated emphasis on their identities as separate individuals through its refusal to acknowledge the partners' relationship. In response, many lesbian couples tend to guard their privacy zealously.[15] When available, privacy offers a crucial space in which the partners reaffirm their individual and shared lesbian identities. As the partners move in and out of direct contact with society's view of lesbian relationships as illegitimate, they return home with a mutual need to demonstrate the central importance of their sexual and emotional bond.

Many couples protect their relationships by moving close together and creating rigid boundaries between themselves and the outside world.[16] While this intimacy is a prized source of satisfaction for many lesbians,[17] the couple must often shift between intense closeness with their partners at home and a facade of greater distance when functioning in the mainstream community. The partners must somehow preserve for themselves and for their relationship a sense of consistency even when behaving in inconsistent ways.

Achieving this sort of relational flexibility is often difficult.[18] Many lesbian partners find that they cannot suddenly shift out of their public mode and into their private identity immediately upon returning home. Homophobia encountered in the outside world may result in reluctance in one or both partners to express emotional and sexual intimacy openly at home. Therefore, just as homophobia increases the partners' need to demonstrate their mutual bond, it may also interfere with their capacity to do so. This tension creates some of the most frequent complaints among lesbian couples seeking therapeutic help.[19]

"What do you mean you're going out with Barbara on a Saturday? You see her all week at work. Doesn't her husband want to be with her on the weekends?" Rosa asked Lois. Lois knew she was breaking new ground. She and Rosa did everything together on the weekends. Their unstated but clear expectation had always been that the weekends were time to see their joint friends or to be alone together. But Lois had been so struck by how easily Barbara had proposed they meet for lunch on Saturday. Lois knew Rosa was afraid they were opening some kind of floodgate

*where the couple would end up without enough time alone at home. She
wondered why this was such a tense negotiation between herself and
Rosa, while Barbara and her husband didn't seem to cling to each other
on the weekends at all.*

Without society's assistance, lesbian couples must clearly articulate
for themselves how their relationship will remain unique and go
beyond each partner's outside friendships. Because intimate friendship is often such a central feature of lesbians' couple relationships,
incorporating other friendships into the partners' lives can be complex. In a study of lesbian friendship, the majority of study participants had difficulty distinguishing between the terms *friend* and
lover.[20] The respondents repeatedly returned to the concept of intensity to describe the couple relationship, but they acknowledged that
even that could be shared with outside friends.

Not all couples can use unrestricted privacy to generate a strong
sense of couple identity. For example, working-class lesbians unable
to afford their own apartments may have to live with roommates.
Lesbians of color, whose cultural norms may value more permeable
relational boundaries, might be expected to open their homes to relatives and friends more continually than do middle class white lesbians. Lesbians with children frequently have very limited privacy and
must elicit support from their home environment—as well as provide
it for their children—without much time alone as a couple.[21]

Like other kinds of couples, lesbian couples employ numerous
agreements or symbols (such as rings) to signify the closed nature of
the couple relationship. For example, many (although not all) couples
vow monogamy as a major boundary-keeping device. Couples may
keep secrets together, or reserve weekly times they will always spend
alone. They may agree to certain restrictions on outside friendships as
an external demonstration of their desire to be uniquely close and
involved with each other.

Frequently the couple keeps their symbols clear to each partner and
deliberately unclear to the outside world.[22] For example, lesbian couples show more diversity than do heterosexuals in decisions they
make about wearing rings. Some couples may purchase identical
rings and wear them on the ring finger of their left hands, while others may deliberately select different rings for each partner. Still other

couples will choose matching rings but will wear them on their right hands, either to avoid social recognition as a couple or to signify that their relationship is different than a heterosexual marriage. The level of negotiation and consideration lesbians must invest into these decisions illustrates how seemingly simple and common acts are often far more complex for lesbians.

> *Kate and Melissa hosted Melissa's family for dinner. Afterwards Melissa's ten-year-old niece, Callie, started playing with Kate by tickling her hand at the table. Suddenly, Callie exclaimed, "Hey, you and Aunt Melissa are wearing the same ring!" Kate tried to stay cool as she frantically slipped the ring into her pocket and tried to redirect Callie's attention. Kate couldn't believe she had forgotten to take off her ring before the family arrived. Melissa was right; it would have been much simpler to buy different rings.*

Differences as Sources of Stress

With so much riding on lesbian couples' abilities to emphasize their intimate closeness at home, areas of difference or conflict between the partners can feel particularly threatening. Because conflict and separateness are integral and repeating elements of any couple's life, the couple may frequently confront these fears. The more the couple relies on maintaining a conflict-free environment, the more disruptive anger, differences, and desires for separateness will become.[23] In this way, stress originally (and continually) imposed on the couple from outside their relationship creates tension within the relationship as well. In extreme cases the couple may find themselves perched on a precarious ledge, forced to function inauthentically as separate individuals in public and in an equally untenable state of continual connectedness at home.

Lesbian couples seeking therapy frequently report difficulties in moving back and forth between intense intimacy and separate identities.[24] Unlike heterosexual couples, lesbians face a loaded challenge: their fears that acts of separation can threaten the couple relationship are valid interpretations of a socially imposed danger.

> Because same-sex couples often must spend greater amounts of energy defining boundaries in order to maintain their relationship and private

couple space and, because for same-sex couples, differentiation is not countered by external forces supporting the survival of the partnership, any energy spent on more individuated behavior may been seen as tipping the scales toward dissolution.[25]

Establishing Relational Roles

Our society presents clear gender roles to all males and females. The culture works to persuade and to prepare both males and females to base couple relationships not only on the existence of gender difference between the partners, but on the relational roles that society associates with appropriate male and female behavior.

Various ethnic, racial, and religious groups adhere differently to these socially proscribed gender roles. For example, Asian-American families encourage a strict compliance with gender roles,[26] while African-Americans often create considerably more flexibility both in women's roles and in the degree of equality between heterosexual partners.[27] Despite these distinctions, it remains true that all groups differentiate family roles and status based on gender, and all groups have been influenced by the dominant society's unequal valuing of male and female roles.

Lesbians cannot base their assignment of relational, sexual, economic, or parenting roles on gender differences between the partners. As two women, lesbian couples build from a clean slate, negotiating from scratch all aspects of the partners' roles. Individual abilities, interests, and tolerances form the basis for the complex construction of these couples' relational roles.

As lesbians approach this task, though, they are confronted with a serious, socially imposed obstacle. As a result of the sexism pervading American society, typically male roles are connoted as being specially skilled and important, while typically female roles are evaluated to be more universally performable and of secondary status. Therefore, when lesbian couples divide up everything from domestic work to their decision-making process to the emotional work of the relationship, their efforts are tainted by the unequal status assigned to some tasks and abilities relative to others.[28] For example, if one partner's work hours are especially long while the other returns home in the late afternoon, it may be practical for the latter woman to make dinner and to tend to the domestic tasks which arise on weekdays. Because this arrangement smacks of traditional male-female role divisions, however, the partner handling the domestic duties may feel subservient, while the longer-working partner may feel differently entitled or empowered by her position.

Another example is the couple's efforts to extricate their roles as sexual partners from the common dichotomies between men and women. Research indicates that lesbians typically work hard to avoid establishing fixed, traditional roles of the sexual aggressor and the sexually pursued; instead, they expect partners to initiate sex equally.[29] In this and other areas of their relationships, many lesbians work hard to free themselves from pervasive social training, perhaps especially those lesbians who have been influenced by feminism. The couples, however, live in a cultural context of unequal, hierarchical, and sexist role distinctions for women and men. Lesbian couples are commonly, though not identically, stressed by this bias.

While the difficulty of needing to design each partner's role in the relationship causes lesbian couples ongoing stress, this call to creativity offers them a special opportunity as well. The additional originality lesbians must bring to creating their relational roles allows each partner to sculpt the specifics of her coupled life beyond the parameters heterosexual couples commonly follow. While many heterosexual couples are also working to redistribute power and responsibility within their relationships, lesbians are operating from much farther outside the traditional model. This additional distance from gender-based relational roles may make it harder for lesbians to fathom desirable alternatives to the only model they have seen, and in that sense may make their task especially difficult. After all, lesbians cannot settle for minor revisions in existing role distinctions, since those roles are based on a gender difference between the partners that does not exist for them. At the same time, they may feel freer to consider radically different—and more personally satisfying—relational patterns.

Lesbian couples frequently place great value on achieving equality between the partners in all aspects of their joint lives.[30] Commonly, partners expect that each of them will provide emotional caretaking within the relationship, without this task being relegated disproportionately to one partner or the other.[31] Partners frequently view each other's lapses in providing this sustenance as a problem, and work to rebalance their contributions to the relationship.[32]

Lesbians' efforts to establish equal partnerships with other women are often a primary source of their relational satisfaction and are often perceived by them as an important improvement over what they see in heterosexual relationships. At the same time, the culture they live in teaches that relationships are hierarchical, with one partner holding more of the power, and that couple relationships cannot be legitimately formed outside of that paradigm. The absence of alternative models increases the likelihood of conflict and uncertainty between the partners in negotiating this huge and unfamiliar task.

The creation of roles becomes even more complex when the partners are also parents.[33] Practically every aspect of heterosexual parenting roles is associated with either masculinity or femininity. Yet if all female parenting behaviors are part of the role of mother, who is the second female parent? The lesbian couple must construct a clear set of dual female parenting roles, within a social frame that suggests this cannot be done.[34] The partners may find themselves vying for very similar roles. Similar parenting behaviors hardly make two parents identical, however, nor do they necessarily indicate that other parenting functions are being overlooked. Lesbian parents may be in an especially advantageous position to demonstrate to the rest of society how needlessly dichotomous traditional parenting roles have been. Lesbians must transcend powerful social messages, though, in order to more creatively design their relationships to their children.

The Impact of Power and Money on Family Roles

Virtually all couples battle for power within their relationships, and lesbians are no exceptions. While lesbians do appear to achieve relative equality more often than heterosexuals,[35] no partnership is equal all of the time; all partners—of any sexual orientation—periodically seek to prevail in important disputes. Female socialization hampers lesbians' attempts to grapple with these ongoing tensions. Girls and women frequently meet with powerful resistance when they attempt to compete or dominate in any area of their lives. As adults, many women have difficulty directly pursuing various kinds of power; they therefore work to obscure or to deny these forbidden desires.

Lesbian couplings face even greater impact from this residue of socialization. A partner's desire to support equality within the relationship may conflict with her desire to win a particular argument or force a particular course of action.[36] Moreover, the feminist beliefs common in many lesbian communities frequently equate dominating actions with male behavior. Lesbians connected to such communities tend to attempt to avoid demonstrating typically male attitudes and behaviors.[37] Power struggles in a relationship may become submerged with one or both partners trying to avoid acknowledging "inappropriate" feelings.

> Soon after she and Sarah pooled their money, Dana found herself shopping frequently. She would go to the mall, always buying items for herself despite the nagging guilt she felt. She drove home rehearsing for the fight she expected from Sarah; Dana heard herself declaring that combining their money didn't mean she couldn't do what she wanted. She didn't want to consult Sarah on her purchases, and she was afraid she had somehow lost her autonomy by agreeing to the joint account. Dana then recognized that she was reaffirming her power when, as a woman, she should be striving for cooperation and equality. Feeling guilty, Dana vowed not to tell Sarah what was really going on.

Lesbians tend to work especially hard to equalize relational power in the financial arrangements between the partners.[38] As women, many lesbians have personally experienced financial obstacles resulting from the culture's reserving the majority of its resources for white men. Already schooled in the link between money and power, lesbians commonly grapple with how to allocate the family's money, with both partners being aware of these decisions' symbolic importance with regard to the balance of power between the partners.

While heterosexuals typically combine all of their assets immediately following their wedding, lesbians do not have one normative timetable for arranging the family's finances. As a result, lesbian partners demonstrate greater diversity in their selected financial agreements than do married couples.[39] A sizable number of lesbian couples choose never to pool their money. These couples value the individual identity and decision making this option offers, and they select different arenas in which to blend their lives. Other couples blend a certain portion of their income and maintain separate accounts for the remainder.[40] Still others eventually combine all of their resources, but more gradually than heterosexual couples usually do.

Frequently lesbians struggle to have financial agreements demonstrate their simultaneous commitments to the partners' independence, equality, and interdependence. While lesbian couples do typically expect both partners to be employed (unless there are small children at home or there are other extenuating circumstances), they may not bring home equal paychecks. Nevertheless, lesbians commonly strive to break the traditional linkage between income size and relational power seen in heterosexual couples and to reject the concept of there being a head of the household. As Blumstein and Schwartz report, "Lesbians do not expect to support another adult or be head of a family in the same way a husband expects to take on the position of breadwinner. A lesbian sees herself as a worker, not a provider or a dependent."[41] These researchers found sufficient distinction among lesbians to report that "money establishes the balance of power in relationships, except among lesbians."[42]

Lesbian couples with children often experience a particular challenge in creating nontraditional financial arrangements between the partners. Studies indicate that lesbian mothers live on lower incomes than either heterosexual mothers[43] or gay male parents.[44] For these families, the additional economic strain may affect other role and power-related decisions, including those about the roles of income earner(s) and primary child-care provider, as the partners strive to support their children adequately.

Lesbians experience both additional stress and an opportunity for creativity in establishing their roles concerning their financial arrangements. All of a couple's negotiations, however, take place against the backdrop of a dangerous insecurity inflicted on them by society. Because lesbians cannot achieve joint legal status as a couple, the court system typically refuses to assist partners in dividing up joint assets in the event that they decide to break up. Blending their assets therefore constitutes a substantially greater risk for lesbian couples than for heterosexuals and likewise reflects a deeper trust between partners.[45]

Poor and working-class lesbian couples (with disproportionately high representation of lesbians of color in these groups) may face particular stress in balancing the financial resources and power within their relationships. Not all women earn enough money to achieve financial self-sufficiency. In many working-class and poor communities, people pool resources not as a demonstration of trust or commitment, but as a means of survival. The interdependence this reflects is not an individually selected arrangement but an imposed and unchanging economic reality. For these lesbians, the timing and attached relational significance of combining their money may be even more complicated than for their middle-class peers.

Sexuality

Like most other people, lesbians derive great pleasure from sexual expression and view it as a source of appreciation and pride in their lives. Many lesbian couples experience powerful emotional and physical intimacy through sexuality and have worked extremely hard to protect this realm of their lives from outside challenge.

Due to the twin influences of homophobia and sexism, though, lesbians often are unsure what their own natural sexuality is. The male-dominated perspective of our culture views nongenital sexual touching as foreplay rather than a complete sexual experience, frames sexual infrequency as dysfunction, and defines sexual functioning as a central measure of the couple relationship's overall success. Objective inquiry about women's natural sexual interests, preferred frequencies, and selected touch is discouraged or obscured. As couples composed of two women, lesbian couples are powerfully affected by this absence of information and, like all other women, are encouraged to evaluate their own sexual normalcy against standards based on male experience and desire.

Seen through this distorted lens, many lesbian couples sexual lives fail to reflect the required patterns. While the amount of available research remains insufficient, findings indicate that lesbian respondents report having sex less frequently than either heterosexual or gay male respondents.[46] Lesbians describe significantly higher levels of nongenital physical affection than other kinds of couples, and they are more likely to consider this contact to be a complete experience instead of foreplay to orgasmic sex.[47] In addition, lesbians' evaluations of their sexual satisfaction appear less linked to sexual frequency than is true for nonlesbian populations.[48]

As all-female couplings, lesbians are profoundly affected by the fact that no one knows what women's natural sexual desires, expressions, and ways of relating are outside the influence of sexism. Lesbians are further compromised by the lack of information about normal *lesbian* sexual patterns apart from heterosexual women. The development of accurate generalizations about lesbians' sexual lives is complicated by researchers' lack of access to the large closeted segment of the lesbian population. Because so many lesbians must hide, one is unable to determine whether a study contains a representative research sample of lesbians, and accurate information cannot be gathered on how their sexual expression does or does not vary from other kinds of couples. Nonetheless, lesbians are the women whose sexual relationships are most clearly independent of male influence.[49] Further exploration of lesbians' sexual patterns can offer greatly needed understanding of not only their own sexual natures but those of females in general.

Specific social influences obscure accurate observation of women's sexual natures. With some variations among racial, ethnic, and religious groups, it remains generally true that girls are encouraged to repress their own sexual urges and to consider sexual feelings as shameful and unfeminine, except in the service of satisfying male sexual desire.[50] For lesbian women to recognize their desires, they must at least partially transcend this prohibition, pursuing sexual interest with no accompanying aim of including or satisfying a man.[51] Because in so doing lesbians disobey a central social tenet, most people define them in terms of not only their involvement with women but also their refusal to be involved with men. (Bisexual women involved in lesbian relationships face a related charge by failing to offer men the exclusive attention needed to prove sexual "normalcy.")

Because lesbians refuse to adhere to the sexual restrictions inherent in the socially sanctioned female role, society places an exaggerated emphasis on the sexual aspect of lesbian identity. As Loulan points out, "because the culture identifies lesbians by whom they have genital contact with, sexual activity becomes more than behavior, it becomes an entire identity." Social condemnation of and exaggerated emphasis on lesbian sexuality frequently results in couples becoming sexually constricted.

Many gay men and lesbians have learned to inhibit sexual desire at an early age because of a conviction or an impression that such feelings for someone of the same gender are wrong. . . . While sex gives us pleasure, it can be preempted by the need to avoid pain, which demands a higher priority in our psychological functioning.[52]

The result is that lesbians are forced to extricate themselves from powerful contradictions. As lesbians, they are told that their sexuality constitutes a tremendously important and defining feature of their identities; as women, though, they are taught to de-emphasize exactly this realm of their lives.[53] Frequently their internalization of this distorted perspective on their sexuality creates shame and leads lesbians to inhibit or avoid this now-tainted aspect of their personal identities.

Lesbian sexual expression is further compromised by the prohibitions against women taking on the role of sexual aggressor.[54] Lesbians' reluctance to initiate sex on a regular basis appears strongly linked to gender socialization and to the perception that initiating sex is male behavior. For feminist lesbians, this practice may also be negatively associated with the mainstream male role. Blumstein and Schwartz's findings led them to hypothesize that many lesbians' discomfort with the role of sexual aggressor contributes to the relatively lower sexual frequency among these women. Roth concurs:

Lesbians, especially those who are younger or who came out after the women's movement, are in a particular bind, since they usually place a high value on equality; neither partner can readily take on the role of the initiator or aggressor on any regular basis.[55]

Lesbians' positive sexual self-images are challenged yet again by this culture's ongoing assault on women's body images. As women, both members of a lesbian couple are challenged by this misogyny and must work harder to generate the confidence in their attractiveness needed to pursue desired sexual contact. In addition, lesbians are often accused of turning to other women because they are not attractive enough to win a man's attentions. In a perverse twist, some lesbians may feel particular pressure to be attractive by mainstream standards in order to legitimize the idea that they are with female partners by choice.

Finally, lesbian relationships will be disproportionately affected by the high incidence of women who have experienced sexual abuse.[56] There is no evidence that such abuse is more common among lesbians per se; however, because most sexual abuse is directed at females, lesbian couplings are more likely than heterosexual or gay male couplings to include a partner who has survived sexual trauma.[57] As sexual abuse can often complicate a woman's efforts to access her own sexual desires and capacities, it is likely that many lesbian couples are coping with the sequalae of this trauma and that it further restricts their sexual lives.

As each generation of lesbians liberate themselves further from the influences restricting their full sexual expression, the stresses associated with lesbian sexuality may abate, leaving these women to decide for themselves how and when to share sexual expression with their partners. Due to the enduring nature of both homophobia and sexism, though, lesbian sexuality will continue to present couples with not only the fulfillment it is intended to provide but also with socially imposed duress.

Sexism

The patriarchal tenet that males deserve preferential treatment over females permeates virtually every aspect of our social structure. Barriers to women's economic and social equality and society's continuing tolerance of violence against women are but the most obvious results of sexism that continually restricts the lives of all-female couples. The residue of this bias on women, both concrete and less tangible, has been articulated beyond reasonable rebuttal.[58]

Sexism heightens the other stressors common to lesbians' lives and contributes to the devaluation of their families. For example, the social withholding of recognition of lesbian families is based in part on the absence of men in such partnerships. Patriarchy defines families that do not include a male adult as failed or incomplete units. Women parenting without men hear their families described as "broken homes" or "female-headed households" (not families), and they are depicted as "unwed mothers." Lesbian families are similarly disqualified, in part because of the women's "failure" to secure male participation in the family. Even after a woman has divorced or been widowed, her previous connection to a man remains the defining factor in her social status. Men, as the more prized gender, are the focal point of society's evaluation of family units, even when they are not members of the family at all.

Sexism permeates lesbian couples' attempts to create relational roles for each partner because it values some roles and behaviors over others. Both partners have been exposed to the social message that tasks associated with the role of wife or mother are less highly esteemed than those typically adopted by men. This divisive influence may taint the partners' attempts to delineate their roles in the family, adding further stress to a task the couple must already accomplish in the absence of models or guidance.

A further example of sexism's impact on lesbian families is found in the partners' attempts to construct their public and private identities. Lesbians must consider their capacities to ensure their own safety in a social climate that renders them vulnerabe to physical assault both as lesbians and as women. As they continually weigh when to acknowledge their identity—and when, as noted earlier, they must often separate their public and private lives—society's refusal to protect women figures heavily into their decisions.

> *Everyone had heard about the assault over the weekend. Jaime was accepting phone calls, Myra had been told, but she was still too shaken up to have visitors. "The newspaper article made it sound like the guy really went after her," Myra commented to Sheila. "What was going on?" "It's really hard to tell," Sheila told her. "She was the only woman around, and that might be why he picked her. Also, I have no idea if he sensed she was a lesbian or not. It could have been either, you know. You just don't know in a situation like this."*

Sexism also invades lesbians' experience of their private sexual lives. Our culture socializes both genders to believe that the penis is the ultimate sexual organ, singularly capable of providing sexual ecstasy to women. Psychoanalytic theory, elevated for decades to the level of supposed fact, has destructively articulated this vision, defining women as sexually inferior beings who seek sexual relationships with men to compensate for their physiological inadequacies.[59] This still-influential perspective has provided "scientific" justification for an unending assault on the potency and attractiveness of women's bodies. Lesbians therefore must develop a sexual life against the backdrop of a society that tells them that both they and their partners are sexually incomplete. It is impressive that so many lesbians are able to achieve sufficient distance from this sexist social mythology to create fulfilling sexual lives.

Armed with an increasingly well-articulated feminist rebuttal to these biases, many lesbians are successfully purging themselves of some of sexism's influence. Because this thinking continues to be imbedded in so much of mainstream culture, however, it is unlikely that any woman can truly rid herself of its deleterious effects.

Racism

Beyond the challenges commonly confronted by all lesbian couples, lesbian couples of color face specific, additional stressors that are enduring realities of life in this culture. Manifestations of racism created by the mainstream culture include (but are not limited to) threats to physical safety, restricted access to economic and social opportunities and rewards, and imposed social invisibility and exclusion. Facing frequent discrimination in educational and employment opportunities, powerfully negative social images of all people of color, and greater vulnerability to a range of social problems, lesbians of color have particular reason to distrust the dominant culture and to monitor their dependence on traditional social institutions as best they can.

Lesbians of color commonly struggle with competing loyalties and group identities. They must defend themselves against living fragmented lives, pulled in opposing directions by affiliations they deeply value. Layers of oppression compound their challenge as racism, sexism, and homophobia combine and direct the responses these women receive from various important peers and family. Lesbians of color therefore are called on to generate enormous strength, relying on support networks of their partners, families, communities, and their own inner resources to create meaningful, self-determined lives.

In almost every part of their lives, lesbians of color face the experience of being in some way different from the people around them. Indeed, in their relationships within the white-dominated mainstream culture, their own racial communities, their families of origin, or the lesbian community, some crucial aspect of these lesbians' identities is not only different but devalued. Many lesbians of color devote continual energy to preserving these vital relationships, tolerating the ongoing anxiety that frequently accompanies their insider-outsider status.

While the influence of racism has frayed the relationships in many families of color, their shared minority-group membership often also builds special bonds. Lesbians of color who come from close families bring this experience to the challenge of adopting lesbian (or other nonheterosexual) identities. This important example, provided by their own relatives, may prepare lesbians of color to confront homophobia in ways less familiar to lesbians from unoppressed or more detached family backgrounds.

While lesbians of all backgrounds commonly fear being shunned by their families upon coming out, the consequences of being cut off carry particular weight for many lesbians of color. Because the mainstream culture specifically devalues nonwhite heritage and cultures, these lesbians' ties to their families and their cultural community are irreplaceable. The risks of being ostracized due to their family's homophobia are especially serious.[60] As the likelihood of suffering social rejection increases as a result of their claiming a lesbian identity, the security of their lifelong support networks also comes under fire.

Many lesbians of color are accustomed to turning to their (often multigenerational) families and community for guidance when they are experiencing some kind of race-related oppression within the dominant culture. These lesbians may find it both foreign and painful to need to protect their couple relationships from the very people who have supplied their self-esteem and protection from oppression throughout their lives. The stress of this difficult position may manifest itself as tension between the lesbian partners, and one or both may feel a particular isolation as they grapple with whether to bring news of their lesbian identity and partnered status to their primarily heterosexual families.

For many lesbians of color, then, coming out contains particular risks. In the last couple of decades, when the predominantly white lesbian feminist movement has encouraged lesbians to come out, many lesbians of color questioned whether these women fully understood the full risk they faced in answering this challenge. Many lesbians of color conclude that the potential losses associated with coming out are simply not worth it for them.

> In a homophobic world . . . coming out is suicidal. . . . If you're barely surviving, and then you're going to take the risk to lose the respect, and the love, and the sense of place that you have with your own family, you have nothing. . . . So, why add more stigma to yourself? Why take one more horrible risk to be further disenfranchised from society? You have no place to go.[61]

While middle-class white culture places particular importance on fully developing individuals' personal identities, some other racial and ethnic groups de-emphasize the values of separation and individuation espoused by the dominant culture; instead, they value interdependence above personal fulfillment.[62] Asian-Americans offer a particularly clear example of a group whose traditional values have espoused doing what is considered best for the family unit over the individual happiness of any particular family member, especially female members. Clearly the family is unlikely to consider a woman pursuing her lesbian identity as doing what is best for the family, and her insistence on continuing her lesbian relationships may be interpreted as a profound act of disrespect for closely held cultural values. The lesbian's family may be particularly unpersuaded by her claims that she must explore her own personal identity; in fact, they may be further offended by this attempt to explain her feelings.

In addition, the family of a lesbian of color may interpret her lesbian identity to represent an abandonment of their also-oppressed male peers. Relatives may also assume that lesbians will not bear the children that are so important to the group's future. Finally, lesbians may be viewed as bringing additional emotional suffering upon family members who already have more than their share of pain.[63]

Despite these and other obstacles, though, some families of color may be more reluctant than white families to ostracize a lesbian family member. As many families of color are keenly aware of the dangers of lost group membership, they may have particular reason to worry about the impact of cutting their lesbian relative adrift. While families of color are not devoid of homophobia, the family's shared minority identity may cause them to resist actually breaking crucial family ties.

The commitments of lesbians of color to their racial and ethnic communities may occupy a similarly central place in their social networks. Many lesbians of color rely on access to their communities, which offer not only needed protection but also inclusion in cultural rituals and traditions, for affirmation of their racial identity. While often deeply rewarding, these ties may complicate a lesbian's decision about coming out, as endangering these special connections would be particularly costly. At the same time, lesbians of color may understand or tolerate their community's unexamined homophobia, as Trujillo notes: "Maybe it's too early to expect tolerance [for lesbian and gay Chicanos] from my culture as well, since all of our energy must be directed toward the war we must fight."[64]

Many lesbians of color cope with the stress of simultaneously recognizing their communities' preoccupation with battling racism and the need for it to pay attention to sexism and homophobia. These lesbians face much pressure to compartmentalize vital aspects of their own identities—on top of whatever divisions they have already made either as lesbians or as members of a racial or ethnic minority—in order to preserve potentially conflicting memberships in key relational arenas.

In addition, all lesbians confront the work of forming an internally consistent sense of their own lesbian (or nonheterosexual) identity. While white lesbians' and lesbians of color's experience of this process have much in common, some lesbians of color may follow a somewhat different path than middle-class white lesbians, based on different norms concerning family connection and personal privacy.

Particularly during the earlier stages of adopting a lesbian identity, many lesbians delay "coming out" until they have achieved some level of internal acceptance and understanding of themselves. Whether closeted or not, many white middle-class lesbians distance emotionally or physically from their families and immediate social circles during this time. The buffer provided by this space allows crucial development to proceed before (or apart from) fully confronting others' reactions to their lesbianism. The higher levels of familial and community contact typical of some racial, ethnic, or religious groups, however, may complicate the lesbian members' efforts to achieve this space, as they must simultaneously develop the identity they share with their families and one that separates them from most or all of their relatives. As a result, a lesbian of color may struggle with an increased sense of responsibility toward her already-burdened family, whether these feelings originate within or are presented to her as expectations of her family or community. The family of origin may even attribute their daughter's distancing to her new "friendship" with a lesbian partner, further complicating the couple's efforts to secure the support and trust of those closest to them.

Some (though not all) lesbians of color want the support and social opportunities offered by the lesbian community. Their experiences within their racial communities have often served as examples of how coming together with others like oneself can support and enrich the entire group. Because women active in lesbian communities are predominantly white, however, lesbians of color often experience not only shared group membership with other lesbians but additional alienation as well. White lesbians are no more free of racism than people of color are free of homophobia. Lesbians of color therefore risk feeling supported but also marginalized within the lesbian community.

Relations between lesbians of color and the lesbian community were particularly aggravated in the late 1970s and early 1980s, when many lesbian communities encouraged separation between lesbians and men. Many white lesbians confined their primary affiliations to relationships with other women (or other lesbians), sometimes based on the belief that patriarchal oppression could not be dismantled while women continued to nourish relationships with their oppressors. This political analysis often sounded simplistic to lesbians of color, given that white lesbians not only do not share minority group identity with men in their racial group (as lesbians of color do) but also belong to a group that continues to oppress people of color. The resulting breach further isolated lesbian couples of color from a supportive resource they needed as much as any other lesbian couples. The relationship of many lesbians of color with the lesbian community is further complicated when they look to community activities as a way to meet potential partners. While white lesbians looking to the community for this purpose will primarily meet other white women, lesbians of color are likely to encounter fewer women from their own racial group at community events. Lesbians of color are therefore more likely to become involved in interracial lesbian relationships than are white lesbians, and therefore they risk experiencing the additional stresses that often accompany interracial relationships.

There is, of course, great variety among lesbians of color in virtually all aspects of their personal confrontations with stress. The catchall term *lesbians of color* does not describe one homogenous group, and no easy generalizations can apply to such a diverse population. All lesbian couples of color in this county, however, are exposed to racism and must respond to this ongoing stress in addition to the others previously presented. The families they form must respond to the varying ramifications of this social condition in ways not shared by white lesbian couples. As these couples develop their own personal lesbian identities, make decisions about coming out as a lesbian family, and choose strategies to simultaneously secure their most important personal and social relationships, lesbian couples of color experience both common and unique lesbian stressors.

White lesbians and lesbians of color alike create adaptive responses that work to protect the individuals and their couple relationships against these central stressors. It is testament to lesbians' relational capacities that many couples weather these stressors, building lives that contain a great deal more than simply effective responses to painful stress. Such an accomplishment requires particular strength in themselves and in their couple relationships.

4

Lesbian Couples'
Strengths and Coping Mechanisms

LESBIAN COUPLES CAN PROVE THAT NECESSITY *IS* THE MOTHER OF invention. Many of the strengths common to these couples are inventions made necessary by the stresses of homophobia. Heterosexual couples (with a few exceptions, such as interracial couples), rarely experience the near-complete absence of social approval or even simple acknowledgement that their relationship exists. Lesbians have made specific adaptations to these stresses that have protected their relationships and fostered their growth.

Lesbian couples need what all couples need from their social environment: basic boundaries around their relationship that are socially recognized and respected; social validation that the family unit is a legitimate and viable grouping; and a sense of membership in a group of similar families that make up the surrounding social community. While heterosexual couples are granted these necessary elements as a matter of course, however, lesbian couples are deprived of them and must generate them alone.

The problem lesbian couples face is that each of these central supports is inherently social—that is, each ingredient requires the participation of people outside of the couple relationship. Couples cannot fully create their own relational boundaries in the absence of anyone to acknowledge and respect them. Likewise, social validation requires that an outsider communicate approval or acceptance to the couple. Similarly, membership in a larger social group of families requires an invitation to be part of the group. In all three cases, the couple is left to supply for itself something that was never intended to be self-generated.

While there will always be coping mechanisms and strengths unique to each couple, some common strategies used by lesbian partners to nurture their relationships are becoming more clearly visible. Fusion, a pattern of intimate relating typical of many lesbian relationships, is a strategy the couple can develop and employ strictly on their own, if necessary. Increasing use of family rituals allows lesbian couples to determine how much to keep the rituals to themselves and how much to risk sharing these supportive acts with others. Finally, brave efforts over the past two decades to create a rich and supportive sense of lesbian community have provided couples with the inherently social aspect of the validation their relationships require. Taken together, these strategies offer couples purely private, private or social, and clearly social methods of nourishing and validating lesbian relationships.

Fusion

Lesbian couples need high levels of family cohesion not only in temporarily stressful circumstances but throughout the family life cycle. To provide this strong connectedness in their relationships lesbian couples frequently develop patterns described in the psychological literature as *fusion, merging*, or *enmeshment*. Used commonly in interactions ranging from lesbian comedy routines to couple support groups, the term *fusion* is familiar to many lesbians and is characterized by high levels of interdependence and blending of the two partners' individual lives.[1] The partners place a high value on emotional closeness and time spent together as a couple, they emphasize their commonalities, and they may experience anxiety around areas of persistent difference.

With a continual lack of support from the external environment, lesbian couples' pattern of emphasizing their connectedness serves clearly adaptive functions. Couples' perceptions that their relationships are always in danger are all too accurate, adding credence to their sense that they must insulate themselves from homophobic social influences.[2] Making their identity as a couple a centerpiece of their lives undoubtedly helps to stave off the forces aimed at breaking their relationship apart.[3] Lesbian couples' widespread use of fusion is testament to its usefulness in protecting families from the impact of social homophobia.

Joy's parents had refused to welcome her partner, Denise into the family. Yet they continued to expect Joy to return home frequently for weekend visits. For two years, Joy had succumbed to this pressure, unable to risk losing her parents if she refused. Now the toll this was taking on the couple was becoming clear, and Joy was able to resist the family's pressure more directly. "I won't come if Denise isn't invited," Joy told her mother. "We're not going to stay apart all weekend, feeling insecure with each other because I'm agreeing to let you exclude her." "You sound like you're joined at the hip," Joy's mother countered. "You can't get through just two days apart to come visit your real family?" "For the moment, we are not leaving each other's side until this battle is settled," Joy said. "For now, if you want to see your daughter, you'll have to include Denise, too. We're not budging."

However, there is clearly more to the story. As Elise has pointed out, gay men are subject to similar homophobia-related duress, yet fusion is less common in their couple relationships.[4] This often observable contrast between gay male and female relationships suggests that lesbians' typically intense relational bonds are related not only to their homosexual identity but to the fact that the partners are both women.[5]

Feminist writers, researchers, and clinicians have argued persuasively that women naturally prefer close emotional relationships characterized by high levels of self-disclosure, expressed emotion, and mutuality and a sense of their personal identities unfolding within, not outside of, the relationship.[6] Miller, Jordan, Surrey, Stiver, Kaplan, and others have claimed specifically that women's growth hinges on ever-deepening relational ties, not on separation from others. Other authors add that female socialization may particularly develop women's capacities to derive a sense of identity from within their relational connections.[7] Girls' childhood experience of the mother-daughter bond may further prepare some women to form emotionally close connections with each other.[8] These central features of female experience, culminating frequently in the ability to develop very intimate relationships without feeling an overwhelming threat to one's individual identity, may have special relevance to lesbian couples.[9]

> *"Let's spend the entire weekend alone," Ariel whispered to Johanna. "Let's not answer the phone, or go out anywhere, or invite anyone over. I want to be together every minute and not stop touching. The world can't have us this weekend. We can keep them all out and just get lost in each other."*

These typically female patterns of intertwining personal identity and interpersonal closeness have been framed by both the individualistic, competition-oriented mainstream culture and the field of psychology as evidence of female inferiority or personal deficit. Many people still view women's frequent preference for high levels of closeness and interdependence as an indication that they have insufficiently developed their personal identities apart from relationships. While it is true that female socialization often gives short shrift to girls' individual identities, this argument seems especially ironic when applied to lesbians. As women whose entire adult family lives require a dangerous deviation from what would ensure social acceptance and approval, lesbians can hardly be accused of lacking personal autonomy. Rather, the emotional connectedness typical of their couple relationships provides balance for such autonomy. Seen in this light, lesbian couples' embracing of fusion demonstrates a major strength and embodies a drive toward wholeness needed by lesbians and nonlesbians alike.

As Mencher[10] and others demonstrate, when lesbian relationships are evaluated by looking at nonclinical samples of lesbian couples themselves, a very different—and far more positive—picture emerges that substantiates their normative use of fusion and the special value they assess to this connectedness. The lesbian respondents in these studies repeatedly identified the profound closeness and intentionally blurred boundaries between the partners as a primary source of satisfaction in their couple relationships.[11] As Mencher reported,

> The women interviewed accounted for the success of their relationships by naming as relational advantages the very same traits which often are labeled fusion. The intense closeness of the partners and the placement

of the relationships as an axis around which their lives turned were cited as significant advantages of these relationships.[12]

Lesbian couples' tendency to form particularly close, intense, and intimate relationships therefore stems from several motivations. First, this relational style is uniquely effective in giving couples some measure of security in the face of ongoing homophobic challenge. Second, as women, lesbians may be naturally drawn to intense emotional closeness. Women in general appear to be particularly capable of and interested in forming close interpersonal relationships. Third, female socialization creates the conditions that would explain this choice. As the culture's dichotomizing of autonomy and intimacy leaves all people needing to reintegrate these twin core aspects of themselves, lesbian couples' lives often demonstrate particular success in this task. Their relational choices do not stem from social obedience, since their lives overall do not reflect the norms of patriarchal dependency.

The Dangers of Fusion

For fusion to support and protect lesbian couples, the partners must be able to move flexibly between higher and lower levels of closeness. This movement allows for the ongoing nourishment of both the partners' separate identities and their couple relationship. As many lesbian couples know, insufficient closeness can result in a shaky relational foundation.

> *Regardless of the therapist's probing, she could elicit little from this couple. They spent time together, but in rather routinized ways, with little new discovery about each other emerging from their experiences. They reported little fighting and had difficulty naming the particular joys of their partnership. Clearly invested in continuing their relationship, the couple appeared stumped about why they felt this detachment, apparently unaware of how little real intimacy they wrested from their daily lives together.*

Inflexibly high levels of fusion, though, can create serious problems as well. For example, prolonged patterns of merging can leave partners overly attuned to each other's needs at the expense of attention to their own individual experience. Too much focus on immediately relieving each other's anxiety can cause the partners to find themselves intolerant of normal, minor conflicts that exist between them.

Couples who maintain particularly high fusion levels may find it difficult to sustain their unique identities within the relationship, instead forming an exaggerated base of commonality in behavior, style, and communication patterns. These problems manifest themselves in a variety of ways, including partners speaking for each other and using the pronouns *I* and *we* as if they are interchangeable. In addition, excessive fusion can lead to sexual dysfunction, as physical intimacy comes to feel threatening when added to the merging that already exists between the partners.[13] These partners may inhibit their involvement in separate pursuits and outside friendships, gradually limiting themselves to activities that can be experienced jointly.

> *"They're even starting to look alike," Dana said. "I know!" replied Debra. "Have they cut their hair differently, or what is it exactly?" Dana sighed. "The thing that worries me is that I can't seem to talk to them individually anymore. I call for Georgia, and the first thing she does is call for Sandy to get on the extension." This comment made Debra roll her eyes. "Yeah, I know what you mean. I left Sandy a message the other day that I wanted to meet her for lunch on Saturday, and she called back to say they couldn't make it because Denise had some other appointment. I like Denise just fine and all, but I was calling for Sandy, not both of them." Dana shook her head. "I wonder what's going on between them. I don't remember them being so inseparable before. It seems to be getting worse over time."*

It is impossible to know how many lesbian couples experience difficulties maintaining a flexible level of fusion in their relationship, since a large segment of the lesbian population is inaccessible to researchers. Lesbian therapists do report, however, that problems related to managing closeness and distance are behind many of the complaints presented by lesbian couples seeking therapy.[14]

While certainly lesbian couples have no monopoly on these struggles, the frequently heightened levels of intimacy present in their relationships may be sufficient to trigger problems less frequently reported by heterosexual or gay male couples. After all, if female socialization particularly develops women's capacities to embed their personal identities within intimate relationships, this same training also creates the potential for an overdependence on relational contexts. As Burch suggests, "Women raised in a patriarchal culture inevitably have trouble with issues related to sense of self, and, as we have seen, sense of separateness. It does not seem unlikely that most women would encounter some of these conflicts in an intimate relationship with another woman."[15]

Our understanding of fusion must clearly distinguish between different interpersonal situations. When lesbian couples marvel at their emotional closeness, they are not endorsing relational patterns that keep the partners from expressing key aspects of their individual identities. For couples caught in such patterns, the strength of their fusion has indeed become problematic. Instead, lesbian couples value a situation in which two distinct individuals welcome most aspects of each partner's separate self while still maintaining levels of emotional closeness that deviate from patriarchally determined relational norms.

The fact that so many couples develop this relational style without knowing that many of their peers are creating similar relationships indicates how natural these patterns are for many women. The intimacy common to lesbian partnerships supplies the couple with many of their most valued rewards for living outside of basic social support.[16] It is, for many couples, the hallmark of lesbian relationships.

Rituals

Fusion offers lesbian couples ways of strengthening their connection on a daily basis, and it helps them compensate for the usually absent social recognition of their family status. To complement this, lesbians have created ways to mark what society ignores, highlighting important relationship milestones and underscoring fundamental family traditions.

Family ritual strengthens families' sense of themselves as cohesive, successful, and moving through stages over time.[17] "Rituals bring delineation of beginnings, middles, and ends. They signal key successes in a family, they flag moments of important passages, and they imbue the time between a family's formation and its dissolution with . . . [important] punctuation."[18]

Such rituals, however, also powerfully sanction certain families within our culture. Particular families are invited to celebrate their passages in public, with actions specifically designed to bring others' attention to the ritual. Local newspapers invite families to send announcements of weddings, births, deaths, and other family events so that the news can be shared with the entire community. Families burying a member turn their car lights on in an act understood by all to indicate what has occurred and to keep outsiders from interrupting the procession.

Families send written announcements of various highlighted moments in their family life cycle to a wide variety of people in their lives. Across the life cycle, families ritualize key moments such as engagements, weddings, the birth of children, children's various progressions from year to year, wedding anniversaries, retirements, and deaths.[19] They know what moments they will be invited to ritualize, what those rituals commonly consist of, who can be expected to witness and validate the event, and what ritual will come next as they look ahead to further progression through their family's continued development.[20] For these families, the rituals profoundly validate their family life and demonstrate society's support for the boundaries needed to secure family cohesion.

Because the particular transitions and accomplishments that are reinforced through ritual are culturally determined, society exerts much control over the collective understanding of what constitutes a family and of how family life is supposed to proceed.[21] Family ritual is far from apolitical. Our heterosexist society invites *heterosexual* families to participate in the series of celebrations and shows of public support that rituals offer. Lesbian families are deliberately excluded from society's definition of family and, hence, are barred from virtually every ritual designed to support and congratulate family life.[22]

In addition to identifying the members of families, rituals also mark important changes or progressions as family life proceeds.[23] They underscore the family's sense of itself as a vital, growing unit that moves through particular challenges and achieves a series of accomplishments. This image is in stark contrast to society's vision of lesbian families as static couples who do not progress through stages or reach significant milestones.

Finally, rituals highlight every family as being both unique and also like other families. The family's unique identity is underscored by members' participation in designing life cycle rituals themselves. Brides-to-be often devote an entire year to designing the unique aspects of their weddings, and they identify greatly with the individualized aspects of the final event. Simultaneously, the traditional aspects of transition rituals or holiday celebrations allow each family member to feel linked to a greater group, and to feel the connection and security that goes with this belonging. Clearly, lesbians' exclusion from these rituals carries a destructive message that neither the family's individuality nor their common membership are accepted.

Daily Rituals and Family Traditions

How, then, do lesbian families use ritual to strengthen their families? Fortunately, there are forms of family rituals that do not require the participation of anyone outside the family. In fact, many of these ritualized acts occur completely within the privacy of the couple's family life. *Daily rituals* and *family traditions* are terms used to describe such everyday acts that become filled with important and affirming symbolism, signifying to the couple not only that their family exists but that it is strong and vital.[24] Seen in this light, many of the everyday acts lesbian couples devise to strengthen their sense of being a family can be described as rituals.

Every family, of course, has rituals, often without noticing that what they are doing constitutes ritual at all. These daily or weekly habits communicate continuity and stability to a family.[25] What time the partners return home at night, how dinner is prepared, and how the couple spend their evenings can all serve as important rituals. The lesbian couple who takes a walk after dinner each night, or the partners who meet nightly in their daughter's room for "story time," are supporting their relationship and generating the validation for it that society continually withholds.

Imber-Black points out that "membership rituals" (those that identify the members of the family) occur in all families and are associated with parting and reentry, meals, socializing, and sexuality.[26] The Thursday night outings to the movies, or the Saturday morning ritual of going to the bank, symbolically underscore a couple's dependable patterns. As the couple establishes these ongoing habits they become family rituals, not simply because they are repeated but because they come to symbolize the recognizable life—the signature—of a particular couple.

Jan always got home first on Friday nights, so she was the one to order the pizza. Friday was the one night of the week the partners didn't need to discuss dinner arrangements: they knew what kind of pizza they would get, and Jan knew to set the table in the kitchen rather than the dining room. The partners looked forward to this favorite beginning to their weekends, and they counted on being alone on Friday nights to reconnect before beginning their other weekend plans.

Because these repeated behaviors occur behind the closed doors of the couple's home, this form of ritual has been more available to lesbian couples than the more social traditions associated with life cycle transitions and holidays. Performing these rituals does not require that the couple be publicly identified as a family. Therefore, even couples who need to remain somewhat hidden can reap the stabilizing influence these rituals have to offer. Couples who do not live together probably have a harder time establishing daily patterns, but they may be able to create some similarly symbolic rituals of their own.

Establishing ritualized ways of conducting their home life adds significant validation to lesbians' couple relationships. These patterns provide a structure that reassures the couple of boundaries around their relationship. Each time they spend an evening in a "traditional" way they have personally created, their signature goes onto their family life one more time. Daily rituals connect couples to their relationship's past and present, and they make it possible for the partners to envision their future. Each act of daily ritual rebuts the social claim that they are simply "roommates" with no joint family life at all.[27]

Lesbian couples can also use family traditions to strengthen their relationships. These traditions involve how the family chooses to celebrate birthdays or anniversaries, spend vacations, and engage in other selected events integral to a particular family's life.

Every year we devote one summer weekend to a family camping trip. The kids come with us, and we go to the same campground every time. We rent a canoe one of the days and go on a long ride, and we always tell stories around the fire at night. We don't always know what else a particular summer will bring, but we all count on that one weekend away.

Lesbian couples often expand family traditions, marking more events than heterosexual families might select. Often there are several anniversaries lesbian couples observe: the beginning of their being a couple, the day they moved in together, the day they bought rings for each other, and other highlighted moments. They may ask each other, "Guess what we were doing last year at this time?" and take particular pleasure in marking their continuance as a couple since certain significant events occurred. Knowing that "We've done this X number of times now" or "We always spend this day in this way" provides powerful reassurance and relational security for many lesbian couples.[28] These conversations allow the partners to become the subjects of a developing family story with a past, present, and an implied future. In this way, the family members serve as affirming witnesses to their unfolding life together.[29]

Membership rituals become complex when families have been reconstituted. Instead of simply delineating a single family unit as separate from the outside world, there are sometimes several family groupings with overlapping functions and shared membership. For example, because lesbians often come to consider their ex-lovers as extended family members, family membership rituals will sometimes include previous partners. Also, if separated lesbian couples jointly parent children, the ex-partner may be included in some family rituals and excluded from others. Likewise, the new family of creation may face complex choices about when to make the new couple the central membership group, and when the co-mothers of the children constitute the most relevant family grouping.

"Jonathan said he wants to go out with his parents and his sister for his birthday," Megan told Rachel lightly. "That's perfectly understandable," Rachel heard herself say, somehow silenced by the legitimacy of the boy's desire to gather together his now-separated mothers and family. She felt torn, understanding Megan's desire to maintain her connection to Jane as the children's other mother, and knowing that this first year in her own relationship with Megan was still a tentative and transitional time. Yet as the kids celebrated their birthdays for the first time since their mothers' breakup, Rachel struggled with her status as outsider—Megan's lover but not the children's parent, the newly forming unit confronting the permanence of the one that came before.

Unlike other kinds of rituals, daily rituals and family traditions are intended not to mark a change but rather to demonstrate the continuity of a couple's relationship over time. Lesbians frequently view a ritual's repetition as a symbol of their relationship's success and strength. They learn to supply themselves with the boundaries and validation that are not provided by outsiders.

> *The couple always rented the exact same condo on the beach for vacation. Every year they brought the same activities with them: Jaime's poetry journal, Denise's knitting project, and the couple's favorite recipes. They loved that they could picture the whole vacation in advance and know that no matter what had changed since they were there last year, they could keep their vacation the same and feel how uniquely it reflected who they are.*

Family Life Cycle Transition Rituals

Lesbian families are claiming their right to ritualize the major transitions in their family lives. With and without the approval of their heterosexual peers, lesbians are celebrating their families' milestones and are inviting others to take part in the ceremonies.

Unlike daily rituals and family traditions, family life cycle transition rituals are about change. They are ceremonies that mark important passages from one life cycle stage to the next, and they ease the normal stress that accompanies these transitions. These rituals acknowledge the impact of a transition on various levels, including changes within each individual partner, within the family of creation, in the couple's relationship to their families of origin, and in the relationship between the family and the community at large.[30] Public rituals are well recognized for their power to support families.

> Even at times when the family feels unformed or fragmented, the power of ritual is so strong that it can, for better or worse, substitute external validation for internal cohesion. . . . Ritual, and the knowledge of which ritual comes next on the horizon, generates momentum that moves a family through life.[31]

Likewise, when crucial life experiences are not adequately celebrated, people are left feeling disappointed and somehow incomplete.[32]

When all members of one's own group are collectively barred from these important rituals, the negative effects are compounded.

As more lesbian families are coming out, fewer are content to tolerate being excluded from every supportive ritual society provides to heterosexual families. Lesbians instead are taking the lead and designing rituals on behalf of their own families.

The couple spent months designing their commitment ceremony. They labored over every detail, from what they would wear to whom they would invite to the ritual. From their selection of rings to their writing of their vows, the couple completely invested themselves in creating the perfect expression of who they were as a couple. They borrowed from traditional weddings and they designed brand-new symbols, weaving together their desires for their ceremony to be both like and unlike the weddings of heterosexual couples. The result was purely their own, and they were filled with pride as they took their places at the homemade altar.

In marking the major achievements and transitions in their family life, lesbians are contradicting society's primary charge: that lesbians cannot create family units, and that their relationships neither progress nor develop over time.[33] Commitment ceremonies that announce the creation of a new lesbian family, as well as rituals celebrating the birth of children into these families, spotlight the creation and progression of lesbian family life.

Similarly, the increasingly popular ritualizing of key anniversaries (such as a couple's ten-year anniversary) mark not the creation of a lesbian family but its progression over time. In addition to infusing the celebrating couple with well-earned congratulations, these rituals offer the guests a supportive message that lesbian relationships can endure and thrive. In this way, the new lesbian family life cycle transition rituals support not just the family conducting the ceremony, but all lesbian couples.

Unlike daily rituals and family traditions, these rituals typically include witnesses who represent the couple's surrounding community and open the couple to social response to their event. While they therefore run the risks of rejection or disapproval, these lesbian couples are convinced that the benefits justify the dangers. Even lesbian couples who cannot risk the exposure of having their transitions witnessed are having private ceremonies. Creating life cycle transition rituals without witnesses may be another lesbian adaptation of existing social norms, in this case allowing closeted families to share the benefits these rituals have to offer. Couples who can risk social exposure, meanwhile, are creating powerful ceremonies that bring together sometimes very diverse segments of the partners' parallel systems.

> *Never had I been to such a moving ceremony. The partners looked beautiful as they faced each other to exchange their vows. Both partners' families attended, as did their coworkers, heterosexual and lesbian friends, former lovers, and childhood buddies. Unable to contain my emotion any longer, I cried when the couple asked us all to sign their scroll, each signature a promise to sustain them in their new commitment. How often do lesbians see their friends, mothers, fathers, and bosses sign up to nourish a lesbian family?*

Research chronicling lesbian commitment ceremonies shows tremendous creativity and diversity in the ceremonies designed by particular couples.[34] In an unintended twist, lesbians may benefit from being excluded from existing rituals, in that this encourages a level of creativity not required of (or encouraged in) heterosexual couples. As Butler notes, "The creation of women's rituals has come to be seen as a way of affirming our own identity, a way of creating our own symbols and traditions."[35] Sullivan adds that "lesbian commitment ceremonies are not imbued with the same sense of inevitability that often is felt at heterosexual weddings. Not one person at my friend's [lesbian] wedding was overheard saying 'I knew they would get married someday.'"[36]

Lesbian family life cycle transitions claim our right both to use existing, culturally important symbols and to deviate from heterosexual traditions and form ceremonies of our own making. Butler's study found some lesbian couples borrowing heavily from heterosexual weddings in their commitment ceremonies.[37] For them, the political act of "marrying" despite social prohibitions was the element of the ritual they most desired. Other ceremonies bore little resemblance to heterosexual weddings, with the couple deliberately rejecting the traditional, socially prescribed ritual. In both cases, the resulting ritual could not help but be individually designed, with great care taken to craft a ritual that expressed the precise identity of the partners being joined.

Because lesbian family life does not precisely mirror heterosexual family life, lesbians may need to design rituals to mark moments not experienced by heterosexual families. For example, because the process of coming out is especially difficult and unmarked, lesbians may want to celebrate this important, lesbian-specific journey. The following account of an actual event is offered in the spirit of stimulating our collective imaginations.

All were requested to dress formally. The occasion was the first annual "coming out" ball for women in the community who had come out for the first time during the past year. Each "debutante" was announced by the master of ceremonies; as her talents and hobbies were read aloud, she was escorted down the stairs in evening gown and long white gloves. Lesbian escorts, complete with tuxedos, accompanied each ingenue to the applause and hysterics of her friends waiting below. Whatever else awaited these women for their decision to come out, this was a moment of celebration and welcome. The laughter notwithstanding, everyone felt the power of this event.

Celebration/Holiday Rituals

For fortunate lesbian couples, holidays such as Thanksgiving, Passover, Christmas, and Easter are times to be together with friends and extended family, as well with each other. These partners can absorb the validation inherent in families coming together, with everyone welcome and included as a family member.

"Jema!" Marny yelled downstairs. "My mother's on the phone, and she wants us to come to their house for Thanksgiving. She's invited my sisters and their families, too, and we're all going to go to New York and see the parade." "That sounds good," Jema yelled back. "Tell her hello and send her my love."

Major holidays have the potential to highlight many families' feeling of inclusion in a larger social group. The Jewish holidays, for example, are made more special by each family knowing that Jews everywhere are commemorating the holiday at the same time and in the same way. Each Jewish family feels like they are not only their own complete unit performing its own ritual, but also part of a larger group that recognizes and welcomes each family.

Many national and religious holidays are very public events, from the lighting of the Christmas tree at Rockefeller Center in New York City to the public consensus to celebrate Thanksgiving with a turkey dinner. While the rituals themselves may actually take place within private households, these holidays are not simply private moments, but linking experiences that accentuate the family's membership in the larger culture.

For many lesbian families, though, these holidays are a considerably different experience. These families are often painfully reminded of their social exclusion during such times of celebration. For couples who cannot come out, the major holidays can be wrenching times filled with separation, not togetherness. These families must find ways to both mark an event and remain an unmarked family. Since family celebration rituals bring attention to the existence of the family unit, this is no small task.

As in so many other areas of their lives, lesbian couples have found useful and creative responses to this challenge. For example, many partners have learned to redesign holidays, turning what are supposed to be social celebrations into especially private rituals instead. They may celebrate a particular holiday on a day when only the family is aware that a ritual is taking place.

> *"When are you and Anne celebrating your Christmas?" asked Roberta. "Probably on the twenty-third," Jennifer replied, "since she is leaving the next day to go to her parents' house." "Do you ever think you'll get to be together on Christmas day?" pressed Roberta gently. "I hope so. Anne just doesn't dare come out to them. She feels sure they would disown her. They already challenge her about spending so much time with me; Spending Christmas day here with me would really make them suspicious."*

Holidays cause many lesbians to consider coming out to their families of origin, since the tug-of-war between the needs of their couple relationship and the expectations of the families is accentuated at these times. Simply telling the partners' families of origin of their relationship, however, does not necessarily reduce the tension between the family groupings. These choices, awkward at any time of year, bring attention to the difficult circumstances of many lesbian couples' lives and demonstrate the strength and creativity behind the adaptation many have made to the stresses of social holidays.

To help offset the often negative impact of social holidays, lesbian couples may design special celebrations of idiosyncratic family holidays. Couples may elaborately commemorate their anniversary and the partners' birthdays, since the surrounding culture is not collectively aware of these milestones and does not make special demands on the couple on those occasions. Many lesbian families have learned that choosing socially unmarked days for their family celebration rituals helps them tolerate the stress of having to spend special days in painful and invalidating ways.

For heterosexual families, special times often can be celebrated publicly. Many lesbian families, however, have learned to make these special (or holiday) times private instead. As in many areas of their lives, lesbian couples' homes become pivotal in their efforts to protect themselves from social stress.

As a group, the lesbian and gay communities are also beginning to ritualize moments of their own choosing. For example, in the 1980s, a major lesbian-owned record company celebrated its tenth anniversary with a concert at Carnegie Hall. Formally dressed lesbians filled the nearby Manhattan sidewalks and cafés, as each woman took part in a ritual powerfully relevant to her own life, if ignored by the surrounding culture.

The scene inside the restaurant was amazing. Incredibly dressed-up women almost literally filled the place. The bathroom was bursting with the elevated voices of women telling each other where they were from and sharing their excitement about tonight's anniversary celebration. Finally, the waiter approached us with a question: "Is something special going on tonight? I've never seen so many women dressed like this and seeming so excited." In his life this was a typical, unmarked Friday night—nothing special or worthy of comment. To the growing crowds of lesbian women making their way to Carnegie Hall, however, this was a special milestone night that was all our own.

Some rituals aim not only to celebrate a moment, but also to express a group's beliefs and to strengthen the sense of group membership based on this shared worldview. Now that there have been several national marches in which lesbians have come together with gay men and supporters to voice shared beliefs and to celebrate gay lifestyles, these civil rights marches are taking on the function of repeated social and political rituals. The 1993 march found many participants speaking of the previous national demonstration in 1987, with people wanting to link the two events and share stories of their experiences at each one. The fact that these marches are specifically about lesbian and gay identity—and pride—multiplies their power and makes them the next in a series of affirming, supportive responses to lesbians' exclusion from mainstream social ritual.

In conclusion, ritual has a great deal to offer lesbian families. While the creation of public rituals that explicitly affirm lesbian family identities is a relatively new social phenomenon, lesbians have been using private, daily rituals behind closed doors for a long time. As is true in so many aspects of their lives, these women have turned what could be simply a source of stress and invalidation to their own advantage. While lesbians' exclusion from social rituals continues to assault them, their success in using this same tool on their own behalf demonstrates their resilience and relational capacity. As more lesbian couples choose to come out, their adaptations of social rituals will increase, affirming their family life cycles and generating ever more effective rebuttals to social homophobia.

Lesbian Communities

No matter how well a lesbian couple validates and builds sustainable boundaries around their union, no couple can fully nourish a relationship all by themselves. The advent of lesbian communities offers couples unprecedented access to the social supports long absent in the mainstream community.

In the past, lesbian couples' primary choices were to come out to an overwhelmingly hostile mainstream culture or suffer the consequences of forced secrecy and invisibility. While supportive personal friendships can greatly enrich lesbian couples' lives, they cannot undo the effects of the overall societal reaction directed at such couples. Lesbian communities, however, provide an alternative to these drastic and stressful trade-offs. Participation can offer couples a partially public identity and some of the benefits of being part of a supportive larger group without the dangers associated with revealing their lesbian identity to the mainstream community.[38]

Most importantly, involvement in a lesbian community offers couples information about what is normal and typical for lesbians. Couples can help each other to identify stresses that normally accompany particular family life cycle transitions. They can also help each other to identify persistent stressors caused by homophobia and to distinguish between such normative reactions to oppression and personal relational deficits.[39] Group wisdom can develop, and couples can learn from each other's experience without constantly having to start from scratch. Without this,

> the wheel . . . gets invented, invented again, and then reinvented as the solutions found by a couple in Seattle fail to find their way to a couple struggling in West Virginia or another pair in upper New York State. Because of their isolation, couples are forced to depend on idiosyncratic solutions to problems that are, in fact, universal.[40]

As couples discover that some of the primary difficulties within their relationships are caused by forces outside of themselves, their sense of themselves as competent and normal is restored. Without appropriate acknowledgement of the impact of homophobia, partners will frequently overpersonalize responsibility for their problems and further internalize the homophobic message that lesbian relationships cannot thrive.[41]

> *The two couples met at a get-to-know-you potluck at the local lesbian bookstore. Now that they had gone out socially together several times, they began to open up and share more vulnerable confidences about how their couple relationships were going. "I'll bet you two never fight," Tiwanda began tentatively. "Well, actually, we were fighting right before you came over tonight," admitted Rhona with a glance at Dana, her partner. There was sudden silence between the couples. "What do you two fight about the most?" Dana ventured. "Maybe it's the same as what happens between us." "I guess I'd say we fight about who we're going to tell about our relationship. Tiwanda never wants to tell a soul about us, but I can't always live like that," offered Malika. "Well, that's not really true," Tiwanda rebutted. "We wouldn't have gone to that potluck if that was true." Suddenly, not wanting to demonstrate their conflict, Tiwanda and Malika again got quiet. "We fight about that all the time," Dana responded. "You won't believe it, but that's what we were fighting about before you came."*

Contact with other lesbian couples can powerfully change how couples view their own relationships. When couples come together and exchange notes, their sense of isolation breaks down. They can each correct their images of their own partnerships and can experience a resulting boost to the partners' confidence in their relationship. In addition to sharing problem areas, lesbian couples can witness and congratulate each other at moments of important family life cycle transition or other important accomplishment. As these women often cannot rely on other sources of praise and affirmation, each participating couple is strengthened by their ability to receive this from their peers.

Many moments lend themselves to sharing this support, including when a couple receives word that one of the partners is pregnant, when they announce their decision to move in together, or when one partner finds the courage to come out to an important friend or family member. As lesbians find ways to come together, they can more easily create family life cycle and celebration rituals, enjoying the support and camaraderie social groupings have to offer.[44] Only other lesbians can offer couples a full sense of shared commonality with couples around them.[42] It is the unique and irreplaceable contribution of lesbian friendships.

The Evolution of Lesbian Communities

For longer than can be accurately documented, lesbians have been risking arrest, physical violence, and loss of jobs, family, and friends to meet each other. While dark and secluded bars—sometimes in unsafe neighborhoods—provided lesbians with their only public meeting place for many years, the need to break their social isolation and come together with others like themselves was strong enough for some lesbians to persevere. Del Martin and Phyllis Lyon charted groundbreaking territory for future lesbian communities when they founded the Daughters of Bilitis in 1955. This first exclusively lesbian organization moved a few daring women beyond barrooms and gave them their first taste of what social connections could offer their otherwise-isolated lives.

As the civil rights movement of the 1960s and the women's and gay rights movements of the 1970s challenged many of the oppressive conditions affecting their lives, many lesbians forged initial coalitions with gay men and heterosexual feminists. At the same time, lesbians seized the opportunity to develop an exclusive group identity, and they greatly expanded the sense of community started in those frequently raided bars on the outskirts of major cities.

The explosion of openly lesbian social events that began in the mid-1970s greatly expanded the ways in which lesbians came together. In a few particularly liberal geographic areas, the collective lesbian presence and range of activities grew sufficiently to earn the description of an actual lesbian community. The surge in group activity that characterized the 1970s and 1980s convinced many women that they had finally found their "home." Suddenly, there were openly lesbian performers writing songs about lesbian experiences for lesbian audiences. Lesbian-owned restaurants, bars, and stores opened in some areas. Lesbians were writing books, staging plays, and advocating women-oriented social services reflective of the burgeoning feminist consciousness of the time. Increasingly, they were daring to come together—individuals and couples alike—and define a shared group identity on a larger scale than ever before.

Some lesbians experimented with separatism, participating only in all-women events and working to create the possibility of living their lives exclusively in the presence of other women. "Lesbian music" proclaimed the intoxicating feeling that women together were coming home to a safe haven of lesbian support and collective identity.

In this atmosphere of understandable euphoria, many lesbians gave great license to their fantasies of profound commonality among all who shared their sexual identity. Many women envisioned that "the community" would provide them with numerous close personal friendships with other lesbians. Individuals and couples attributed great meaning to their being lesbians together and wove intricate hopes around this basic, ambiguous common trait.

"You'll never believe who the new clerk is at work," Michelle excitedly told Jane. "She's a dyke! Can you believe it? Finally, I'm not the only one! Let's have her over for dinner Friday so we can get to know her. I'll bet we'll really like her. I can't believe it—after five years, I'm working with a dyke at last!" Michelle didn't seem to notice that she knew virtually nothing about this woman. Instantly she felt a profound camaraderie and

assumed this would lead to immediate friendship. She felt so relieved to have another lesbian at work. Who could blame her for leaping in so fast, even if it was fraught with the possibility for disappointment?

Lesbians' assumptions of great sameness came in part from their history of deprivation and social ostracism. In truth, though, lesbians as a group share neither racial identity, religious affiliation, ethnicity, class background, chosen lifestyle, or intergenerational family membership. The formation of group identity is extremely complicated for any such group. Many lesbians made their task even more complex by assuming a common feminist identification, political affiliation, and shared worldview as part of their identity.

As the community-building process began to challenge these untenable wishes for sameness, many lesbians became angry and afraid. They pressured each other to minimize differences by toeing a party line and maintaining an impression of total group cohesion.[43] As Pearlman notes,

> feminism beyond the idyll of its sisterly beginnings, its idealizations and sense of oneness, began to prescribe a purity of analysis, philosophy, and behaviors. There was now a political right and a political wrong, a correct and an incorrect lesbian-feminist line.[44]

Each difference came to feel like a further unraveling of a critically needed connection. The pressure was very much like that which fusion exerts on couple relationships, pushing individuals toward avoiding and distrusting areas of difference and instead clinging to similarities to hold the connection together.[45]

Lesbians of color and those from oppressed communities of affiliation tended not to get so lost in these fantasies of oneness and did not typically share the idealized image of the lesbian community.[46] Weston describes the different experience of lesbians of color:

> Whites without a strong ethnic identification often described coming out as a transition from no community into community, whereas people of color were more likely to focus on conflicts between different identities instead of expressing a sense of relief and arrival.[47]

For these lesbians and others, the lesbian community was both a needed and a problematic affiliation. These women again felt pressure to fragment their identity into aspects the lesbian community would recognize and affirm, with other components of themselves remaining unvalidated. Greene's comments on the result for African-American lesbians apply to other lesbians of color as well:

> Because of their isolation from the mainstream, both black people and lesbians form distinct cultural communities of their own. Black lesbians, then exist within a subgroup of two subgroups, where elements of each group may be rejecting of the other group.[48]

For couples composed of women of color, the lesbian community more realistically represents both a support and a stress. Lesbian couples of color could most benefit from a community of affiliation that replenishes what the mainstream community constantly drains from them. Yet although the lesbian community may be the best source of support for lesbian identity even for women of color, the racism and resistance to diversity present in the mainstream culture also exists within the lesbian community. For these women, active participation in a lesbian community forces them to maintain a vigilance many other lesbians can more easily relax.

Lesbians have learned over the past few decades that no one community can fully compensate for their painful, homophobia-related losses or make fully safe a world still dedicated to oppressing lesbian women. Yet a community can provide special activities, institutions, and supports not available anywhere else. Lesbian communities have already provided an array of crucial services, including bookstores, concert producers and musicians, theater groups, record companies, writers, publishers and women's centers and hotline services.[49]

As for close personal friendships, the community offers lesbians opportunities to meet each other without guaranteeing that intimate one-to-one relationships will result. The earlier disillusionment over this painful distinction has, for many lesbians, now given way to a deepened maturity and acceptance that nothing in their lives will fully supply what the mainstream culture denies them. At the same time, community events have led to profoundly important friendships for some lesbians, keeping alive the hopes of many others for attaining a similar experience.

Participation in events produced within the lesbian community may vary depending on the partners' degree of internalized lesbian identity, as well as their stage in the lesbian family life cycle. Partners may not always require the reinforcement of their lesbian and family identity that seems more essential in the early years. Gradually partners may rely primarily on private, personal friendships, replacing more active group participation with an internalized awareness of the community's existence and support. Now more able to generate independently the affirmation all couples need, these partners' increased development allows them to develop more complex impressions of particular members and of the community's social mores. In the process many couples may draw back, investing themselves in developing their particular family life and in cultivating the informal friendship networks apart from larger group experience.

> *The two couples met for pizza and to begin designing their dream retirement home. They had been friends for many years, having met at a one-day workshop for lesbian couples in 1978. Now they were all in their mid-fifties, and they were serious about their desire to buy a duplex house and live together. They considered each other extended family members, and they knew how precious this friendship would continue to be as both couples reached their later years.*

While such well-established and private friendships can truly nourish couples who have shared years together, this privatization of social networks leaves younger and needier couples without obvious role models. Less dependent on the lesbian community for social connection, well-established couples may not be a readily visible presence at community events. As a result, the newer or less stable couples may primarily see couples who are in similarly early or tenuous stages of family life, which may reinforce the damaging notion that enduring lesbian couples are rare.

> *The therapist had worked with this couple for six months now, watching them try to solidify their relationship and searching everywhere for couples to guide their way. The partners attended virtually every event catering to lesbians within the community, inevitably returning home feeling disappointed not to find more couples to look up to. The therapist thought to herself about her own lesbian couple friends, and about how often their socializing now happened in each other's homes. Now raising children or building a home, the therapist and her friends lived family*

lives that rarely included unknown couples or partners just getting started: With time so limited, the friends reserved their energies for each other. The therapist's heart went out to the women sitting before her, as they struggled to find friendships like those the therapist now relied on.

Despite these personal and stage-related fluctuations in community involvement, lesbian communities also offer supports that couples continue to need. As a collective rebuttal to societal homophobia, these communities can work toward social and political gains relevant to all lesbians' lives. Lesbians' sense of personal safety is buoyed by the presence of an identifiable community of others, as is their sense of commonality with others in their immediate surroundings. The communities of today represent a clear improvement over the dangerous and limited contact available to lesbians in years past and promise to ease the experience of coming out for many lesbian partners in the future.[50]

Conclusion

Oppression causes fundamental harm, not only by robbing people of material and social equality but also by invading their most private visions of their own worth and identity. Lesbian couples, like many other groups, continue to suffer the consequences of societal oppression and struggle against its insidious, pervasive influence. Yet these couples have also responded with great creativity, finding resources within themselves and their relationships. Excluded from existing models for family life, lesbians have freed themselves to construct their own family paradigms, choosing their daily patterns, relational priorities, and very definitions of the word *family*.

Although value may be drawn at times from oppression, this does not justify society's homophobia. Like other oppressed groups, lesbian couples extract from their situation the positive potentials it contains without losing sight of the motivations of their oppressors. Out of this situation, lesbian couples have shaped self-defined family lives and emerged from the battle with more courage, greater resilience, and deepened commitment.

5

Lesbian Families with Children

NOT LONG AGO, MOST PEOPLE BELIEVED THAT THE CONCEPT OF LESbian motherhood was an oxymoron: One could be either a lesbian or a mother, but surely no one was both.[1] If a woman was attracted to other women, she faced enormous pressure to marry a man, have children, and repress her same-sex longings or express them in a highly secretive way. While mothers who were revealed to be lesbian faced almost certain loss of custody of their children, many lesbians avoided detection and were believed socially to be heterosexual wives and mothers. Ironically, then, the generations of lesbian women about which we know the least may well have been the most likely to be both lesbians and mothers.

At the same time, all females in this society—regardless of race, ethnicity, or religion—are socialized to revere the role of mother and are aggressively taught that the ultimate success a woman can achieve is to bear a child. This message is so strong that other pursuits by women are still often viewed as doomed attempts to compensate for the inner emptiness of not having a child. In addition to charges that childless women are responsible for ending the "family line" and depriving their parents of the chance to be grandparents come these threats as well:

> Women who never had children are considered empty, barren, selfish, peculiar. Until they reach their mid-thirties or so, others will tell them

they will change their minds; that it's just a stage; as soon as other aspects of their lives are established, they will want children. As the "biological clock" ticks, women without children are told they will be sorry, sorry, sorry.[2]

In direct contradiction, mainstream society declares that lesbians are inherently unfit mothers whose children must be rescued from their influence whenever their lesbian identity is discovered. Lesbian women are left, then, to believe simultaneously that as women they *must* mother, and as lesbians they must *not* mother. In this continuing social climate, lesbians' consideration of whether to become parents is necessarily distorted.

While earlier, more closeted generations of lesbians may have been especially likely to have children, lesbians coming of age in the 1970s may have been especially unlikely to become mothers. With the reemergence of the women's movement coinciding with the creation of an increasingly accessible lesbian culture, many lesbians exercised the newfound option of charting childless adult lives. Before donor insemination or more progressive adoption policies, many women in this time period equated coming out with not becoming a parent, a belief that moved the concerns of lesbian mothers further to the margins of the political agenda. Unwittingly, these young, politically active lesbians continued to adhere to the socially imposed dichotomy between being a lesbian and being a mother. Framing liberation as freedom from the earlier requirement that women become mothers, lesbians left unchallenged the accompanying social oppression of women who reintegrated their dual identities as lesbians and as mothers.

On the heels of these two earlier groups—lesbian women who entered motherhood through socially required heterosexual marriage, and those who extricated themselves from the social imperative that women mother at all—came a vastly different next generation of lesbian women. For the first time ever, lesbian women began to conceive children without having sexual intercourse. While donor insemination had existed before, women who were unmarried or known to be lesbians had typically been barred from using the procedure. Beginning in 1982 with the Sperm Bank of California, though, feminist health providers established insemination programs that did not disqualify women based on marital status or sexual orientation.[3] Likewise, lesbians have gained greater access to adoption, although typically they must present themselves as heterosexual women and settle for achieving so-called single-parent adoptions.

Lesbians may also have been galvanized by watching lesbian mothers lose custody of their children in epidemic proportions throughout the late 1970s. While until 1974 there were few publicized custody battles involving openly lesbian or gay parents, the second half of this decade saw many more examples of lesbian women fighting to retain their custody rights in divorce situations.[4] As the courts consistently refused to grant these women custody rights, an organized lesbian response to these rulings began to emerge, supporting lesbians' rights to their own children at exactly the time that technology made lesbian motherhood more possible.[5]

The impact of these advances on lesbian families is tremendous. For the first time, lesbians (individually and in couples) can build two-generational families in which the children are not products of previous heterosexual marriages. While losing custody remains an ever-present danger, lesbian couples now bring their new infant home from the hospital as their child's original parent figures—a possibility that would boggle the minds of many of their lesbian predecessors. This opportunity for lesbians to mother their own children openly is decidedly new, and constitutes a powerful step in the push for lesbian rights.

They had been in the delivery room for what seemed like days. Lena was close to delivering, and Joanne had never seen her lifemate look anything like this. She was so intent, so utterly absorbed, bravely continuing on despite the pain. Joanne heard the doctor say it would be just one more push—and before she could even process this information, the baby was being born before her eyes. As the couple's new daughter was laid on Lena's stomach, the doctor and nurses congratulated both women, clearing a space for the couple to enjoy their first moment with their baby. The partners held each other and their new little girl, soaking up the excitement in the room, feeling safe, supported, and forever changed.

Lesbians' newfound excitement about the advent of donor insemination, expanded (although still problematic) access to single-parent adoption, and the gradually increasing social awareness of healthy lesbian parenting is extremely healing. It is perhaps natural that for a while parenting will be the talk of the town, the new social trend, the latest new development in lesbian family life. Even this obvious step forward, however, presents lesbians with some serious challenges. As stigmatized women, lesbians may be particularly motivated to challenge society's disapproval, perhaps by succeeding at exactly the tasks they are charged with being unable to perform. With this newfound expansion of the option of parenting, having children must not become a symbolic act designed to prove lesbians' ability to conform to prescribed social dictates for women's lives, or to affirm their oft-challenged capacity to raise healthy children.

   Critics of lesbian parenting charge that lesbians' children will show confusion related to their gender identity, that they will fail to demonstrate "appropriate" sex role behavior, and that they will grow up to be gay themselves. In addition, popular myths erroneously suggest that gay people are more likely to sexually molest their own and others' children. Research efforts, though, have demonstrated the fallacy of each of these charges. Studies comparing children raised by lesbian and heterosexual mothers repeatedly find little or no distinction in the children's gender identity, sex role socialization, or personal sexual orientation. Overwhelmingly, the research indicates that lesbian parenting closely resembles the child-rearing practices of heterosexual families.[6]

Some lesbians, however, are concerned with the campaign to present lesbian parenting as identical to that of heterosexuals.[7] Particularly for those who consider themselves feminists (or womanists), the goal is *not* to conform fully with the stereotyped, misogynist models of gender-typed girls and boys, in which the lesbian parent vigorously steers her children towards heterosexuality and works to ensure that her lesbianism has no influence on her children. These parents must often choose between safeguarding their custody of their children and abandoning the very values they wish to offer them. Polikoff explains that

> a study comparing heterosexual and lesbian mothers concluded that the two groups have similar sex-role behavior and attitudes towards ideal child behavior. My immediate response as a lawyer was to be elated— one more piece of evidence to help convince a judge that our clients are not really "different" kinds of mothers at all.

But as a lesbian, a feminist, and a mother with a vision of an entirely different way of raising our children, I was horrified. I am not pleased to discover that my lesbian sisters pose no threat to the perpetuation of patriarchal child-rearing.[8]

Lesbians' challenge now is to embrace a spectrum of lesbian family forms, neither precluding nor mandating the inclusion of children. In order to support the full range of decisions made by lesbian families concerning children, I include a discussion on lesbian parenting here without locating it with the generalizable stages of lesbian family life (Part II of this book). Lesbian family life cycle models must separate relational junctures reached by most or all couples from those that only particular couples may include in their journeys. The inclusion of lesbian parenting in a model that aims for widespread applicability would contribute to the oppressive suggestion that all women must or should consider becoming parents. Lesbians must demand the basic right to parent their own children; at the same time, though, their right to not even consider parenting requires equal support.

The Circumstances of Lesbian Parents

The circumstances under which lesbians become parents vary considerably. From couples jointly deciding to give birth to or adopt children to those in which one or both partners already are parents prior to the beginning of the couple relationship, some aspects of life as lesbian parents are common in most families. Lesbian parents work to nourish and harbor their children, to establish desired rhythms of private intimacy between the partners, to sculpt relationships between the parents and the children, and to interact carefully with both the children's and the parents' social communities. In addition, the partners must at minimum devise a parenting role for the nonbiological or nonadoptive lesbian parent; in cases where the partners have children from previous lesbian partnerships, they must create three or even four distinct female parenting roles within a culture that offers lesbian parents no validation for these unique relationships.

Despite the particularities of a specific family's circumstances, several general categories of experience characterize lesbian family situations. For partners who first come together as a couple and later decide to raise children, the child is the new member being incorporated into an existing family unit. Partners who become first-time parents together are likely to more similarly share the changes, joys, and losses attendant to the child's arrival and to identify more easily with each other's reactions. Nonbiological or nonadoptive parents in these situations are not replacing a previous parenting relationship; their bond with the child does not come on the heels of the child having lost an original parent. The partners may be freer to enjoy moments of unprecedented intimate connection that bolster them during the also-likely times when the rigors of parenting temporarily pull them farther apart.

The family's challenges are different when one partner comes to the couple relationship already a parent. In these instances, the new partner—not the child—is the new family member. Although the parenting lesbian's role is already firmly established with the child, the new partner's role is especially vague. The parent works to make a space in the family for the new partner and to share areas of parenting she has previously handled either alone or with another partner. As the new partner finds her way into an already-formed family, she may initially feel especially dependent on the voluntary invitation of the family members, as she holds neither an official nor a relational parenting tie to the children. At the same time, she must also maintain her own identity as she takes her place in an established household she did not create.

The circumstances of parenting lesbian families frequently demonstrate particular complexity. For example, the partner who comes into the couple relationship with children may have had these children within a previous lesbian partnership. In such instances, frequently the parent's ex-partner also occupies the role of nonbiological or nonadoptive female parent in the children's lives. With no models, the new partner must distinguish her role not only from her partner's role as the children's biological or adoptive mother but from that of the children's other lesbian parent as well. In other situations, the partner bringing the children may herself be the nonbiological or nonadoptive parent from a previous lesbian relationship. In these situations, the couple is made up of two parenting women, neither of whom has a direct biological or legal tie to the children. An additional variation on this theme exists when *both* partners bring children to the new

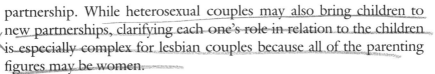

partnership. While heterosexual couples may also bring children to new partnerships, clarifying each one's role in relation to the children is especially complex for lesbian couples because all of the parenting figures may be women.

Regardless of the circumstances in which the family comes together, parenting both profoundly bonds and also further separates partners. The intimacy of shared parenting can at times rival any other possible bonding experience by cementing the partners' recognition that they are, in fact, a family. The ongoing and willing dependence their children demonstrate to both parents can reinforce the essential importance of the couple's enduring relationship and can deeply strengthen their intimacy and stability.

At the same time, parenting requires a large portion of each partner's emotional resources, and these demands frequently prevent the romantic, one-to-one interaction more readily available to couples without children. The partners must learn to sustain their intimacy with less time, less uninterrupted attention, and less energy available for their connection as lovers. These stresses are familiar to most parents; however, since lesbian partners often build their relationships on exactly these elements—much time alone together, reciprocal emotional nurturing, and an intense exclusivity within the couple relationship[9]—the latter couples may especially feel the impact of the relational changes that accompany parenting. Interviews with parenting lesbian couples illustrate these common feelings.

> The lesbians in the role of co-parent presented themselves as feeling isolated as their partners bonded with the child. They talked about feeling left out, not knowing what role to take, and feeling jealous of the closeness their partner had with their child. They wanted more frequent sex and affection and more time together as a couple . . . [and] they struggled with their needs for inclusion, time and attention. Both mother and co-parent were looking for ways to reconnect, to re-merge. Co-parents were on the outside trying to get in; biological mothers were somewhere in the middle with their child, searching for their partners.[10]

While no universal or simple solutions exist for these challenges, lesbian couples frequently work hard to reinforce the sense of family among themselves and their children, using family traditions, special family-only outings and events, and private family jokes and stories to cement all members' sense of family identity. At the same time, these partners often maintain particular awareness of the importance of also safeguarding their separate relationship, stealing time and private ways of underscoring their bond apart from their roles as parents.

The Second Lesbian Parent

In most cases, whichever lesbian partner does not give birth to the couple's child or does not serve as the supposedly single applicant for adoption has no legal parenting role at all. Without a name, role, or legal protection, these lesbian parents are especially exposed to the social vulnerability imposed on parenting lesbian families. The family knows clearly who the second lesbian parent is *not*—neither mother nor father—but must invent for themselves who she *is* or will be to the children.

Not even the partners themselves know what to call the second lesbian parent. Some couples encourage the child to use the partner's first name; others create a special nickname to be spoken only by the family of creation. Some families present the parents using twin terms for mother, such as "Mom" and "Mama," or "Mommy" and "Ma." Some wait for the child to choose, listening for a special name to emerge and reinforcing it when the situation arises.[11]

Often lesbian partners refer to the other lesbian parent in the family as the "nonbiological" or "nonadoptive" mother. While technically accurate, these descriptors define the second parent by who she is not, and therefore they do little to describe her unique relationship to the children.[12] The term *co-parent* offers some recognition of her parenting role, but does so by obscuring the lesbian partner's gender.[13] This term erroneously suggests that male and female, heterosexual and lesbian co-parents are virtually interchangeable; once again, it does not accurately define this woman's unique role within the immediate family. Lewin and other authors use the term *second mother* to describe this lesbian parent.[14] While this description may offer some important recognition of her primacy to the child, it also reduces the role of this other lesbian parent to seeming mimicry of the other, "primary" mother.[15]

When families must struggle simply to name one of the family's two parents, creating this second parent's actual role is bound to cause similar confusion. Parenting roles are socially constructed along gender lines, with expectable kinds of authority and nurturing behaviors for the two roles of mother and father. Lesbian partners must at least partially extricate themselves from powerful social prescriptions about the role of the female parent in order to envision a second, central parenting role for a woman. Because social conceptions of the role of a female parent are so circumscribed, each member of the family will confront their own internalization of these teachings as they maneuver to make room for a new and foreign approach to shared parenthood.

> As I thought about parenthood throughout those months, I felt I would always be between worlds. I wondered where I would fit in this child's life. As a woman, I could not play the role of father, nor did I want to. My child would have a mother. What would she need with me?[16]
>
> *agree* 3

In the eyes of most heterosexual people, the nonbiological or non-adoptive parent is simply not a parent at all. With no legal or biological claim to the children, her role is widely viewed as redundant, since the only parenting role recognized for women is "already taken" in the family.

> *Linda was home when her son, John, came running in the door, bleeding and screaming in pain. She took him immediately to the car and raced with him to the nearby health center. His fear was evident as they wheeled him in to the emergency room, with Linda right behind him. The nurse stopped her at the door and asked her if she was John's legal parent or guardian. As she admitted she was not, Linda frantically tried to get across to the nurse that she was in every way John's second parent. "I'm sorry," the nurse responded, "but we will have to contact his real mother to get her permission to go ahead. I understand you're very connected to this boy, but your signature will not enable us to treat him."*

The absence of a clear role for this parent extends to virtually every central arena of the family's life. Speaking of these lesbian parents, Crawford states:

> No matter how strong her presence and involvement in the family, it is she who bears the brunt of invisibility, it is she who is disenfranchised by the school, by both families of origin, by the outside world.[17]

The second female parent is routinely excluded, beginning early in her partner's pregnancy. Likewise, in cases of adoption, the couple often must actively hide her—literally—from the first contact with an adoption agency. In childbirth classes, the couple will usually be viewed as platonic friends, and doctors are far less likely to invite lesbian partners into obstetric visits than they are to include fathers. At the birth, the lesbian partner's participation may be restricted, since she is often not seen as immediate family.[18] In situations where the couple is not "out" to their families of origin, the nonbiological or nonadoptive parent also forgoes all family support, as the grandparents misperceive her as being a family friend.[19] Similarly, in the workplace, the second parent may be forced to conceal the huge new role she has entered into, if disclosing her lesbian identity would jeopardize her job. It is painful to silence natural impulses to share her new experience, though, and typical moments of sharing between coworkers require restraint and self-protection.

> When other parents display photographs of their new babies, this woman must keep quiet. She cannot trade stories about the birth or the baby's exploits, nor can she commiserate about sleepless nights.[20]

Despite the recent spate of inquiry into lesbian parenting, even supportive researchers reveal their confusion concerning the other lesbian parent in the family. Researchers frequently study lesbian mothers in comparison to other groups, and they typically select single heterosexual mothers as the appropriate group for comparison.[21] The prevailing thinking is that because both groups of mothers share an unmarried legal status, both groups are actually single parents.[22] One group of researchers admits:

> Our naivete in constructing this study led us to define single mothers as mothers who were unmarried. We discovered that half of the study children were living with lesbian mothers who were currently sharing households with lovers in committed relationships.[23]

Another otherwise supportive researcher used the terms *lesbian mother* and *lesbian single mother* interchangeably, as though all lesbian mothers are single.[24] More dramatically, Lewin's recent book on lesbian mothers devotes merely a few pages to any discussion of these mothers' partners, rarely acknowledging that they may be parenting the couple's children. Invalidating these parenting relationships further, Lewin combines her remarks about the mother's partner with other friendships the mother may have, specifically stating that it is "difficult to disengage a discussion of mothers' ties to lovers from the broader context of friendship." Meanwhile, she devotes an entire chapter to fathers, whom she repeatedly recognizes as the children's parents.[25]

Whatever term is used to describe them, lesbian co-parents dramatically illustrate the outlaw status of all lesbian families. Without title, social status, basic safeguards of their relationship to their children, or specified parenting roles, these parents clear particularly uncut paths, highlighting both the stresses and calls to creativity common to all parenting lesbian families.

Regardless of how the couple addresses this ongoing stress, the second parent's precarious status creates a power imbalance between the partners that influences their relationship, whether subtly or directly. In times of struggle between the partners, the second parent's position in the family can feel especially tenuous, dramatizing the different positions of each parent vis-à-vis their children.

The couple fought in the session, demonstrating the problem that had brought them to therapy. They complained of never reaching closure when they fought, which left each feeling that disputes hovered over them and never actually got resolved. During the fight in the session, Bette suddenly became quiet, no longer working to make Karen see her point. The therapist stopped Karen and asked her if she had noticed Bette's withdrawal. Karen said yes; she was aware that Bette prematurely ended arguments, and she added that the pattern had become worse in the last few years.

While initially resistant to discuss this topic, Bette finally admitted what silenced her: Karen's habit of saying during a fight that perhaps they should just break up. Crying now, Bette angrily asked Karen if she had any idea how this felt. "You would only lose me," Bette sobbed. "I would lose you and both of my own kids, too. What fight is worth being threatened with that?" This moment in the therapy highlighted the unequal power each partner felt in relation to her role as a parent.

After many discussions, the partners decided to have Bette adopt the couple's children, as they lived in a state that had granted similar adop-

tions to lesbians in the past. Equalizing the power between them as much as possible, the couple reported back a year later that the adoption had freed them up within their relationship and had left both parents and children feeling more firmly rooted within the family grouping.

Adoptions relevant to lesbian (and gay) families allow the second parent to achieve a legal tie to the children without the other parent needing to relinquish any of her own rights to the children. With precedent in at least eleven jurisdictions, these adoptions are presently a rare but growing option for lesbian families.[26] In years to come, they may significantly improve parenting lesbian families' capacities to form more equal, stabilizing family units.

The Role of Fathers

Many, if not most, lesbian mothers gave birth within the context of an ongoing heterosexual relationship with the children's father. While this fact should simply describe the personal relationships between children and former partners, homophobia embellishes the father's power and threat to the lesbian family, as he symbolizes the heterosexual alternative to the couple's children being raised by their lesbian mother. When a custody request comes from the child's own father, judges can rationalize their moral qualms associated with separating children from their mothers. After all, the fathers are the children's parents, too—and usually heterosexual parents, at that. These fathers offer themselves as the "healthy" alternative to having children raised by homosexuals, and they are frequently entrusted to socialize these "impressionable" children appropriately by providing a model of "normal" heterosexual development.

Because the courts have routinely asserted the right to condemn lesbian families per se, with no needed evidence of substandard parenting at all, heterosexual biological fathers enjoy a powerful advantage in court.[27] Since even primarily absent biological fathers therefore represent an enduring danger to lesbian families, many such families' sense of security rests on their hope that the father will not want custody and therefore will not initiate court action. Concerned lesbian parents take a risk in welcoming the father's unlimited involvement with the children, as his increased presence could further endanger the family.

As a result, the father can become an overblown internalized presence within the family of creation, even when his actual contact with the children is quite limited. Along with the court system itself, he hovers as the figure with the power to disrupt or even dissolve the lesbian family, and hence he must be appeased and treated very carefully.[28] His power frequently distorts the family of creation's relationship with him and creates an exaggerated dependence on keeping things amiable between the ex-partners.

This necessary appeasement can infringe on a lesbian mother's freedom to assert her basic rights, including collection of child support payments owed by the father. Legal experts repeatedly advise lesbian parents to stay out of court, since the odds of judges ruling in their favor are so low.[29] These parents cannot afford to bring the court system's attention to their families, nor can they risk provoking the delinquent father into retaliation. Instead, many lesbian mothers assume complete financial responsibility for their children and live with reduced economic security rather than risk attempting to hold the father to his obligations.

Some researchers have observed that while lesbian parents are always up against terrible odds in custody disputes, their chances of keeping their children are reduced still further if they express any pride or positive valuing of their lesbian identity, especially when this includes publicly acknowledging their lesbianism.[30] Judges are not required to protect mothers' rights in these cases, but rather are empowered to determine "the best interests of the children." Judges therefore hold much discretionary authority, and they frequently target openly lesbian parents as particular threats to their own children.[31] Accountable to no general standards for awarding custody in these cases, judges have been largely free to decide that the children would benefit from being moved to the home of heterosexual relatives or guardians. In the name of protecting children from their own mothers, the courts have enjoyed tremendous freedom to act out society's homophobia, creating needlessly ruptured families and punishing these mothers for the ultimate transgression of failing to live as heterosexuals.

Even in the minority of cases in which lesbian parents retain custody of their children following a custody action, the court may reserve the right to reconsider its ruling in the event that circumstances within the lesbian parent's household changes in the future. Effectively keeping these lesbian parents under the court's thumb even following a victory, these "change of circumstances" clauses have often included an order that the parent cannot share a home or even overnight visits with a lover without risking having her custody overturned.[32]

While some lesbian parents maintain successful relationships with their children's fathers, the bonds are necessarily influenced by the ongoing risks to the lesbian family. These fathers are frequently entrusted with tremendous power in exchange for carrying out society's homophobic resistance to lesbian families. Embodying but one of the dangers confronting lesbian parents, the family's relationships with the children's father(s) dramatize lesbians' endless need to monitor outsiders' reactions to the family unit. Returning repeatedly to choices about their private and public identities, these families face concrete and frightening possibilities. The motivation to protect the family often clashes with the desire to foster the children's full participation within their chosen social circles.

Public Versus Private Identities

While all lesbian families grapple with continual trade-offs inherent in choosing secrecy or acknowledging their lesbian family status, lesbian parents must consider additional complexities. These challenges surface repeatedly as parents decide what their child's last name will be, whether to present both partners as parents when registering the child for school, how to introduce themselves to the child's friends and their families, and whether to apply for family benefits such as health care, among many other choices.

Joan immediately took the call when her receptionist told her Janice's teacher was on the line. "I wanted you to know that Janice has been behaving decidedly out of character this week," the teacher began. "On Monday, I told the children we were going to make time lines in class. I asked them to bring in baby pictures of themselves and pictures of the rest of their families. The children were to select a couple of events that have influenced them and draw or describe them in their collages. Janice is always such a good kid, but for three days now she has come to class unprepared to make her time line. Do you know what could explain her resistance?"

Of course Joan knew what the problem was. Janice didn't feel free to complete the assignment and apparently didn't want to discuss it with her lesbian parents, either. After dinner that night, Joan and Sarah talked to Janice about the teacher's phone call. With encouragement, Janice voiced her concerns that some of the other kids wouldn't like her if she let them all know her parents were lesbians. Further, she was afraid Joan and Sarah would be mad at her if she told the whole class. She pointed to an incident that had occurred the previous winter in which the parents had decided to avoid coming out to a group of other adults because of job-related risks for Joan. Janice had interpreted this incident to mean that sometimes her parents wanted to keep their relationship a secret.

Slogging through the difficulty of explaining such complex realities to a ten-year-old, the parents told Janice that in certain circumstances the family would need to protect themselves from people's negative judgments. As a rule, however, Janice was free to tell her friends about the family. While this made the partners nervous, they chose the increased risk of this open stance over enlisting Janice to keep the family closeted. They told her that if there were situations in which she didn't want to tell people, they would like her to talk to them about it. Emphasizing that they could understand her not being ready to let everyone know, they stressed how much the three of them could support each other if they could talk things over as they came up.

Potential custody challenges, whether instigated by the children's biological father or by other relatives or acquaintances, pose the most serious threat to the family of creation. Do lesbian parents encourage their children to speak freely about their family life and hope there are no severe repercussions, or do they protect their children against these reprisals by asking them to keep a dangerous, burdensome secret? This responsibility can shift parents' previous decisions about how to represent their family, bringing some previously more closeted people into a fuller public identity and, by contrast, leading some previously "out" partners to decide to return to a more hidden social position and tolerate the accompanying stress this reversal exerts on both partners.[33]

While the need to protect children may increase the pressure on lesbian parents to be secretive, the increasingly social nature of their children's lives presents them with constant challenges to this position. Because they are frequently called on to identify the members of the family, preserving the family's privacy may require the partners to misrepresent themselves as a single-parent heterosexual family. The second lesbian parent is presented simply as a roommate or family friend with no familial tie to the mother or to the children.[34] Colluding in the family's invisibility in exchange for sometimes necessary protection, the parents must explain these misrepresentations to the children and often must engage them actively in maintaining the family secret. The resulting burden on the children often includes confusing messages about pride and lying and leaves them insecure about the family's basic safety.

Parenting partners are also confronted with the children's own preferences about decisions to affirm or hide the family's lesbian identity. The children's ages particularly influence their perspective on the family's predicament. Older children who are more aware of the family's difference may want the parents to remain primarily closeted, as they do not yet feel ready to "come out" themselves as the children of lesbian parents. Given a choice, many older children (particularly adolescents) wish to present themselves as just like the other kids, choosing to manage the stress of the family secret in exchange for being able to control personal disclosures outside the home.

Younger children, in contrast, tend to be far less aware of social critique and easily disclose virtually anything anyone asks them about their lives. They may readily name their second parent and remain unaware of the ramifications of this seemingly simple disclosure. Too young to understand, these children may construe the parents' anxiety about their random disclosures as an indication of shame, not a desire to shield the family. Situations calling for the family to welcome contact with the surrounding community especially highlight these families' difficult positions.

In addition to protecting their children, lesbian parents must also articulate a clear and affirming family identity to their children. With no clear consensus on what lesbian families' areas of uniqueness and specialness are, the parents must demonstrate their pride in the family to their children. Difficult for any family that mainstream society devalues, lesbian (and gay) families' task is compounded by the fact that not all members of the family are lesbians. While family members within nondominant racial, religious, and ethnic groups all share their minority identity, lesbian parents cannot assume their children will grow up to be gay. In that sense, these are not "lesbian families" at all, but rather families with lesbian parents. The child's likely identification with heterosexual peers complicates naming the family's shared group identity and potentially threatens the family members' experience of belonging.

Acknowledging the parents' lesbian relationship can assist parents in affirming the family's identity to the children. The family can enjoy considerable relief as they experience more consistent public and private identities, and the children are released from the task of precociously helping to secure the family's safety. While coming out does invite more direct social response—some of which will still present the children with society's homophobia—children may also be strengthened by embracing their social nonconformity. "Out" lesbian parents have the opportunity to model independence and pride to their children, and to foster the children's own courage to establish and maintain an identity apart from social approval. In addition, because identifiable lesbian families are easier for other lesbian families to approach, the family is therefore more likely to be invited into lesbian social circles. The children may benefit particularly from such social connections and from the resulting access to other kids being raised by lesbian parents.

Lesbian families' dual tasks of providing both protection and affirmation to their children illustrate the interdependence of their relationships within the family and in the social community. Their presentation of themselves within the privacy of their home will influence their children's preparedness for joining the outside world. Likewise, a particular family's social circumstances and experience will influence how family life proceeds at home.

Parenting Lesbian Families and the Mainstream Community

The mainstream community presents parenting lesbian families with many contradictions. Becoming parents can make contact with the wider social world especially appealing just as the parents realize new dangers of increased assimilation. Similarly, as the family discovers new commonalities with parenting heterosexual families, the distinctions between lesbian and heterosexual families have never been more clear. As the children pull the family into greater visibility through their interaction with the mainstream community, the reasons to conceal the family's lesbian identity are never more compelling. Finally, as the children seek conformity with their friends with heterosexual parents, the parents face new challenges to teach their children about the uniqueness of their family's identity. These incongruent realities—that the family feels more proximity, commonality, call to visibility, and pressure for conformity with the mainstream community just as it also experiences greater need for protection, distinction, and seclusion from mainstream social contact—are ongoing components of life for lesbian families with children.

The experience of raising children is a great equalizer, giving the lesbian parents much in common with heterosexual families with similarly aged children. Their lives look strikingly like those of the other mothers they see arriving at the pediatrician's office, attending parents' night at school, ushering their children into Sunday school class, or taking their seat at the school play. The social institutions set up for families with children suddenly hold great relevance to the parenting lesbian family, and their needs and interests frequently dovetail with those of their parenting heterosexual friends.

Parenting lesbian families see their family lives progress in closer accordance with the heterosexual family life cycle models. Since depictions of heterosexual family life typically follow the development of the children presumed to be present in the family, these lesbian families may recognize themselves in the social images of so-called normal family life and may warm to the implied social inclusion of this resemblance. The predictable periods in child development allow these lesbian families to know that the trials and challenges going on in their home frequently resemble those in the lives of their parenting heterosexual peers, providing a basis for substantive connection and mutual concern. After much experience with feeling profoundly different from heterosexual people, parenting lesbians may experience their own surge of interest in deepening these connections, furthering the family's overall gravitation toward the social spheres of the mainstream community.

The parents stood huddled along the sidelines of the soccer field, wishing either the rain or the seventh-grade soccer game would end. In between cheering the girls on, the parents got to talking. "Tina is going through a stage that just might kill me," Anne commented. "Her moods change faster than I can believe, and I spend most of our time together wondering what I did to make her so mad at me." "Oh, it's not you," Randy assured her. "It's exactly the same in our house. She's my last one to hit this age, and by now I've learned not to take it personally. They're all like that. My husband and I call it 'the stage from hell.'" "That's such a relief to hear," Anne responded. "Sometimes Debra and I fantasize after she's gone to bed that we'll wake up to a note from her saying she's gone off to boarding school and will see us in a few years." The parents laughed together, sharing the moment as they rolled their eyes in mock frustration at their daughters' arrival at puberty.

As the partners absorb this newfound similarity to their heterosexual peers, the children encourage the family's identification with the mainstream culture. The entire family is drawn to the partially accurate impression that the family truly belongs within their immediate social environment.

Children bring rewards that no other experience can provide. The special intimacy that comes from the profound interdependence of parents and children is as special for lesbians as for other parents. The irreplaceable connection between parenting partners, as they shape and nurture their child's development, is a unique and powerful reward known by the vast majority of parents, despite other areas of diversity.

Yet essential differences remain. Heterosexual families will never be dependent on lesbian families for their sense of social belonging or acceptance. Lesbian families, however, often look to their friendships with heterosexuals to help affirm their continually challenged sense of family integrity, giving these friendships additional symbolic impor-

tance.[35] This asymmetry is compounded when the lesbian couple is primarily secretive about their relationship outside of these chosen friendships. The heterosexual family's openness about their sexual identity in no way increases their vulnerability and is not a particular act of trust between the couples. For the lesbians, however, the simple act of identifying themselves as a lesbian couple unbalances the friendship immediately, leaving them in a permanently more vulnerable position.

In addition, heterosexual family life does not challenge the existing power structures in this society. Lesbian parents propose that family life even family life with children can be complete without a father in the family of creation.[36] This profound threat to patriarchy does not go unnoticed. Lesbian parents experience continual dangers as various organizations and individuals work to oppose social acceptance of intentionally all-female families.

Lesbian parents must also face the ongoing concern that people will ostracize or harass their children to protest the parents' lesbian identity. Every parent's nightmare is that they will be unable to protect their children, and society's homophobia leaves lesbian parents preoccupied with this worry. While no easy solution to this terrible problem exists, Benkov offers a description of many lesbian parents' attempts to protect their children:

> For many parents . . . the idea is to establish a strong foundation—one in which kids develop high self-esteem, good family relationships, and an appreciation of diversity. From this base, parents can actively teach children about prejudice even before they encounter it as a problem in the world, rather than internalizing its destructive messages. Sobered by the thought of how much hatred their children may be exposed to over the years, gay and lesbian parents of young children are [often] hopeful about their capacity to cope when the time comes.[37]

Lesbian families of color are especially familiar with this ongoing strain, as they must protect their children from the double dangers of racism and homophobia. As Clausen reminds us, "Black children are still being shot down in the streets in this country. That's something Black lesbians have to discuss when we talk about parenting."[38]

Lesbian families' relationships to the mainstream community frequently remain contradictory. As children increase the family's involvement in their surrounding social community, the parents' responsibilities to monitor and at times limit these relationships grow correspondingly. While the children's friendships and community activities naturally change as they age, fortunate families can balance this expectable change with relatively unchanging supportive relationships with the partners' friends and families of origin. When positive, extended family ties can strengthen lesbian families and, at their best, can be a safe haven for the family as they make their way through the varied experiences presented by the mainstream community.

Relationships with the Partners' Families of Origin

Having a child, changes the relationship between the lesbian couple and their families of origin. Upon hearing of the couple's intentions to raise a child, members of the family of origin reexperience their reactions to their relative's lesbianism. Usually, family members discover their internalization of the social teaching that parenting is reserved solely for heterosexual families. Again the lesbian relative asks her family to embrace her nontraditional choices, challenging them to extend their recognition and support to now include the couple's roles as parents.

Beyond this common first reaction, however, families of origin's responses to the lesbian couple vary considerably. In some families, the arrival of a child serves as a lightning rod for homophobic feelings. These families do not move beyond their initial reactions, often increasing or solidifying their distance from the family of creation and refusing to develop family ties with the child. This moment in the family life cycle, which they had envisioned so differently, exacerbates their pain and disappointment at their family member's lesbian identity. Some families never progress beyond this point, with family relationships remaining hostile or disengaged.

Many families will question how fair it is to involve an "innocent" child in a family life that will be stressful and socially difficult. In these situations, the concern for the children serves as a container for the relatives' residual resistance to the women's lesbian identity itself.

John and Madeleine got up to see what the children were squabbling about. John's daughter had been playing with a toy first, and Madeleine's son had apparently tried to take it away. Madeleine returned the toy to her brother's daughter and explained to her son that he can't take what doesn't belong to him. Assured that the situation was resolved, the brother and sister rejoined the rest of the family in the living room.

Throughout the day, Madeleine could sense that John was mad at her. When she approached him about it, he eventually admitted that he couldn't let go of the incident between their children earlier, but he didn't know why. "It's something about the way you parent," he admitted. "I always end up mad at you at these family visits." Madeleine felt her own anger rising. She suspected it was the fact *that she parented more than the* way *she did it that angered John. He had never owned up to any objection to her lesbian relationship with Marty, and he had kept silent when they announced that Madeleine was pregnant. Still, something between them had changed, and it always came up around the children.*

Intrusive or Underinvolved Families of Origin

One way homophobic families of origin may express their opposition to the lesbian family of creation is by failing to respect basic family boundaries and private family matters. At worst, members of the partners' families can and have sued for custody of the children, claiming that the latter should be removed altogether from the partners' care due to their lesbian relationship. This most extreme form of intrusion influences some lesbian families' decisions about whether to come out to their families of origin, as protecting themselves and their children sometimes requires forming as impenetrable a boundary around themselves as possible.

In less extreme forms, lesbian parents may find their relatives showing a lack of respect for their authority as parents by attempting to influence decisions that heterosexual couples would be left to make for themselves. Likewise, the lesbian partners may have difficulty regulating the comings and goings of their relatives who may enter the family home at will, as though no intact family life existed within its walls.[39] In heterosexual families there is far less room for debate about whether a family unit exists, and there is social support and precedent for the family of creation's objections to any violation of their needed privacy and authority.

Other families respond by remaining underinvolved with the lesbian partners and their children. Rarely visiting or calling the family, or discouraging attempts by the partners and their children to establish close family ties, these relatives remain largely unavailable due to the homophobia they feel toward the lesbian family. Even when there is not a total cutoff within the family, such underinvolvement robs the lesbian family of needed support. For example, while new mothers typically enjoy the assistance and guidance of their mothers and sisters, lesbian parents may not be offered these increased connections, further stressing their family unit at an already overwhelming moment in the family life cycle.[40]

Perhaps the most formal extended family ties are between the grandparents and the grandchildren. Circumstances may greatly influence the extent of these relationships, as will the particular individuals involved. Unlike in heterosexual families, however, where grandparents are expected to maintain contact and some family connection with their grandchildren, there are no formal social expectations for grandparents of lesbians' children. The grandparents are unlikely to experience social censure if they choose to remain underinvolved, and the lesbian parents will have little recourse when their own parents refuse to participate in the family.

The teacher had had all the kids make holiday presents for their relatives in school. Jonah had followed the lead of some of the other children and made them for his grandparents as well. Rhona cringed as she envisioned the scene on Christmas Day. Her parents would make a brief stop at the house, and Jonah would proudly present them with his handpainted hat. They would have nothing for him in return and would barely say thank you. She would have to convince him to give the hat to someone else; she couldn't watch him be rejected by them even on Christmas Day.

When there are blood ties between the grandparents and the children, there may be less leeway for the grandparents to completely disown their bond with the children, although even this disconnection is within their range of options. For example, when the children are the result of a previous heterosexual marriage, the grandparents may have established relationships with their grandchildren that are independent of their feelings about their daughter's lesbian relationship. The

parents of lesbians who actually give birth to their children may similarly feel more direct ties and may therefore maintain a closer relationship with the lesbian family. By contrast, the parents of the nonbiological or nonadoptive parent may feel free to identify or not with the
role of grandparent, potentially withholding an important family connection from the lesbian family of creation. Because there are a variety
of circumstances under which lesbian couples parent children, the
range of responses from grandparents is considerable.

Frequently the second lesbian parent bears the brunt of her partner's extended families' reactions to their being parents. Because she
is vulnerable to claims that she is not "really" related to the children,
relatives may feel free to dismiss either the relationship between the
parents, their own ties to the children, or both. While this invalidation of the family of creation creates stress when it comes from the
mainstream community, it is often particularly painful coming from
the partners' own families. The resulting loss to the children is equally
obvious.

Often the grandparents' motivations for limiting their involvement
with the family are related to a desire to hide their daughter's lesbian
identity. The parents of childless lesbians are relatively free to pretend
to others that their daughter is an unmarried heterosexual woman.
When asked how she is doing, they can discuss her work situation,
where she lives, or her involvement with social activities. Friends can
be left to assume that although she has no lover, the daughter is nevertheless heterosexual.

Once the parents acknowledge to others that their daughter has a
child, however, they are confronted with additional personal questions: Where is the father? Did she get married? Ready or not, the
lesbian's parents find themselves under new social pressure to explain
their daughter's personal life.

*"I wanted to die, I was so mortified," Freda exclaimed to her hus-
band. "There I was at the community center, and Jean Drummond
walks right up to me and says she hears I have a new grandchild. There
must have been ten people within earshot. Mary is the only person I told
about this; she must have blabbed the news. I'm not ready to have every-
body know about Janey and the baby. For years I've told them she's got*

this great boyfriend, and now this baby is going to make a liar out of me. I can't handle this, Ben. I'm just not ready to handle this."

Supportive Families of Origin

Fortunately, not all relatives are either underinvolved or intrusively present in lesbian families. There are also genuinely respectful and supportive families of origin who work through their heterosexist socialization to form meaningful and healthy connections with their lesbian relative and her family. Research indicates what one might expect anyway—that lesbian parents very much want these connections and prefer to garner needed support from their families than from any other source.[41]

Lesbian families with children experience their relationships with their original families differently than either heterosexual families or lesbian families without children. As noted above, they face particular risks of both rejection and intrusion and must tolerate an ongoing power imbalance that endangers the new family and distorts their relationships with their relatives. Their needs are influenced by their social status as a lesbian family with children, and their families are called on to respond to these particular needs for support and recognition.[42] For couples who are not "out" to their families, though, an additional layer of complication exists, making it even more difficult to ensure the integrity of family boundaries and to be seen as a two-parent family unit.

At the same time, the presence of children offers at least three potential incentives to the original families to maintain supportive relationships with their lesbian family member. First, children's open demonstration of their desire for family connections can persuasively touch the hearts of otherwise rejecting and homophobic parents and siblings. The ultimate ambassadors between estranged factions of a family, children frequently accomplish a family reunification the adults have failed to broker.

Four-year-old Emily led the way, sneaking into her grandparents' house in her red Christmas dress with a present hidden behind her back. She got as far as the dining room before her grandpa discovered her. As she threw her arms around him and handed him the present, Emily gave him little choice but to return her sustained hug. From the foyer, her parents watched his stern face melt into a rare smile. Emily did for them all what they could not do for themselves, oblivious as she was to the idea that any family feud could get in the way of a family holiday.

Second, the arrival of a child allows the family to share with their lesbian relative the life-changing experience of being parents and living with children. Relatives in such cases will find it harder to harbor notions that the lesbian partners' lives bear little similarity to their own. Third, many original family members may be drawn to the child (and hence the couple as well) by the biological tie or shared last name of the new family member. Relatives may recognize their kinship ties to the child in a way they have not achieved in their view of their lesbian relative's partner. In this way, strains and distance within the family can be eased, and the entire extended family can move to a new level of relationship.

Few families of origin see their relationships with lesbian relatives remain unchanged when the latter become parents. As in so many arenas, having children changes things—for better or for worse—and presents the opportunity for these family relationships to become especially central ties for lesbian families.

Lesbian Parents and the Lesbian Community

Both parenting and childless lesbians have struggled to ensure that the lesbian community addresses their primary needs and affirms their life choices. Necessarily bringing powerful needs for validation to this sometimes lone source of social support, many lesbians maintain high hopes that "the community" will offer substantial emotional backing to otherwise very undersupported groups of lesbian women.

Yet lesbian mothers often express disappointment or anger at what they say has historically been an inadequate response by nonparenting lesbians to the child-related needs of lesbian mothers.[43] These women argue that nonparenting lesbians seem to view their parent status as some kind of artifact from their previous existence as heterosexually involved women. As a result, lesbian parents may feel ignored by the community as they see their needs and agenda superseded by those of childless lesbian women.[44]

Parents require from the lesbian community some concrete accommodation of their needs. The couple's participation in community events, for example, requires either that they have access to child care or that the event includes the children. Many community events are geared toward either political action or adult-focused entertainment, neither of which easily lends itself to the inclusion of small children. Financial constraints on many lesbian families with children also require that activities be accessible to parents of limited financial resources.

In addition to these considerations, lesbian parents can be greatly supported by the unique validation the lesbian community can offer them. Parenting greatly increases any family's interaction with the mainstream community (such as through school systems, day-care programs, and various child-focused recreational and social groupings), where lesbian mothers can easily experience both invisibility and disapproval. These lesbians may spend much of their time compartmentalizing their identities, being identifiable as parents in child-related settings and as lesbians in others. The nonbiological or nonadoptive parent particularly is forced to cope with this pressure, as her identity as a parent is so often ignored by the mainstream community. The lesbian community can offer these women validation of their joint identities as parenting and as lesbian families, providing an inner synthesis rarely offered in other social circumstances. Therefore, any way in which the lesbian community fails to extend this affirmation can be especially painful, as it mirrors the rejection and invisibility these lesbians experience elsewhere in their lives.

Within the lesbian community, parenting couples may find themselves shifting their focus toward other parenting couples. They may find new basis for connection with these couples and may also find themselves struggling to sustain previous friendships with nonparenting lesbians. Lesbian parents of color experience even more layers of commonality and difference within their numerous primary communities, further reducing the available groupings of others who share each of these essential personal identities.

Lesbians Without Children

Lesbians deeply value the community's power to affirm their nontraditional choices, and many look at the liberation of being a lesbian as directly connected to this invitation to authenticity and nonconformity. The recent rapid advances in lesbians' opportunities to bear and to adopt children apart from men is clearly one manifestation of this social nonconformity, as it furthers the integrity of lesbian individuals and families. It is an advance of unimagined social importance.

Yet many childless lesbian women are also wary of the new phenomenon of widespread lesbian parenting. For these women, the high visibility within the community of lesbians without children has been profoundly validating, demonstrating that lesbians can create rich and full adult family lives not centered around the narrow definition of heterosexual nuclear families.[45]

Some nonparenting lesbians therefore fear that they will now come to feel more different not only from heterosexual people but from some of their most intimate lesbian friends as well.[46] As lesbian parents reposition themselves within their changing social networks and absorb themselves more fully within their own families of creation, these lesbian friends fear they will be left behind. Often keenly aware of how society isolates and pathologizes women who do not have children, they fear they will now experience a similar distancing from lesbian parents.

> *The two couples had been friends for many years. With the recent arrival of Hana and Kristan's new baby, the couples confronted the quickly apparent changes this meant to their long-standing friendship. "Our lives are completely changed now," the new parents tried to explain for the hundredth time. "We can't just get up and go out on Friday nights anymore; we are exhausted. We have to be here when the baby doesn't sleep on schedule. Can't you just come over? We really do want to see you, and this is a way we can do it."*
>
> *Terry could feel herself getting angry. "We've come over there every Friday night for the past six weeks. Twice you had to change the time, and it was really clear last week that you weren't into having us there at all. We seem to be doing all the accommodating. When did it happen that your having a baby meant you would now call all the shots?"*
>
> *"You don't understand," Hana tried again. "Our lives are all differ-*

ent now. You're taking this too personally. We're putting out tons of effort to still see you every week; we're sure not doing that with anyone else. But it can't be exactly the same as it used to be. We're totally absorbed in the most amazing thing we've ever done. We don't want to have to apologize for that."

"What about the family you already had?" Terry asked, crying now. "Suddenly it's some huge effort just to see us once a week, while you devote yourselves to your real family. What ever happened to all our talk about being each other's family for life? How come we now feel more like just friends who should be grateful for whatever time you can find for us?"

"Well, we don't feel terrifically supported by you right now, either," Hana admitted. "This great thing has happened for us, and you are the people we most want to share it with, but all we hear is how we're letting you down. You have to support what we need now, too. Being each other's family is a two-way street."

Specifically, many childless lesbians argue that the desire to have children has replaced implicit earlier commitments for lesbians to be each other's families—different from mainstream nuclear families, and marked by primary commitments and a shared long-range future. These women express feeling suddenly more alone as their lesbian friends redefine their immediate families, more closely emulating heterosexual family life and replacing the primacy of their previous friendship commitments. Felman speaks especially directly to the fears and pain of some childless lesbians:

> When my friends, lesbians who swore they never wanted children, gave birth, I felt hopelessly abandoned. These friendships—our sisterhoods—have not survived the birth of children; our once shared vision of being family for each other—our own longevity as friends—has ceased to be relevant since my friends have been able to replicate the nuclear family model either by alternative insemination or adoption.[47]

The lesbian community must and does strive to embrace diversity, validating the increasingly common experience of lesbians who choose children while also according full family status to those who make other choices. Lesbian families who do have children deserve the increased recognition they are finally receiving within the lesbian community: They have long been relegated to the outskirts of lesbian social life, and have suffered the effects of the community's disidentification with parenting. At the same time, nonparenting lesbians offer an important warning to the community to safeguard its long-standing support for life outside of nuclear family models.

Conclusion

There have always been lesbian parents. Lesbian couples, however, have not always been able to decide to have a baby and become a child's original, two-parent family. While the responses from others often remain threatening and unsupportive, new ground has been broken. As lesbians claim their right—and now their capacity—to conceive children apart from heterosexual intercourse, the parameters of potential family life options for lesbian couples have been forever expanded.

As always, lesbians do not merely survive the stresses and barriers of lesbian family life. In the absence of established paths, lesbians are charting their own courses, creating their family lives as they go along and expanding all lesbians' options in the process. As lesbians join together to support their right to create two-generational family forms, every lesbian family form is strengthened.

Ever the creative nonconformists, lesbians have and will continue to imagine a particularly wide range of lifestyle options for themselves and their couple relationships. Parenting their own children is an essential component of this freedom, as is the right to choose childless paths of equal validity and reward. In embracing lesbian parenthood without requiring it, lesbians achieve an irreplaceable freedom and endorse in the process one of their most highly prized ethics—a courageous and profoundly creative self-determination that greatly enriches all lesbians' lives.

PART TWO

Stages of the Lesbian Family Life Cycle

6

Stage One:
Formation of the Couple

She repeated: "I have a lover! I have a lover!" delighting in the idea as if a second puberty had come to her. . . . She was entering upon a marvelous world where all would be passion, ecstasy, delirium. She felt herself surrounded by an endless rapture. A blue space surrounded her and ordinary existence appeared only intermittently between these heights, dark and far away beneath her. [*Madame Bovary*][1]

There is a little of Madame Bovary in most people. Romance can awaken such excitement, vitality, and abandon, as new lovers are often acutely aware of their emotional cravings, and their capacity to give to another is frequently at its peak. Bystanders frequently appear lifeless and uninteresting during this period; the invigorated passions of the new partners make ordinary life seem colorless and insufficient. Associations between falling in love and spiritual awakening become easy to understand, as the universal quest for meaningful connection—always present in some form—takes command of new lovers' lives in unparalleled ways.

The mesmerizing experience of becoming a couple leads many new partners to attribute unprecedented emotional significance to a barely formed relationship. As they idealize the mysterious stranger they believe they already know, the partners can maintain greatly distorted projections about each other, persuading themselves that the relationship is actually far more solid than could possibly be true yet. Rationality is simply no match for such forceful emotional states, as the partners use their simplistic but compelling impressions to propel themselves swiftly ahead. The bliss of these imaginings can so intoxicate the partners that they come to believe what Madame Bovary believed—that life has suddenly been transformed into pure "passion, ecstasy, [and] delirium," sometimes even before virtually any substantial contact has occurred between oneself and one's would-be lover.

Entering into a new love relationship is a wonderful and terrible risk. Through joint experiences that will include both euphoric moments of merging and terrible moments of unwelcome conflict, the partners will be exposed to a vast amount of information about each other. In response, most people—lesbians and others—attend only selectively to what they see, highlighting the bliss of their coming together and postponing difficulty for later. In time the partners will revisit the fuller picture, and they will have to distinguish between the enduring connection of authentic love and the illusory and temporary experience of passing attraction.

Love Versus Limerence

Not all sexual attraction leads to love. The complexity and the consequences of mistaking other feelings for real love have long provided a central theme for everything from literature, theater, and music to professional debate within psychology. Of virtually universal relevance, the topic appears inexhaustible. For its part, psychological literature offers the distinction between love and something referred to as *limerence*, which masquerades as genuine other-oriented caring but actually falls far short of authentic love.[2]

The appeal of new attraction lies both in giving to the new person and also in receiving back validation of one's attractiveness. In the moment, the motivations to give and to receive become indistinguishable, and the newly attracted person seldom fully understands the complex nature of his or her newfound excitement. While both real love and limerence seem based on feelings for the other person, however, limerence actually is primarily a self-involved quest to receive validation from someone else. The pursuit of basic affirmation of the self is easily confused with more mature caring, as the two manifest themselves so similarly in this early relational stage.

Leah had only met Sandra twice, but already she could think of little else. She somehow knew Sandra was exactly who she had wanted—beautiful, smart, athletic. Sandra's apparent interest made Leah feel special, attractive, compelling. Leah felt high on being singled out as she ignored her workload and schemed ways to ensure their next encounter. She could hardly wait to feel that flush of excitement again, already feeling bigger, prouder, and bolder than she had in a long time.

While limerent attraction does not proceed to the development of substantial genuine caring for the partner, it can propel the couple into a new relationship. Yet although the beginning stages of love may sustain couples through initial periods of conflict or emotional upheaval, limerence alone will not allow the partners to tolerate interruptions in the affirmation they receive. The foundation built between the partners in such cases will be faulty and insufficient at best.

Lesbians' social position may make them especially vulnerable to developing limerent reactions. The critical conditions for limerence to emerge include the mixture of a powerful hope for an affirmative response combined with reason to doubt that this confirmation will indeed be forthcoming. Limerence increases when the object of the attraction remains slightly out of reach and when the risks of pursuing the relationship remain high. Homophobia creates exactly these conditions for many lesbians, since demonstrating lesbian sexual interest is fraught with the dangers of potential social censure and personal rejection.[3] Lesbians may feel particular dependence on each other for personal validation, as well as freedom from the additional loneliness common to socially isolated groups. These socially created circumstances, combined with the basic insecurities and wishes for intimacy experienced by all people, may further complicate lesbians' task of discriminating the beginnings of love from the fool's gold of limerent attraction.

The Fast Track to Couple Formation

An old joke frequently shared in lesbian circles asks, "What do lesbians bring to their second date?" The punch line: "A U-Haul." As women and as targets of homophobic oppression, lesbians have much reason to want to move quickly into partnered status and, as a group, seem particularly to abbreviate the initial period of couple formation.[4]

Not all lesbians, though, are equally likely to rush the beginning of relationships. The partners' ages and their previous experience with lesbian couplings may influence their pacing, as younger or newly lesbian women may be considerably more vulnerable to idealizing potential partnerships than their more seasoned, experienced elders. In addition, the partners' access to social support and to a lesbian community, the personality traits of each partner, whether either woman is a parent, and other factors may further influence the speed of particular women's entry into new love relationships.[5] Various influences particularly pressure lesbians toward moving quickly, however, and few women are immune from them all.

Academic scholarship increasingly has illuminated a common pattern of women developing their personal identities not by separating themselves from others but by cultivating increasingly intimate relational connections.[6] Two women forming an intimate relationship, then, may particularly associate the relationship's beginning with a powerful boost to each partners' perceived sense of her individual identity. As the partners feel more and more connected to their truest selves, they may credit the new relationship with this invigorating feeling.

While lesbians frequently say their awareness of their lesbian identity began with their first interest in a particular woman, few heterosexuals date their heterosexual identity to the moment of their first kiss. Many lesbians frequently blur two experiences into one: falling in love with another woman and falling in love with their newly accessible, authentic lesbian selves.[7]

> *"I met Joanne and my whole world changed," Jessica exclaimed. "Suddenly my very sense of myself shifted, and everything in my life finally came together. With her, I could be my real self. She gave me the courage to love a woman and, in the process, she helped me find my true identity. I came into my own through loving her."*

The unromantic truth may be that part of what Joanne is attributing to the relationship has little to do with her new lover. Actually, her euphoria is a complex mixture of becoming excited about her potential new partner *and* finally coming into her own as a lesbian.[8] Even for women who have already come out as lesbians, new relationships offer a potent and otherwise largely unavailable boost to their under-validated lesbian identity. Lesbians may be especially quick to credit the new relationship with the sudden infusion of lesbian pride and freedom from inhibition they experience. This feeling persuades women to develop their relationship hastily and move toward being partners.

Lesbians' movement into relationships is also propelled by a specific effect of female socialization. Despite contemporary improvements, girls are still primarily raised to feel shame about explicitly sexual desire.[9] In order to de-emphasize the sexual nature of their attractions, girls and women frequently reframe sexual interest as *relational* desires. Lesbians may feel particular pressure to distance themselves from their sexual feelings for two reasons. First, the nature of their urges is additionally prohibited due to its lesbian nature.[10] Second, with two female partners, neither is socially sanctioned to play the supposedly male role of initiating sex.[11] Agreeing to break these taboos in order to begin a relationship may cause lesbians particular anxiety and thus encourage them to formalize new relationships prematurely.

Lesbians' social isolation also accelerates many beginning relationships. Particularly for primarily closeted women, opportunities to meet potential partners take on great importance. These often sporadic social events invite lesbians out of their aloneness, encouraging single women to develop interest in each other prematurely as they assign exaggerated significance to even superficial commonalities. Moreover, just the women's presence at the event reveals the closely guarded secret of their lesbian identity. The initial and delicate unfolding of a relationship is necessarily distorted when it begins with such a vulnerable and private disclosure. Already these lesbians are way ahead of themselves, depending on a stranger to keep a potent secret.

The social position of lesbians also increases the chances that their relationships with their families of origin are strained or unsupportive. Compromised family connections may significantly increase some lesbians' desire to find a partner and create for themselves the family lives they cannot elicit with other relatives.[12] The combined effect of all of these factors has been described as the lesbian pattern of "meet and marry," where partners move swiftly from their first date into coupled status.[13] Mencher has described this tendency to move quickly as

> the collapsing of the tasks of couple formation to such an extent that there is little or no discernible process between becoming sexually involved and making or assuming an indefinite couple relationship. . . . [But] in meeting-and-marrying, a lesbian couple may be neglecting a basic task in family development, leaving behind a fundamental fracture that may either be mended over time or left to widen until it is irreparable. While the fiery passion and whirlwind rush of early lesbian couple relationships contribute much to the ecstasy of this period, this rapture has its dangers if it is interpreted as representing unquestioned compatibility for long-term couplehood.[14]

While moving more slowly would offer couples the advantages of time and a fuller picture of their potential partners, moving quickly into coupled status is not purely a dangerous or ill-advised path for lesbians. Because lesbian couples face continual pressures to break apart, the power of this initial coming together can help bond the two and create what Pearlman has described as "couple glue."[15] She points out that the bliss of this initial period creates connection that helps couples hold together during the later disappointments and conflict inevitable in all couple relationships. Similarly, Mencher points out that the "jumpstart" of this intense style of beginning serves as a "super-charged boost" which becomes a reserve for later periods of stress.[16]

The Tasks of Forming a Couple

It takes courage to enter this stage. Never will the partners know so little about each other (despite their feeling that they know a great deal), and they operate with only a minimal relational foundation between them. With their passion spurring them on, the partners agree to lean into an as-yet unformed relationship with no reliable safeguards. The desire to protect themselves will grow at times of conflict or disappointment, and each woman will find herself running for cover. Some women will want to retreat back to their prerelationship position of autonomy, while others will attempt to lean too heavily on a still-fragile relationship.

As women, and as lesbians, many lesbians may tend to underplay the frighteningly tentative quality of the new relationship at times of insecurity and look too soon for assurances that the partners' bond will hold. Partners may lose track of the fact that they have virtually no shared past and no dependable future, and therefore they have only their present experience of each other to rely on. Because of this reality, couple formation is actually a far more complex task than new couples' starry-eyed visions would suggest. With no guarantee of success, couples must recognize that they are in danger of being abandoned or disillusioned by their new lover, yet agree to proceed nonetheless.

A couple's first task is to build a beginning sense of themselves as a unit. To accomplish this, the women must emphasize their points of similarity and cultivate what brings them together. Closeness comes from their sense of personal overlap, and individual identity takes a temporary back seat to the feeling of interconnection they enjoy.[17] The partners must agree to relax the boundaries around themselves as they tentatively blend selected aspects of their lives. New lovers frequently forgo time alone or time with separate friends in favor of increased time together. The partners make various personal compromises in order to supplement the connectedness between them.

Later in the relationship, these personal boundaries will return to a position of prominence, regaining some of their earlier firmness. The partners will return to wanting distinct lives despite the more blended relational space they will continue to inhabit. For now, however, they each must welcome the intrusion of the other into their previously personal space. They must use their passion for each other to pull them into this new state, where their fears about "losing" themselves to another often remain temporarily at bay and their deepening intimacy can feel safe, possible, and desirable.

"I can't believe how much we have in common," Vicki told her sister. "We like to go to the same places and spend our time in such similar ways. We think alike on so many topics, and it feels so easy for me to be with her. I can't get close enough to her. It suddenly feels so easy."

The obstacles associated with this task will vary considerably among lesbian partners. The partners' past experience will influence the meaning they ascribe to temporarily loosening their personal boundaries to allow a new partner to move closer. For example, if one or both women have experienced sexual abuse (or other physical or relational intrusiveness) in their pasts, they may experience a great deal of anxiety as they increase their vulnerability to someone they do not fully know. For these couples, the task of becoming a unit may require particular focus on building trust, and the relationship may need to develop at a slower pace. For example, affected partners may need particular reassurance that the new relationship will not cost them their privacy and individual identity. They may also need more fluctuation in the couple's sexual relationship, as this closeness may feel more and less possible at various times. Further, the interdependence that begins as the partners become a couple may have complicated meanings for women who have been hurt in past relationships; sorting through these layers of meaning may affect the pace at which these partners can proceed with the new couple relationship.

The more cautious pacing one or both partners may require need not indicate that the relationship cannot succeed. However, these couples may particularly have to grapple with themes of closeness and distance in order to bolster the partners' confidence in both the relationship and its capacity to support their additional needs for personal space.

The couple reported that their first three months had been a particularly exciting and wonderful time between them. Spending increasing amounts of time together, the new partners welcomed opportunities to come closer to each other, with neither partner experiencing undue anxiety in the process. More recently, however, Pat had become fearful and began asserting her need for time apart, frequently reiterating her need for a separate daily life. Both partners were upset by the resulting tension between them, and they had had numerous fights about it in recent weeks. Pat felt increasingly encroached upon by Jane, and Jane reported feeling rejected by Pat.

As the therapist asked the couple to share more of their individual histories with each other, Pat's fears of being intruded upon became understandable. In her early relationships with both parents, Pat was allowed little privacy or distinct identity. Both partners could more fully see how she might associate closeness with a threat to her separate self, which she responded to by pushing others away at those times. With help, Pat was able to better distinguish Jane's desire for closeness from the experiences of her early childhood. This allowed Pat to again experience the couple's emotional closeness as satisfying and primarily unthreatening. The therapist prepared the couple for the likelihood that they would need to emphasize this distinction repeatedly over time.

Next, the therapist helped the couple devise ways for Pat to reassure herself of her separate identity without triggering Jane's feelings of rejection. The couple planned to spend four nights apart each week, and the therapist urged them to choose the same nights each week so both partners would know in advance when these nights would fall. In addition, the partners discussed Pat's desire to keep two particular friendships separate from the couple relationship, and Jane agreed to remain uninvolved with these two women. In exchange, Jane asked Pat to call her on two of their four nights apart, saying that this gesture would ease her worries that Pat no longer wanted to be close to her. The therapist suggested that these conversations occur regularly, but also that they be brief.

The therapist suggested that the couple lower their expectations concerning sexual contact for the next several weeks as well. She noted that the partners' needs for space, at the present time being voiced by Pat, in the long run were essential for Jane as well. As they recognized their union's capacity to support this space, sexuality would again feel safer to Pat, and the couple could resume additional sexual contact. At the same time, the partners needed to learn how to reassure each other within the relationship; at this moment, for example, Jane needed help in not personalizing Pat's need for distance. For now, though, it was important for both of them to cultivate the individual elements that would ultimately maximize their ability to engage intimately with each other.

Other couples may come to a new relationship with histories of insufficient closeness with primary caretakers or previous partners. For them, the task of forming a couple unit may require them to resist the temptation to move too quickly, as the new coupling stimulates their hopes of compensatory intimacy with their new partner. These women may need to remind themselves that their desire to commit prematurely comes not from certainty about the new relationship but from insufficiencies in past relationships. No new love can shoulder the burden of the partners' past collective disappointments.

As the new partners come to define themselves as a couple, they begin to develop shared methods of coping with the common stresses of lesbian relationships. Typically, fusion is the coping mechanism most in keeping with the relational situation of new couples. Because this early stage is marked by the partners' emphasis on their private interaction, with social involvement not yet fully developed, the partners' capacity to hold close together often develops significantly during this time. This dynamic can be of great use to the couple, but it may also complicate another of the couple's primary tasks during this stage: the development of healthy management of conflict between the partners. Often equated with trouble in the relationship, conflict is something many new couples strive to avoid; they need outside verification that intense closeness and painful disagreement can and do coexist in couple relationships. Managing these two contrasting experiences constitutes a significant challenge to many couples in this early stage.

By embracing the spectrum of emotional experiences occurring between the partners, new lesbian couples achieve another central task of this first stage of the family life cycle. Couples hoping to be able to commit themselves to their partnership must replace their early, simplistic views of each other with more realistic and complex understandings. The women must puncture their initial projected fantasies and learn what angers, scares, touches, and excites each partner. Conflict is an essential ingredient in this exploration, as the spontaneous emotional expression it generates is filled with information about the partners' special sensitivities.

As women, and as socially vulnerable individuals, lesbians may have particular difficulty inviting—or even tolerating—recurring conflict. Particularly in this first stage, conflict disrupts the couple's needed notion that the two partners are consistently compatible. Even relatively minor disagreements can take on exaggerated significance, as they challenge the partners' subconscious fantasies that their bliss can remain uninterrupted. In addition, the partners often cannot put a particular conflict in its proper perspective, because they do not yet know who their lover *typically* is or how their relationship typically goes.[18] Assessing the magnitude and importance of a given argument is therefore most difficult in this beginning stage, with much opportunity for the partners to exaggerate or to underestimate what is being revealed.

As certain conflicts become more prominent over time, couples begin to witness each partner's core fears and primary defenses. For both partners, the relationship will periodically reopen unresolved childhood traumas, causing each to confuse her present partner subconsciously with other, earlier loved ones. Partners wade through both their actual interactions and also the symbolic, distorted meanings attached to selected moments by each partner. As recurring conflicts are revealed to contain familiar and problematic themes for each partner, enduring dynamics of the relationship begin to become clear. Therefore, to state simply that the couple must now establish ground rules for managing conflict belies a complex and emotionally loaded challenge faced by all couples.

"What brings you here?" the therapist asked the couple. "Joan told me on the phone that you have been involved with each other for six months, and that you find yourselves repeating a particular conflict with each other. Can you tell me about it?"

As the therapist listened to each woman describe the situation from her own vantage point, it became clear that the partners were fighting about how much time together and emotional commitment they expected of each other at this point in their relationship. Struggling with this uncertainty, the couple felt their growth as a couple had stalled. The recurring argument highlighted Sandy's reluctance to expand their present expectations, and Joan's resulting feelings of insecurity and fear of the relationship ending.

To further illuminate the couple's struggle, the therapist helped the couple listen to each other's childhood stories. Joan had experienced a repeatedly insecure relationship with her parents, who separated and reunited several times while she was young. The therapist helped the partners relate Joan's difficulty in tolerating the unavoidable lack of guarantee about the couple's future to this traumatic past. Over time, Joan more fully recognized that she and Sandy were still at the beginning of their journey as a couple, making it impossible for the new couple relationship to heal this old injury. Joan then could see the fluctuations in Sandy's ability to reassure her as more normal for their early stage of relationship, and not necessarily indicative of an enduring problem.

Sandy, too, was able to examine her childhood's contribution to the couple's present problem. The nature of connection in her family had frequently felt suffocating to Sandy, which she typically responded to by reasserting her individual identity apart from significant others. Sandy could recognize that she at times overreacted to Joan's requests for reassurance, assuming that Joan was seeking the clingy, frightening attachment she remembered from her childhood. Sandy acknowledged that she sometimes overdramatized her needs for individual space, and that she probably could offer Joan more empathy when Joan became unduly insecure.

As the partners distinguished their relationship from their childhood experiences, the couple was freed up to explore further their developing connection. While certainly their pasts would continue to emerge within their relationship, the partners felt ready to resume enjoying the excitement and unknown future typical for this early stage of a relationship.

No couple can accomplish the work of this first family life cycle stage without directly addressing the task of developing trust between the partners. As each partner offers the increasing self-disclosure required throughout this stage, partners must offer each other empathic responses that encourage further risk and deepened intimacy. Particularly on the heels of conflict, the partners confront many situations in which one or both must apologize or otherwise initiate a reconciliation. Both partners' past experiences with similar vulnerability will influence their capacity to forge a reconnection. For partners with histories of being frequently blamed or humiliated when they offered apologies, reuniting after a conflict will be especially challenging. Couples must learn early how to accept both defeat and victory in ways that protect the partners' egos and build trust between them.

Specifically, each woman must demonstrate over time that she can refrain from using her partner's particular vulnerabilities against her in moments of intense conflict. While partners cannot promise that their interpersonal dynamics will be free of any association to each other's unresolved (and often childhood-based) traumatic memories, trust depends on each one demonstrating some capacity to avoid repeating these earlier injuries. Clearly, no couple fully masters this task, especially not early on in their relationship. Lack of knowledge of each other's full history, as well as defensive strategies for preserving their own sense of self, leads partners to reinforce one another's recurring fears, further inflaming the present conflict. The damage done by this lasts well beyond the particular disagreement and can hamper the couple's development of trust in serious ways.

"How dare you call me abusive for yelling at you?" Celia shouted. "Yelling is part of fighting, and I am sick and tired of you making such a terrible accusation. I've never been abusive to you, and I don't ever want to hear you say that again!" Joan was ready with a quick and emphatic reply. "Look," she said, "in our last three fights in a row you have called me every name in the book, screaming into my face and insisting that I don't know what I'm talking about. That is abusive!"

Celia was silent a moment, then responded slowly. "Joan, I grew up in a family where none of that was ever considered abusive. I am used to yelling when I am mad, but maybe I can see how it could seem abusive from your perspective."

"You see," Joan exploded, "even you think you're abusive!"

Reconciliation requires at least one partner taking the considerable risk of empathizing with her partner's experience. Agreeing to move beyond defending oneself to feel the experience of an angry lover is critical if couples are to use conflict productively to deepen their understanding of each other. When a partner cannot join in the softened tenor of beginning rapproachment, they instead use their partner's gesture to launch a new attack, opting to shore up their sense of personal security instead of contributing to interpersonal reunion.

While no one escapes moments of feeling acute personal vulnerability, if these responses are chronic between partners early in a relationship, trust does not form. Instead the partners develop the pattern of each one choosing self-protection over bridge-building in times of conflict, and the residue from these experiences then lingers in their interpersonal dynamic. Long-term patterns of conflict resolution begin to be developed during the couple formation stage. The content of these early battles may or may not always contain especially significant material for the couple to address. The *process*, however, of how they treat each other is extremely important and warrants special attention by both partners.

To review, the primary tasks of the lesbian couple formation stage include building an initial foundation for the couple as a unit, developing methods of managing needed conflicts within the relationship, creating increasingly complex views of each partner and of the couple's particular relationship, and building trust between the partners. Regardless of the couple's circumstances, these achievements allow the partners to consider the themes of later relational stages and to form a relational foundation that can weather the challenges ahead.

Kinds of Lesbian Couples

As long as homophobia exists, we will never have a complete picture of how lesbians find each other and begin romantic relationships. Many lesbian couples are simply not free to share the stories of their coming together. What we do know is that lesbians find romantic partners in many different ways. In contrast, heterosexual couples can take advantage of established and oft-repeated opportunities to meet each other and to date.

While some aspects of couple formation are experienced by all people attempting to form a new romantic relationship, there are also some influential distinctions among lesbians that deserve attention. In many instances, women become involved with each other after they have already established a close and private friendship. These women friends may have previously identified themselves as either lesbians or as heterosexuals. The gradual unfolding of lesbian identity within a long-standing friendship represents a very different path than that of the woman who first acknowledges her lesbian identity to herself and then finds a partner.[19] In addition, as in other kinds of couplings, some lesbians enter the couple formation stage as a result of an affair with a person who is committed to someone else. Each of these circumstances uniquely influences the process of couple formation.

This stage of the lesbian family life cycle does not begin with a couple's first or second date. No twosome can be viewed as on the road to being a family that quickly. For lesbians, in fact, the demarcation of when this stage begins is especially ambiguous. Lesbian couples could benefit from distinguishing more fully when they began to show interest in each other as opposed to when they began an actual couple relationship.[20] Even that distinction would retain much uncertainty, though, both because lesbian couplings are formed out of an especially wide variety of situations and because lesbian dating is a still unclearly defined concept. This murkiness is sufficiently uncomfortable for many lesbians that they escape it by moving very quickly into self-declared partnered status.

Unacquainted Lesbians Begin Dating

"I met someone," Susan told her friend excitedly. "I know, I know, you're going to tell me not to move too fast. She's really intriguing, though—very self-assured, really bold about her attraction to me, very lesbian-identified. We met at an organizing meeting for the gay rights march, and we're going to have dinner together Friday."

Some lesbians are learning how to date. As growing numbers of lesbians publicly identify themselves and search openly for potential partners, dating has begun to emerge as both possible and acceptable within lesbian social circles. Unlike lesbians from previous generations—who were forced to rely on clandestine, dark bars to provide even a modicum of safety for women to meet other women—younger lesbians are more able to attend at least some mainstream social activities with a female companion. In addition, lesbians in many communities have created social activities of their own, from country and Western dancing to softball leagues and lesbian-oriented theatre. Lesbians now depend less on alcohol-related activities than in previous years and can meet prospective dating partners in a wider range of situations. These social opportunities increase the chances that the two women will have something in common when they begin dating.

Women face particular obstacles, though, when they attempt to pursue and respond to each other in the rituals of courtship. There are no models or mentors teaching women how to date other women, and there are no commonly understood mores about the do's and don't's of seeing several women at a time.[21]

Great ambiguity exists about when a social outing constitutes a date rather than two women simply going out as friends. Society grants heterosexuals a period of time in which to explore various potential partnerships (especially in adolescence and young adulthood) and also encourages particular social experiences (including school-sponsored dances and "boy-girl parties" hosted by schoolmates' parents) designed to facilitate young people's exploration of possible couplings. Clearly young lesbians do not receive similar opportunities, as neither society nor most parents teach their daughters how to pursue another woman romantically or how to recognize when another woman is indicating interest in them.[22] In sharp contrast, girls commonly receive direct or implied social training in how to respond to *boys'* interest in them and how to assume an "appropriately" feminine role in the symbolic dance steps of mating.

In addition, lesbian daters face some very practical problems. Particularly outside of openly lesbian social communities, it is not always easy to identify who the lesbian women are.[24] Pursuing an attraction to a new woman therefore requires a two-tiered task of finding ways to signal first that one is a lesbian, and second that one is attracted to this particular woman. By contrast, heterosexuals rarely devote a moment's thought to how they are going to indicate their sexual identity to each other.

These are formidable challenges to lesbians' attempts to date. Lesbians who searched for a range of potential partners in earlier times, however, faced far greater obstacles. As more women take the risk of coming out, options and rituals related to lesbian dating will continue to expand, and lesbians will be able to select what to adapt from heterosexual dating and what to invent purely from lesbian experience.

Already Committed Lesbians Have an Affair

> She arrived at work looking possessed—her hair strangely standing out, her cheeks suspiciously blushed, her eyes dreamy and otherwise engaged. She seemed to have become an alien, and I watched with a mixture of shock, envy, and pity. I knew she had seen her new attraction last night, and I could only imagine her stealthy return home to her long-term partner. I wanted to help her slow down and to warn her of how transparent her condition was. Clearly, though, she was gripped by a powerful feeling and had lost any ability to evaluate patiently the near-stranger who had so mesmerized her.

It is practically impossible for partners whose couplings began as affairs to have a true beginning to their relationship. Immediately, their connection is infused with danger, guilt, and possible loss of either their existing couple relationship, the new affair, or both. The partners must immediately begin comparing the new lover to their current mate, prematurely asking the new liaison to withstand this competition and raising unanswerable questions of future commitment. The weight of these immediate implications may lead the new couple to slow down as they contemplate the gravity of continuing or to accelerate further as they seek assurance that the new passion warrants the sacrifices it will bring. "I'll leave her for you" is a premature pledge for a barely formed and deeply disruptive relational bond.

Couples in this situation often find that building trust is especially complicated. Their relationship began on a foundation of one or both women breaking a commitment to a previous partner. Each therefore must muster a belief that they will not be the next ones in the unenviable position of the ex-partners. To do so, the women may be very tempted to attribute the failures of their previous unions either to their particular partners or to some dynamic of this previous relationship that does not pertain to the present coupling. In so doing, they run the risk of failing to identify and rectify their own contribution to any problems within the previous partnerships. This denial increases the chances that the partners will repeat—not escape—the dynamics that led to the ending of their earlier relationship.

While heterosexuals having affairs also employ this defensive strategy, affairs constitute threats to lesbians on an additional level as well. Unlike heterosexuals, lesbians must continually rebut society's charge that their relationships are inherently unviable. Lesbians who have an affair and leave their partners must restore their confidence in lesbian relationships in general even as they witness their own participation in the dismantling of a lesbian family. Therefore they must distinguish between their particular failed partnership and lesbian relationships in general. Often the new coupling is the unworthy recipient of this defensive confidence, as the partners prematurely credit the relationship with all that is good about lesbian love.

Women in this situation frequently look for more emotional support from their new partners than is possible in a barely formed relationship. As each woman confronts the difficult choices before her, she may turn particularly to her new lover, as often there are few other people who know of or support their connection. This creates an unfair gauge of the new partner's supportive capacities, where the partners' abilities may either be exaggerated due to their competitive motives ("I'd never do to you what your other partner does") or diminished by the prematurity of the emotional demand ("I can't give you this support yet, but it doesn't mean I won't later be able to").

Unsupportive responses from others in the lesbian community may also test the tentative bond. Lesbian couples already live in an atmosphere of continual threat exerted by the homophobic mainstream society. Affairs between lesbians amplify ongoing couples' sense of vulnerability. Such couples may distance themselves from a lesbian friend having an affair in an attempt to shore up their own beleaguered sense of safety and to disidentify with the turmoil affairs create.

Lesbian Friends Become a Couple

>   *Sharon and Patrice had often joked that if only they could fall in love with each other, they would be spared the horrors of the lesbian dating scene. Each had teasingly told the other there was no way she'd ever fall for her; they knew far too much about each other's quirks and eccentricities. Both were therefore amazed and delighted to find sexual tension developing between them after all this time. Their attraction contained their intimate knowledge of each other, yet brought a new feeling of excitement and anticipation as well. Ever so tentatively, the women edged toward each other, strangely anxious and suddenly vulnerable.*

Lesbians frequently form their most primary friendships with other lesbians. This rather obvious statement clearly distinguishes lesbians from heterosexuals and ensures a complexity to lesbian relationships that heterosexuals seem deliberately to avoid. Heterosexual men rarely form their closest platonic friendships with heterosexual women, especially once they are partnered. Likewise, heterosexual women rarely develop one-to-one intimacy with heterosexual men outside their partnerships. Perhaps heterosexuals as a group limit this intimacy in order to avoid the jealousies, competitions, and likely threats to their couple relationships they expect these outside friendships would cause.

For better or worse, lesbians often make a different choice, taking on the potential complexities of close friendships with lesbians other than their own partners. While in many instances the resulting intimacy does not include sexual attraction, clearly there is potential for such feelings to emerge as the closeness progresses. Couple relationships that arise from previously platonic friendship contain unique features that distinguish these couples' tasks from those of previously unacquainted strangers.

Lesbian couples in this situation must accomplish a particular variation of the task of developing initial intimacy. Their friendship has undoubtedly illuminated areas of substantial commonality for the partners. Even as friends, they have already experienced moments where they have had to draw on these commonalities to support the relationship. Now, however, they are a couple for the first time, and the new partners must reconstruct their bond in a way that allows for the presence of sexual and romantic connection.

Couples with preexisting friendships also tend to manage conflict differently than do partners who were previously unacquainted. Because the partners probably have already argued in the course of their friendship, the avoidance of conflict typical of new partners may be less relevant to these couples. Perhaps less persuaded that their bond cannot withstand anger, these couples may confront emerging conflicts sooner than other new couples. These couples thus may simultaneously develop both the new connection they now need as lovers and their already-developed capacity to tolerate conflict in order to foster further individual identity. Couples without a previous friendship are typically more likely to develop these capacities sequentially, with individual identity being temporarily put aside to foster the new interpersonal connection. The creative ways partners devise to relate simultaneously as a new couple and as well-established friends can shed light on the process of couple formation for all lesbians.

Additionally, all new couples enjoy a particular kind of excitement about their relationship that is tied to its newness and sense of possibility. For previously unacquainted couples, this excitement stems from a wide variety of new areas of exploration of their partner, most or all of which contain surprises and new information. For those who already were friends, however, the newness is more specifically contained within the romantic and sexual realm of their relationship.

There remains much to learn about how the nature of this stage's excitement is affected by the preexisting friendship, as well as about the effect of having the sexual arena of their relationship be called on to supply most or all of the new excitement for the couple.

With less mystery concerning the partners' full identities, lesbian couples with preceding friendships may unrealistically perceive that they can bypass the risk of their now-changed relational status. While they do have better established relational foundations than other new partners, becoming a couple does produce influential changes in the whole of their friendship. Should their romantic relationship later end, they will not simply pick up where they left off as friends.

Because friendship between lesbians is so common, friends becoming lovers is a fairly frequent circumstance of couple formation. The increased complexity this situation brings characterizes many lesbian relationships. As a result, discussions of the tasks for new couples must take into account the particularities of partners coming together with some emotional intimacy already established.

Heterosexual Friends Become a Couple

> *My client had been talking about her friend Joanna for two sessions now. She appeared quite nervous and watched me intently, studying my face for reaction to her anecdotes of their friendship. Patiently, I waited for her to show me where she was leading us. Face flushed with anxiety, she said, "Joanna is actually a very special friend of mine," looking at me to see if I understood the code. "We aren't gay or anything, but we do express our love with physical affection." This was more code. "Are you letting me know that the two of you are sexually involved?" I asked. "I guess so," she said, "but not like actual lovers. We're both quite sure that we're not gay."*

Many lesbians' first same-sex relationships grow out of a close, previously platonic friendship during which both women defined themselves as heterosexual. Mainstream culture allows women to meet certain emotional needs for each other, as long as the relationship remains secondary to each one's presumed involvement in a heterosexual marriage. Many women turn to each other to fill large voids, usually for deep emotional intimacy or for the sense of shared womanness they do not experience with their male partners. Women often describe these relationships as deeply fulfilling, with each woman describing the other as her best friend.

In these scenarios, the women often quickly reject any suggestion that this same-sex physical relationship now suggests lesbian identity. Because formation of the couple precedes the possible subsequent ownership of a lesbian identity, great defensive energy is invested in avoiding a homosexual label, usually through seeing the relationship as a "special friendship."

This category of couple formation is characterized by at least two primary elements. First, because these new partners depend on believing that they are not lesbians, they must continually rationalize their intimacy, usually by attributing their feelings and behavior to the long-standing nature of their preexisting friendship. Second, from the beginning of their couple bond, the women make a mutual pact not to see themselves as being a couple. Instead, they work to occupy the deliberately blurry space between the now-changed original friendship and an unacceptable new status. Ironically, this can aid in the useful process of slowing down this stage, but at considerable expense to each partner since the pacing is achieved on the basis of a deep, mutual homophobia. Moreover, their fears that they would suffer reprisals if they adopted a lesbian identity may be partially or wholly accurate, further motivating them to frame their relationship in vague and unromantic ways.

These couples often experience considerable duress as each partner confronts a massive challenge to her heterosexual self-identity at exactly the same moment that an essential relationship in her life profoundly changes. Like all friends who later become lovers, the partners are in a stage marked by both new and well-established intimacy. In addition, the women may be in committed relationships with men, so that the stresses faced by lesbians having an affair may affect them as well.

When previously heterosexual women come together, they frequently experience the sexual component of their relationship as the site of all the newness. These partners assure themselves that their friendship can contain their sexual "experimenting," and they believe that the risk to the relationship exists purely within the question of whether they will continue their sexual contact. By dichotomizing their relationship, the women can view only the couple bond as experimental and reassure themselves that their friendship would emerge unscathed should they decide to end their sexual involvement. This common formulation serves a very adaptive function, as it allows the women to see some aspects of their identities and relationship as outside the crisis.

Heterosexually identified women exploring lesbian relationships use this defense differently than lesbian partners coming together with a preexisting friendship. The lesbian women are attempting to protect their established friendship from the risks associated with becoming lovers. Heterosexual women, in contrast, are protecting an entire identity that depends on finding an alternate explanation for their present lesbian activity.

> *The two women sitting before the therapist had been best friends for fifteen years, living close to each other and frequently spending time together away from their husbands. Three months ago, the women had become what they termed "special friends." They told the therapist they had begun "expressing their affection physically"—understanding completely, they said, that this did not make them gay, but knowing too that they needed to keep this development a secret. Everyone would come to the wrong conclusion, the women explained. They hated telling this unknown therapist of their relationship, but the present difficulty between them made both partners afraid their precious friendship was in jeopardy.*
>
> *Nancy had recently decided to leave her marriage. Initially this had meant that she and Shawna enjoyed the great new advantage of having private space. But Nancy had begun spending more time with other friends, greatly upsetting Shawna and plunging the partners into painful conflict. "I feel such new freedom being out of my marriage!" Nancy told the therapist. "I feel like a kid again, staying out without having to explain to anybody, making all my own decisions. I can finally stop lying to my husband to grab more time alone with Shawna, or pretending we went out when instead we stayed home together. My friendship with Shawna will always be my closest one, but I don't want to promise to give up the sense of freedom I just now got for myself."*
>
> *The therapist watched Shawna struggle to find a rebuttal to this argument. Nancy's description of her situation was persuasive, but*

Stage One: Formation of the Couple

Shawna's anxiety and insecurity were clearly evident—and not without reason. The couple had protected themselves by keeping the description of their relationship ambiguous. With no special word to describe Shawna's role in Nancy's life, Nancy's increased involvement with other friends felt like a threat. The couple now needed to set firmer boundaries around what they would experience only with each other and what they would share with other people. Yet they needed to see these boundaries clearly themselves without others understanding what was going on between them.

As the therapist helped them articulate how they could keep some aspects of their closeness exclusive, the partners grappled more effectively with the implications of Nancy's getting divorced. Carving out time they would reserve for each other, defining secrets they would keep, and making more explicit that they would not be "physically affectionate" with other friends, the partners paved their own path. Still not calling themselves lovers, the women found a vocabulary and way of life that accommodated both their need to distinguish their relationship from others and their avoidance of adopting a lesbian identity.

Couples in this situation define their foundation together as their shared sense of heterosexual female friendship, not a previously worked-through lesbian identity. Paradoxically, the women point to their presumably retrievable heterosexual credentials as giving them the willingness to continue lesbian exploration. Many women in this situation show remarkable resiliency as they tolerate their own and each other's often lengthy confusion about their personal sexual identities and their particular relationship. These couples' relationships reflect the blending of sexuality and emotional closeness frequently associated with typical female relational styles and demonstrate the inadequacies of present understandings of how some women associate emotional intimacy with sexual identity.

A Heterosexual Woman and a Lesbian Friend Become a Couple

Carla and Emily had been friends for years. Carla and her husband had been great supporters of Emily's lesbian-rights causes, and their different circles of friends had often blended easily. Now Carla came to Emily in tears. "I've fallen in love with you," she said. "I am constantly preoccupied thinking about you, and I just can't keep it to myself any longer." Emily felt tears well up in her eyes as those words released her own long-submerged desire for Carla. Both knew that naming this attraction would change things. Whatever happened from here on would be colored by the feelings they had now acknowledged to each other.

No matter how closely connected these two women may feel as they begin their couple relationship, they are in different positions. Both women agree to take a huge risk by proceeding with the relationship, but the risks confronting each woman are not the same. For the heterosexually identified partner, beginning a same-sex relationship raises questions about her basic sexual identity that are not being raised for her lesbian lover. In addition, she may be facing a divorce, with the emotional and economic strains that typically follow divorce for women.

Unlike couples where both women have previously identified themselves as heterosexuals, this couple does not enjoy the symmetry of each asking similar questions and employing parallel defenses. They may have very different ideas about what the pacing of the relationship should be, how public to be, and what it means to each of them to be lesbian lovers. Without a previously established lesbian identity, the heterosexually identified partner is likely to attribute all or part of her decision to proceed to her feelings for her particular partner. "I've changed my whole life for you" is a romantic but problematic conception of what is occurring. The previously heterosexual woman collapses the thrills and struggles of being in a new relationship together with the changes in her sexual identity. Women in this position often feel as though their lesbian partner has opened a door for them that they could not open alone. As a result, they may associate ending their new relationship with losing access to this newly uncovered aspect of themselves.

Being in the lesbian relationship may require the heterosexual partner to transform a very basic element of her personal identity and to relinquish a privilege she may barely notice until she loses it. Both partners may quickly begin testing the heterosexually identified lover's capacity to bear the stresses of lesbian experience. For example, can she tolerate being suddenly different from even her closest family and friends? How will she manage their reactions if loved ones criticize or distance themselves from her as a result of continuing the lesbian relationship? These are huge weights to place on a barely formed relationship.

The lesbian partner in this scenario may also feel increased insecurity, as she knows firsthand the losses in store for her new partner if the relationship continues. She may doubt that she is worth such a great sacrifice. How can she compete, she wonders, with the constant social approval her partner is accustomed to receiving? Will the relationship still seem worth it when the novelty of falling in love fades and her partner begins to experience homophobic oppression?

In addition, because the heterosexually identified partner is exploring a changed sexual identity, the lesbian may worry that she is serving as a vehicle for coming out with or without her partner's conscious awareness. She may fear that her partner will later need to experience a "lesbian adolescence" where relational commitments take a back seat to independent exploration. Heterosexuals, in contrast, do not have to fear that their partners will have to incorporate the knowledge of a new sexual identity before they can engage in a couple relationship.

The nascent relationship will have to respond to the complex needs the partners inevitably bring to this situation. One problem is the lack of balance; for one partner, the entire experience of being involved with women is new, while for the other the newness is limited only to this particular partnership. In addition, because there are central differences in the positions of each partner, developing the intense connectedness desired during early couple formation is more complicated. Nonetheless, many of these couples weather the difficulties and create healthy partnerships. Whether as temporary or permanent relationships, these unions frequently demonstrate women's capacity to manage complex dynamics and to hold together despite high levels of both externally and internally imposed stress.

New Couples' Social Relationships

Unless the partners choose to, they often do not have to come out as a couple to their families, friends, and coworkers this early into their relationship. During this initial stage, the couple is often free to tell only particularly trusted friends about the new partnership, with relatively little chance that others will find out on their own. As a result, many couples in this stage may not initiate major changes in their social and familial relationships. Instead, the partners may use this initial stage to anticipate peoples' likely reactions—a step that in and of itself may begin to change these relationships, adding a level of tension or incompleteness to the connection. "What would happen if they knew?" is frequently a question that hovers in the minds of the new partners who can foresee a time when secrecy may be harder to maintain or more costly to choose. For the moment, however, many new couples feel a unique willingness to spend most of their time in private and believe they can meet their relationship's needs alone.

Lesbians who are already "out" to these significant others may more easily announce that they have begun a new relationship. Already knowing much about who can respond supportively, these lesbians are more likely to receive selected others' interest and congratulations, and they may be invited to include their new partner in relevant social and family activities.

With or without others knowing of the relationship, many new lesbian couples enjoy a period of experiencing their outsider status as their own choice. Romantically, the partners may attribute homophobia's decreased sting to their new relationship. Their feeling that "When I'm with you, I don't care about the world's reaction" is likely to intensify their relationship.

For women in their very first lesbian relationship, this initial period of privacy may serve additional functions. Especially for women who have not previously seen themselves as socially oppressed, even the glow of their new relationship will not fully insulate them from their first negative judgments from family, friends, or others. Privacy may buy these partners some time, allowing them to explore their new relationship further before facing societal homophobia.

The tasks of the couple formation stage lend themselves particularly well to couples spending much time alone. In addition, the partners enjoy a greater capacity to hide their relationship from outsiders than will become true in subsequent stages, when couples typically blend their lives in increasingly visible ways (such as living together, vacationing together, joint home ownership, or co-parenting).

The dichotomy between many new lesbian couples' public identity as unattached individuals and their private identity as a new couple exerts stress on the barely formed relationship. By contrast, heterosexual couples are typically offered opportunities to announce even very new relationships to the people in their lives. They can, for example, tell their families and friends that they are seeing someone they are excited about. Employees attending work-related social events are often invited to bring a date, just as single people are expected to bring a guest to weddings. Because they are not required to relinquish their privacy as a couple in order to join in these social occasions, heterosexual couples are able to be both out in the world and by themselves at the same time. Lesbian couples often have much difficulty eliciting the same supportive opportunity.

> *Susan and Kate arrived at the restaurant hoping for an intimate, private evening. The host began leading them to a table in the brightest and most traveled section of the restaurant. Disappointed, Susan summoned her courage and asked if they could instead have one of the corner tables. The host replied that they like to reserve those more private spots for couples, especially on Saturday night.*

Lesbian communities offer many fledgling couples a unique opportunity for validation and social connection. Community events sometimes help the couple to meet in the first place: Friends may introduce single lesbians to eligible women, or deliberately include them in lesbian social events. New couples can find congratulatory responses from other lesbians that they may not find elsewhere.

> *"I'm seeing someone, and I couldn't wait to tell you. I thought I would just burst if I didn't reach you soon. I'm so excited I can't stand it. When can I come over and tell you about her?"*

The lesbian community can also share new couples' pain when the partners experience rejection or exclusion in other social arenas. In addition, contact with other lesbians can help new couples access potential sources of support that they may not have known about otherwise.

> *"Did you hear about the new rabbi in town? She's just come, and already she has announced that she intends to extend a particular welcome for lesbians in the community to join the synagogue. She said she'll even officiate at lesbian commitment ceremonies, too. You two should check it out. You might really like it there."*

Clearly not all new lesbian couples will receive the same response, even within a lesbian community. For example, lesbians may respond more tentatively to new couples formed by women with no previous lesbian identity. They may protect themselves from possible loss of these new friends by waiting to see if the lesbian identity lasts over time or if it proves to be a temporary experiment. Lesbians of color and biracial couples must navigate an even more complicated path: They may choose to make use of the resources that are only available within a community of other lesbians, yet they must remain painfully aware of the limitations of what these communities have created so far.

With or without access to a lesbian community, the couple enjoys more control over who knows of their relationship during the couple formation stage than will be true later on. The dichotomy between the couple's internal sense of excitement about the new relationship and the outer world's frequent disapproval or silence, however, propels some couples further into isolation, just as it motivates many others to maintain as much independence from social response as possible.

The couple's perception that they can live relatively fully within this privacy is more persuasive now than at any future stage. While inevitably failing to reach complete social self-sufficiency, many lesbian couples achieve partial independence from social validation, strengthening their relationship against the stresses of homophobia and turning the strain of imposed isolation into the more active choosing of a distinctive relational privacy.

While the partners' relationships to each of the social groupings in their lives will grow more complex over time, this important initial period provides them with confidence that their relationship can support them. With their foundation partially established, couples can now progress into later family life cycle stages. As the challenges and rewards of partnered life evolve, most couples will continue to look to these early days as crucially important and as their initial source of "couple glue."

7

Stage Two:
Ongoing Couplehood

THE FIRST STAGE OF A RELATIONSHIP DOES NOT LAST FOREVER. NEWness, by definition, inevitably gives way to other feelings. No couple remains perched on that initial edge forever, regardless of its rewards.

With stage one comes very disrupted lives. Friends complain that they cannot find their newly partnered friend. The partners themselves no longer feel like they really live in their own home, now that they are not there as often; laundry and shopping somehow do not get done frequently enough, and evening rituals fall by the wayside. Couples feel as if they are living on the run, having relinquished much of their routine to follow the heat of their new love.

Eventually, this gets tiring. Partners begin to miss the exact routines they could not wait to throw aside just a short while ago. They each want to clean their house, to sit down and pay their bills, to spend some time alone. The partners begin to want both the still-fresh passion they feel and a way to integrate their new partner into their previously established lives.

As the partners will soon realize, combining passion and dailiness is a complex task—one that marks the couple's entry into the second family life cycle stage. Stability no longer seems deadly dull, and making love until dawn feels somehow too taxing to keep doing every night. For the first time, the couple can create patterns of being together and can sculpt the beginnings of ongoing connectedness.

149

The partners are not seeking "married" life—just a little more rest, a few more chores completed, and a few friendships restored.

There is no way around the fact that stage two represents a trade-off. Partners exchange the thrill of their initial passion for the deeper and less self-conscious intimacy that now emerges. While this second stage has a great deal to offer couples, the partners are also acutely aware that something from stage one is lost.

It was their first anniversary, and Jaime really wanted to spend it reliving their first night together. She imagined they would go back to the same restaurant and repeat the after-dinner walk that had resulted in their first kiss. As the day grew closer, though, she started to worry about her plan. She somehow knew it wouldn't feel the same a year later—that they couldn't really recapture the anxious excitement that had added so much to that perfect night. Still, she wanted to relive even just one night of that scary, thrilling vulnerability.

For partners who have attributed their relationship's value to the craze of limerence, the transition into stage two is very difficult. Even partners who fully recognize and value the deepening intimacy that becomes possible may find themselves mourning the loss of their love's wild, emotion-packed initial passion. While stage two offers tremendously rewarding possibilities that could never occur in stage one, this truth takes time—and work—to accomplish.

Lesbian couples need to know that the fact that their initial excitement may now be calming down does not signal relational failure. While all couples risk interpreting this transition as evidence that the relationship is petering out, lesbian couples are at particular risk because they have so little information about what is normal for their relationships. In addition, society encourages lesbian couples to expect the worst through its constant messages that only heterosexual pairings can succeed. The slowing down of their initial passion is a powerful screen onto which couples may project these fears. The explanations for their sense of loss seem ambiguous to the partners, raising insecurities that are common in most (if not all) people.

The couple relationship turns an important corner as it moves from unbridled passion to the beginning of stability. While brand-new relationships offer great excitement, they also require the partners to tolerate tremendous uncertainty. Few partners can indefinitely withstand the vulnerability of being chosen only for the present moment. Most need at some point to mitigate the risks and exposure of early romance with a gradually developing foundation of relational security.

Stage two allows this foundation to solidify. The partners take on huge amounts of relational work during this period and have the opportunity to discover powerful truths about themselves and each other. The tasks are unevenly loaded into these early years of the relationship, as the partners take on the enormous challenge of bringing each other into their everyday lives.

The Tasks of Ongoing Couplehood

Throughout this stage, couples find ways to use daily moments between them to symbolize their deepening connectedness. During stage one, the couples sought validation that they were, in fact, new lovers. Now the partners need more. They want to know that they are an ongoing *couple*, and they work to demonstrate this increasing conviction between them. The pair now tends to spend a great deal of time together, sharing secrets and emotions, family histories, and private dreams. Daily rituals and patterns take on particular meaning as the couple begins to shape their unique and blended life together. With the ensuing emotional closeness, the couple begins to assume a short-term future commitment between them. Finally, they can realistically make plans for themselves and can buttress themselves against the ever-present insecurity that the relationship will cool as quickly as it heated up.

> *The couple looked over the large calendar they had hanging in the kitchen. "Hey, we have plans written down for three months from now," Jema noticed. "How do you know I'll still be here?" Ellen knew Jema was playing, and she confidently retorted, "No one in their right mind would want to leave me." Suddenly serious, Jema looked at Ellen deeply and told her she was right: "I already know I'll be here. I feel more sure every day."*

Couples who move in together early into this second stage have easy access to the daily behaviors that symbolize the progress of their relationship. As they develop chosen ways of doing everything from decorating their home to putting dinner on the table, they work at erasing the boundary that separates "I" and "you" from "we." Everything from seeing both of their names on the mail that gets delivered to choosing household amenities reassures the couple that their relationship is real. Sometimes partners will get a pet after they move in together to underscore the new family unit. Gardening in the yard can powerfully connote the growth and development of the relationship, as can having mutual friends over who acknowledge the true nature of the couple's relationship.

Couples who do not live together find other ways to accomplish the increased joining that is central to this stage. Short-range future plans—for example, a joint vacation planned several months in advance—assume that the couple relationship will still be intact, thus offering some demonstration of a relational commitment. For couples where one of the women has children, involving the nonparenting partner in the children's lives may well symbolize increased trust, as well as a belief that the relationship will continue. Entering into a vow of monogamy may also meet this need.

Lesbian couples may wear each other's clothing, allowing it to signify the easy intimacy that exists between them, or start photo albums of their shared experiences. They may institute some rituals, such as going dancing together every Tuesday night, or take a portion of their money and form a joint fund toward future social plans. Coming out as a couple to coworkers or within the partners' social circles may serve to demonstrate that the couple relationship is progressing and that the initial limerence is being replaced by the partners' deeper involvement. Couples may turn to their friends—or, for the very lucky, to their families of origin—to supply some of the needed validation during this stage.

As the couple shares a wider range of experiences, the partners learn facts about each other's personality traits, defensive styles, values systems, and areas of vulnerability that were obscured during their initial contact. In addition, couples now learn more about each other's past histories (in other love relationships and within their families of origin) as the patterns of these significant experiences become manifest in the couple relationship. While partners in stage one typically devote a great deal of effort to deciphering the impact of relevant history on their new partners, they now begin to interpret accurately the bits of information they have accumulated.

When Sue came down with tonsillitis, Kay immediately made plans to spend the evening; she brought juice, magazines, and plenty of stories to keep Sue's mind off her symptoms. Kay could immediately tell, however, that Sue wanted to be left alone. As tactfully as possible, Sue suggested they wait to see each other until she felt better.

Later, the couple talked about what had happened and realized that each was responding to illness in a way that reflected how she had been cared for as a child. Kay was used to being the center of attention, with the family convening in her room to help her pass the time. Sue's family, though, had encouraged family members to recuperate more privately and to place less focus on their being sick. Clearly, the partners had some decisions to make about what to keep from each partner's legacy.

Not all new couples' past histories move aside to make way for their initial passion. For example, sexual abuse survivors may find that the relationship's initial focus on sexuality quickly triggers the effects of their traumatization. It may not be until stage two in the family life cycle, however, that the couple can assess what the ongoing implication of that history will be within the couple relationship, since new passion can temporarily overwhelm the fears survivors experience. Similarly, for women just coming out, the past may emerge right away, particularly if they are facing rejection from their families or friends for going ahead with their lesbian relationship. Likewise, partners from differing racial or religious backgrounds or women forming a couple relationship as the result of having an affair may be similarly encumbered before they reach this second stage. Typically, however, it is during stage two that the partners' pasts become particularly relevant to the work of developing the relationship.

Commitment

Most people prefer sure bets. Few people wager significantly on schemes they know little about, and most do not want to hear that their investment could all be lost. Taking these risks can be even harder when it is one's *heart* on the line. Up until now, the partners have been able to take the relationship as it has come, with few demands for long-range guarantees. Now, however, both partners begin to long for more assurance that their heart will not be broken next week or next month when the newness of the relationship fades.

As each partner realizes the gamble she is taking, the fearlessness of stage one gives way, exposing the fears of rejection, abandonment, suffocation, and disappointment that have remained largely below the surface. Now the partners want to know what they can count on and what they should expect. Does their partner distance herself in difficult times? How far away will she go, and when and how will she reconnect? Does she cling when she feels threatened, and will there be space enough left for each to lead independent lives? How dependable is she not to leave for some new lover? How will she respond to the previously unnoticed blemishes of who the other is? How will each feel emotionally safe?

As couples take in the huge amount of information now available to them, they become able to make realistic commitments for the first time. The commitment must allow the couple to envision a short-term joint future, yet be tentative enough to reflect the reality that the promise is not yet permanent. The couple must maintain a particularly precarious balance between their newfound cohesion and an uncertain future—a balance that becomes even more difficult when insecurities get triggered.

The commitment that is possible in this stage offers an important but incomplete respite from these fears. The partners cannot realistically promise they will stay together through thick and thin. The possibility of one leaving the other remains, and each partner will have to manage occasional escalations of these risks. While the couple will work at this crucial boundary (of commitment versus risk) throughout their relationship, stage two presents them with the first and one of the most powerful tasks related to these challenges. The commitment they make will serve as the trade-off for the now-decreasing limerence of stage one.

Couples respond differently to the insecurities exposed during this stage. Some couples, for example, may prematurely declare their commitment to be permanent. While offering the partners relief from their fears of being abandoned, this strategy creates the false impression that the foundation of the relationship is already built. Unless the partners grapple with the challenges presented by their needs for both closeness and distance, a crucial kind of relational strength may not fully develop. These couples may later discover that their relationship can bear only limited weight.

Other couples may hold back on making a commitment, warding off the possibility of broken promises by making as few promises as possible. These couples emphasize their separate lives as imagined protection against the pain of a possible breakup. Nonetheless, the relationship is moving along, and simply denying this truth in order to ward off the accompanying insecurities provides marginal support at best.

Living Together

In part because of soaring divorce rates, heterosexuals for the most part no longer move immediately from a temporary period of dating to consideration of marriage. To slow the pace of the commitment between the partners, many couples add an interim step of living together without promising a permanent relational commitment. Living together became increasingly socially acceptable beginning in the 1960s; in the 1990s it is a generally—though not universally—accepted option as a relational stage for couples.

This interim stage of living together better reflects the reality of how relationships proceed. It is not reasonable to move immediately from limerence to permanence, and the massive resulting stress on relationships that are not fully formed sooner or later puts the partnership in serious jeopardy.

At the same time, many books and articles have been devoted to the trend among young couples to prioritize their individual needs and desires over their commitment to sustaining the couple unit. Couples are inundated with so-called self-help approaches encouraging them to focus almost solely on themselves. These theories pathologize the compromising and sacrificing that any functioning partnership periodically requires. The resulting public perception that escalating breakup rates are due to young people who cannot commit probably also holds important lessons.

These two truths—that commitment can only be developed gradually, and also that insufficient commitment is an equal danger to the relationship's stability—make up the parallel themes of this second stage. Like heterosexual couples, lesbian partners must hold back the desire to move too quickly while still taking the risk of movement toward an increasingly committed relational status.

Lesbian couples face an additional stress that exerts significant influence on the course of their relationships. While heterosexual couples can use living together as a trial marriage of sorts, trying on the possibility of a permanent commitment and developing much of the needed foundation before moving into a marriage, lesbians have no similar next step to take after moving into the same home.[1]

In lesbians' attempts to identify events that mark the progression of their relationships, living together takes on a tremendous and coveted symbolism. Unlike heterosexual couples, who can use moving in together to slow down their progression toward marriage, lesbian couples frequently move in together to *create* movement in their relationship. Perhaps this is why many lesbian couples move in together relatively quickly, accepting the risks of such a dramatic step in exchange for an indication of their movement out of stage one and into stage two.

The ability of a given lesbian couple to control the pacing of their developing relational commitment will be affected by a number of factors. The ages of the partners are one such influence; younger women probably have an easier time moving slowly in relationships because they are still in an individual developmental stage that is consistent with shorter-term planning. For a twenty-five-year old to be unsure where she will be in fifteen years is frequently more tolerable that for a woman who is fifty-five and is beginning to plan for retirement.

Class differences may also affect this task for couples, particularly those who choose to live together. If the partners envision themselves as future homeowners, then renting an apartment will signify a more tentative movement toward commitment for them than for couples who expect to rent all their lives. Economically privileged couples have the option of moving quickly into fuller commitment if they choose to buy joint property rather than rent an apartment together. Although the relational symbolism of these moves will vary among couples, it will be very significant in shaping the partners' understanding of where they are in terms of commitment to each other.

In addition, for partners in their first lesbian relationship, the development of their emerging sexual identity will affect their pace toward commitment. They may slow down to allow time to incorporate this new self-knowledge, or they may speed toward commitment, since the newfound identity is experienced as being housed in the relationship itself.

Regardless of their circumstances, all lesbian couples must negotiate this balance between allowing interdependence and maintaining their separate identities. The partners grapple with their approaches to developing genuine intimacy, with the relevant challenges presented by the partners' individual stages of development, and to managing the fears that accompany this process. Throughout this stage, couples work and rework this delicate and changing equation, contending with each partner's capacities and deficiencies in creating intimacy as well as the developing dynamics of their particular pairing.

Fusion

While lesbian couples often place great value on achieving fusion throughout their couple relationships, the tasks of this stage especially encourage the couple to create fusion now. During this stage, the partners make the transition from being primarily separate individuals to also becoming an ongoing couple unit. They deliberately loosen the relational boundaries between themselves, allowing the unique features of their relationship to emerge as a result of this closeness. At this juncture, the couple's fusion may feel especially rewarding, as now there is sufficient authentic connection between the partners for each to receive real sustenance from their intimate sharing.

While the interpersonal dynamic typical in stage one tends to consist of charged sexual tension and desire, the quality of closeness possible in stage two reflects the sense of safety and trust the partners are developing. Although the relationship commonly retains its sexuality, the bond is now deeper and fuller, if at times more quiet. The couple repeatedly experiences their connection as endless and without danger, allowing the partners to immerse themselves fully and revel in the intimacy they have achieved.

"I can't get you close enough," Angela whispered in Jean's ear, as the couple held each other as tight as they could physically tolerate. "I want to tell you my every secret, show you my every feeling, tell you my every thought."

For lesbians, the opportunity to intentionally blur individual boundaries and increase their closeness is powerfully enhanced by the partners' both having female bodies. The resulting identification with the other's actual physical experience reinforces the couple's feeling of heightened fusion.

> *Lost in passion, Abbie closed her eyes and felt Emma touch her in deeply familiar ways. With every touch, Abbie knew what they were both experiencing. She knew exactly what it felt like to touch a woman as Emma was, and she could sense that Emma knew exactly what receiving that touch was like. As two women, they could both savor their own sensations and identify strongly with the other's feelings. It seemed so powerfully natural that they would feel so interconnected.*

In addition to the explicitly sexual connection lesbian couples typically share during this stage, they also tend to create and maintain high levels of nonsexual physical affection.[2] With their entry into stage two, lesbian couples may now initiate much physical affection that is meant not as a prelude to sexual contact, but as a complete experience in and of itself. This pattern both reflects the high fusion levels common to lesbian couples and may help to actually create such fusion, as touch reinforces the couple's sense of connectedness and intimacy.

These powerful and wonderful feelings are not unique to lesbian couples. Survey research, however, continually finds that lesbian couples place particular priority on creating this feeling of oceanic oneness with their partners and frequently evaluate their relationships in large part on the basis of their success in creating this mutual feeling.[3] Authors have repeatedly suggested that what distinguishes lesbian couples is their particular success in creating this euphoric and seemingly full connection with their partners.[4] At the same time, lesbian couples may feel especially sharp pain when their fusion inevitably ruptures and the partners' differences and sources of conflict emerge.

Distance

If the welcome intimacy described above constituted the whole experience of the second stage, couples might not perceive this period as especially challenging or work-intensive. Few human beings can tolerate uninterrupted closeness, however, and equally few can consistently offer this full connection to their lovers. This period of intimacy is complicated by the partners' competing strong need to establish limits on their connection, as well as to assert their individual boundaries and needs for separateness. While in reality the partners have always needed both closeness and distance, the limerence of initial attraction tends to disproportionately highlight the partners' moves into ever-increasing proximity. This still-early relationship stage creates a circumstance ripe for partners to experience not only their deepened desire for their partner on the one hand, but their fears related to rejection, abandonment, and failure at the same time. For couples negotiating the work of this stage, the emergence of the partners' needs for distance comes as a rude awakening.

Stage two of the lesbian family life cycle raises powerful, ancient vulnerabilities for the partners. It is all but assured that they will struggle as they try to balance their needs for intimacy and for a separate self. Without enough relational history between the partners, all frightening possibilities seem plausible to them during periods of distress. The women must face the fact that they do not·know enough about each other at exactly the times that they most want some guarantees. While years later, any individual fight will be less likely to convince the partners that the relationship is about to end, breaking up seems a more realistic threat at this time.[5] Especially during the beginning period of this second stage, the partners must sort out what part of their reactions is actually linked to present events and what part comes from the resurfacing of earlier losses. The couple is quite dependent on each partner's degree of self-awareness at this point, as neither has a complete picture of the other's vulnerabilities.

"Why did you erupt like that," Evelyn said, "when all I said was that I couldn't stay over tonight? We hadn't planned to stay together, had we?" Elaine was forced to admit they hadn't discussed it. "Well, you say it like you couldn't care less whether we're together or not. I end up feeling like you would just as soon leave now, for that matter." The couple sat in silence, as each tried to figure out how this exchange had gotten so tense so quickly. Finally, Elaine forced herself to try to bridge the gap. "Look, I'll admit that I bring some baggage with me on this one. When

I was with Jema I never felt like she especially wanted to be with me, and I may be oversensitive because of that. But I can't have that insecurity triggered every time you want a night alone. You have to tell me differently so we don't get into this battle every time."

Early into this stage, the partners begin to see how each defends herself in times of conflict or threat. The relational situation virtually guarantees that each partner will be confronted with some of her worst fears, which usually involve rejection by her partner and/or loss of her independent identity. Lesbians may have to work especially hard to normalize one or both partners' needs for distance in the relationship, since women tend to place their emphasis on creating intimate bonds with their lovers. Also, lesbians' reliance on fusion to protect their relationships against homophobic challenge increases the chances they will disproportionately focus on sustaining the connectedness between the partners.[6] Many lesbian couples must work hard to balance each partner's movement into and away from the developing intimacy of second-stage couplehood.

Sarah had felt tortured all day waiting for Chris to call. Finally she couldn't stand the terror she felt another minute. She dialed Chris's number and became instantly enraged to hear Chris sound so calm, almost cheerful. "How could you leave me waiting all day after the fight we had last night? I've been out of my mind with pain about how you pushed me away. And then you don't even call me to work it out?" Chris said, "I was going to call you. I just think it's best if we take some distance first. I would have called you, probably tomorrow."

"Tomorrow! You were going to leave me this upset until tomorrow? How could you do that? Don't you care about our relationship? Am I supposed to be the only one to worry about it when something goes wrong?"

"Look, I'm someone who always does better if I take some space to myself first. It doesn't mean I'm not coming back, it just means I need a break—a little time to think."

"Well how am I supposed to know if you're coming back? There's no guarantee of that!"

Chris hated these amorphous conversations where they fought over how she should and should not take space. It was true that she had been

feeling kind of burdened by the relationship this week, and she had
enjoyed forgetting about it for awhile. She wished Sarah would just let it
alone and not make such a big deal out of it. She seemed so overly threat-
ened. On the other hand, Chris had heard similar complaints about her-
self from lovers in the past.

Each felt the seriousness of what their relationship was up against.
What if their styles were just incompatible? What if Sarah couldn't tol-
erate the space Chris needed, and what if Chris couldn't move closer
when Sarah needed reassurance?

Struggles related to the management of closeness and distance surface in a wide variety of ways. Often the partners do not agree on
what is occurring, or on who has set the cycle in motion. The distancing partner's experience may be that she is being forced away by her
partner's encroaching or suffocating behavior. Frequently the alleged
smotherer argues back that she is holding tighter only in response to
her partner's efforts to push her away.

Couples must learn to distinguish partners' nonthreatening
requests for the space or separateness needed in any healthy relationship from a more dangerous reliance on distancing in reaction to
stress. Partners who shift their focus and time in order to develop
other aspects of themselves are not necessarily distancing themselves
from the relationship in any problematic sense. This kind of natural
movement toward and away from engagement need not threaten the
couple relationship; in fact, each partner can bring new energy created by outside stimulation. In contrast, when one partner must sever
all sense of emotional connectedness with the other in order to
achieve desired space, the relationship will absorb the reverberations
of this abrupt or exaggerated disconnection. The distinction becomes
clear in the partners' emotional experience: Those who establish distance in a healthy manner maintain some reminiscence of their previous connectedness, whereas those who do so defensively reject the
previous connectedness and create an abrupt change between the
partners.

The couple arrived at the therapy session locked in a stalemate.
According to Sharon, Cindy simply could not tolerate her having sepa-
rate friendships, and she herself was unwilling to live without them.

Cindy countered that if what Sharon was having were friendships that would be fine with her, but these were clear flirtations that posed a real threat to their relationship.

As the sessions unfolded, the underlying dynamic became clear. Sharon's increased contact with other women was almost always on the heels of Cindy doing something new alone. Sue's provocative moves toward other lesbians allowed her to pull Cindy into closer, if conflictual, proximity to her. The partners actually became the spokeswomen for each other's positions, as Sharon now presented herself as the voice for separate involvements and Cindy retreated to advocate continued exclusivity. It took effort to remember that beneath Sharon's cry for independence lay clear fears of being left, and that behind Cindy's pleading presentation the conditions existed for independent actions.

Couples work and rework this distinction, usually in times of conflict or insecurity in one or both partners. The women must negotiate the process for taking space from each other and must reach at least a minimal level of compatibility on how their defensive styles will be tolerated within the relationship. Pairings containing one partner who naturally craves time alone during periods of distress and another who feels a deep need for closeness at those same times will have hard work to do early in this stage.

Differences

A related task for couples in stage two is to recognize and manage the range of differences that are by now becoming evident between the partners. Whether the women actively welcome these differences or unhappily crash into them as they go along, they will confront many reminders that they are two distinct individuals. How they react to this fact will be based on everything from personality factors to their past history to important ethnic and cultural distinctions in how differences between people are interpreted.

"We never talk about things in depth anymore," Susan lamented. "I miss our debating about world events and feminist politics." But Margaret just couldn't do it anymore. Every time they had a so-called discussion of these topics, Susan launched into an impassioned rebuttal of

everything Margaret said. Susan seemed to thrive on this, but to Margaret it was painful.

"I can't stand the arguing," Margaret told her. "I know you love it and that you were raised with it. Your whole family argues with each other and no one seems to mind, but I can't stand it. I keep trying to find our points of agreement. You seem to think that's less interesting or something, but to me it's really important." They both knew they sounded like ethnic stereotypes, with the Jewish partner finding argument stimulating and the WASP partner experiencing it as unpleasant.

Over time, the partners found ways to accommodate each other's needs. Susan found that commenting more frequently on those ideas of Margaret's that she agreed with did not deaden the debate, and it allowed Margaret to stop personalizing Susan's rebuttals. Margaret likewise worked to stop viewing the couple's arguing during these discussions as representative of how the partners felt about each other or how their relationship was progressing. While the difference in style remained between them, the partners learned to anticipate areas of difficulty, as well as the specific concerns that each partner experienced at those times.

Obviously, some disparities are easier for couples to embrace than others. Relationships can be enhanced greatly when the partners are able to welcome their differences. For example, the partners may pursue very dissimilar lines of work, and each may enjoy hearing about the other's work life without necessarily wishing that she herself had such a job. This kind of difference affirms both partners, as each can appreciate or feel stimulated by the other and yet be sure of her own choice. Similarly, one partner may possess a particular talent, interest, or trait that the other one appreciates being in proximity to within the relationship. For example, a musician may provide a nonmusical partner with access to people and things her own life would not otherwise include. A writer may bring her partner into contact with a community of poets or storytellers the latter would otherwise never meet.

Differences can also reassure partners that they will not be engulfed by each other. As two women, lesbian couples may find that they have so much in common that each partner feels threatened. Wanting closeness is not the same as wanting to be exactly like someone else. Clearly visible and enduring differences, or even conflicts, between the partners can affirm each one's unique identity and can actually make emotional intimacy less frightening than it might be otherwise.

If couples believe that their bond comes solely from their points of commonality, though, the partners will experience their major differences as threats. Most couples grapple with some version of this dilemma, particularly at this stage in the relationship, when the partners have little experience in confronting their differences and do not yet feel confident in the strength of their bond.

Younger women's struggles with differences may be somewhat different than those confronted by older women. Earlier in adulthood, a woman's identity may be less fully formed, and thus she may be more easily influenced by her desire to enhance similarities between herself and her partner. She may temporarily avoid facing differences by defensively incorporating core aspects of her partner's identity as her own. This may allow the couple to postpone some of the feared experience of being dissimilar, although they will almost certainly have to return to the challenge of establishing identities both as individuals and as a couple.

Conversely, older women may have more difficulty avoiding or tempering their differences, because their increased life experience has further developed each one's sense of her own personal identity over time. Flexibility or compromise may feel like it is at greater expense to the already intact identities of older partners.

Conflict

Not even limerence can squelch all conflict for new couples. Conflicts do emerge, and the partners must respond to them as they arise. Because stage two of the family life cycle brings large amounts of new information about each partner and about the compatibility of the couple relationship, it is a likely time for couples to confront in earnest the fact that relationships repeatedly include conflict.[7]

Early into stage two, partners must display a growing ability to initiate reconciliation with each other. Each woman must become able to go first, crossing the tense and perhaps angry gulf between them. This absolutely critical skill reflects a partner's ability to tolerate vulnerability in a moment where neither partner feels safe. As trust between the partners develops further, each must demonstrate an increased capacity to take risks in this area. Otherwise fights are protracted and damaging, distorting the importance of the topic involved to the point where the couple will have no way to distinguish major battles from relatively inconsequential disputes.

This difficult balancing of how and when to assert one's own position and/or to empathize with the other's experience requires endless refinement, especially during stage two. When it is time for the conflict to be resolved, each partner must place mending the connection ahead of winning the battle. The couple must develop flexibility in these roles, as healthy growth cannot occur if the partners are in fixed roles—one always arguing, and the other always accommodating. Through repeating this process of conflict and resolution, the couple establishes patterns of decision making and communication that may last throughout the life of the relationship.[8]

While the process of the couple's fighting is important, by stage two the actual content of the conflicts reveals important information as well. The couple now has logged enough time together to identify recurring themes and charged differences between them. Each partner can now glimpse where problem areas reside, and the couple begins to grapple with the meaning of these tensions. For example, if a couple continually confronts differences in their value systems, goals for their lives, or basic views of the world, the partners need to take a serious look at their general compatibility and observe closely how they resolve these matters as they arise.

The partners face a daunting task. They must learn to distinguish the manageable disappointments present in their relationship from the signals of a basic, underlying incompatibility. It is very hard to know how much significance to attach to any particular conflict. Because the partners still have spent only a limited amount of time together, they may exaggerate the meaning of a particular problem and prematurely lose faith in their relationship. In being quick to attach dire implications to a battle, they may fail to realize that a healthy relationship can withstand some enduring areas of conflict. These are specific times when lesbian couples' lives are harmed by their lack of access to role models and peers who could share their own learning and support viable couples through their first experiences with serious conflict.

Conversely, partners may find themselves holding on to an

unworkable relationship, falsely reassuring themselves that the conflict will pass or underestimating the significance of the differences between them.

> *The couple reported that their plans to move in together continually brought them into serious conflict. Barbara wanted to buy a house, knowing the partners would have to increase their hours at work to afford it but feeling that owning a home was a central goal worth extra sacrifice. Penny, though, was unwilling to increase her work hours. Owning a home was not a particularly important goal to her, and she valued her free time far more than she wanted to earn more money.*
>
> *As the sessions progressed, the partners presented considerably different visions of their futures. Barbara wanted to dedicate her thirties and forties to hard work, hoping to earn enough money to afford both a primary residence and a beach house before she reached age fifty. She spoke with passion about the importance of these personal goals as the path she wanted for herself and for a long-term partnership she would be happy in. Penny shared little of this vision. To her, living for the present moment was far more important, as were several central interests she had apart from work. She did not aspire to the more middle-class dreams Barbara held and felt that compromising substantially on these disagreements would be at odds with her true self.*
>
> *As each partner listened to each other, they understood the scope of the difference between them and recognized that it would emerge repeatedly throughout any shared life they might pursue. With great sadness but clear decision, the partners gradually separated, choosing to hold true to their differing life goals and to allow the relationship to end.*

For couples who remain together, conflicts and the need for the partners to negotiate their differences continue through all phases of the family life cycle. The learning that takes place during this second stage, however, is especially rich, and couples can learn to tolerate fighting and to generate a gradually increasing sense of relational security even from some of their most unpleasant shared experiences.

Combining Fusion and Distance

Perhaps if couples could take the tasks of coming close together and of learning to manage conflict and separateness one at a time, the work of this stage would not seem so challenging. If partners could first spend time blending their lives without facing any serious differences between them until their relationship had absorbed all of the stabilizing power fusion can offer, then maybe they would not feel so overwhelmed and at risk of breaking up.

Some models of couple development do present these as sequential tasks, suggesting that conflicts are minimized and denied by the partners until later in the relationship. For example, McWhirter and Mattison's model for gay male couple relationships does not identify dealing with conflict as a task until year four.[9] Likewise, Clunis and Green, in their work on lesbian couple relationships, separate "romance" and "conflict" into two stages.

The real challenge of stage two, though, is that the couple confronts several crucial and difficult challenges *at the same time*. Couples work to sustain a feeling of oneness despite the inevitable and repeated interruptions caused by powerful conflicts and needs for separate space. The couple must manage both simultaneously without a relational foundation strong enough to absorb the stress. The partners work to recapture the sense of fusion, knowing it will again be ruptured and yet again mended. It is precisely this simultaneity of the tasks that develops the foundation between the partners. Neither fusion nor conflict alone can create a reality-based bond between the partners.

Stage two forces the couple to confront several crucial polarities and to incorporate both elements into their relationship. They must establish commitment, but they cannot rely on it to be permanent. They must foster the development of intimate closeness, yet become increasingly adept at managing incidents of broken connection. The partners must look for shared values, interests, and experiences while continually grappling with their central differences.

When these tasks are separated, the partners fail to achieve the bulk of the work. Above all, the couple must develop flexibility in responding to very dichotomous experiences with equal strength and capacity. The aim is not to establish one static balance between these competing variables and stay there. Instead, couples must identify correctly what a given situation calls for and learn how to provide the needed response. Couples who know how to invite great fusion but cannot tolerate the assertion of individual identities may not survive.

Likewise, couples who come well equipped to hold their own in a battle but who cannot allow for vulnerability will also not create a full relationship.

Carly and Debby had come a long way together in their first three years. Both could feel that they were reaping the benefits of what they had accomplished emotionally, and each felt relaxed with their interaction. Tonight they were enjoying both being home: Carly sitting by the stereo listening to classical music, and Debby upstairs working with watercolor paints. It felt like a comfortable balance, both home together yet each engaged in her favorite individual pastime.

Women are socialized to preserve relational ties at the expense of articulating their full individual selves, as if intimacy and individuality are contrasting aims. As a result lesbians, particularly those from certain ethnic and racial backgrounds, have been trained to view closeness as arising out of powerful similarity between two people. Women frequently come to partnerships likely to sacrifice their distinct identities in the service of taking care of the relationship. Because of this, it is important that the work of this second stage not be seen as sequential steps where first women de-emphasize their separateness and build cohesion, then incorporate their differences later.

Perhaps in a model depicting gay men's couple relationships (such as McWhirter and Mattison's) it is possible to treat delays in asserting separate identities as normal until after the couple has emphasized blending for a period of time. After all, men have been socialized to hold on to their individual identities, and temporarily understating these distinctions may be a manageable risk for them. Lesbians, however, face additional obstacles to resuming this focus on individual identity later on. Closeness and separateness must be equally incorporated into the original mix in order for lesbian couples to view their differences not just as frightening but also as resources in their relationship. Postponing recognition of differences may be a natural tendency for many couples, but it is far from neutral for couples who bring a double dose of social training in avoiding these inevitable components of a relationship.

Joanne and Beth had looked forward to this vacation for months. Now, on their first night, they found themselves on the verge of a big fight. Both struggled with the competing desires to express their anger and also to preserve the mood of excitement both wanted to feel.

"Look, we have to get this out of the way if we're going to salvage this night," Joanne said. "I think we should give this an hour and really say what we need to, then agree we aren't going to hold on to it and ruin the start of our vacation together." Beth cautiously agreed, thinking about how hard it might be to let it go in an hour. We could never have pulled this off a year ago, she thought, when we had no idea how to be both angry and close.

In addition to all that is occurring privately between the partners during their transition into ongoing couplehood, their relationships with the world around them change as well. While many new couples welcome a good deal of distance even from family and cherished friends, the couple's privacy shifts into isolation if it does not bend to the changes brought by entry into the stage of ongoing couplehood.

As the partners bring each other into their daily lives, they address the range of existing relationships each partner brings with her. For partners who have come out to their family, friends, and/or coworkers, this is a time in which there are significantly more visible signs that the couple relationship has become an ongoing partnership (especially for couples who move in together.) The partners now absorb the various responses these significant others offer to the couple and to their relationship.

Even couples who feel they must remain secretive about their relationship reach the point of wanting a softer boundary around themselves. These couples may jointly pursue some activity or community involvement, or they may introduce their partners to people who the partners were already close to before the relationship began. While the dangers of homophobia curtail many couples' opportunities to interweave their personal networks, it seldom takes away their desire to broaden their involvement as their relationship becomes more established.

Not only do couples want to reconnect with the other people in their lives at this point, but those others typically demand their return as well. Jobs, families of origin, children, friends, and community commitments all require the partners' attention. Children, for example, do not wait until their parents are more in the mood to include them. Job-related demands do not coincide with the partners' readiness to be pulled farther away from each other. Gatherings, rituals, anniversaries, and crises in one's family of origin occur without regard for where the new lesbian couple is in their stage of development and how the couple will feel about being called into fuller participation at this moment.

The couple's social relationships in stage two are shaped by competing tensions. The couple now reaches out for more inclusion in the world around them, just as others exert pressure on the partners to resume their individual participation in previous commitments. These outsiders' demands however, often come with no corresponding recognition of the new family unit. The increased involvement they request is frequently for the partners separately—often requiring the partners' collusion in others' refusal to see them as a couple. Clearly this taints the invitation to the partners, and it complicates each option open to them. Over time, this homophobia becomes internalized as well, as the couple's temporary immunity to society's opinion of them wears off.

> *Fran finally said what she had been holding back. "I haven't wanted to tell you this before, but I cringe every time you take my hand in public. I've never shown my relationship with my lover in front of strangers before, and I notice myself trying to avoid situations where you are going to touch me." Mya was visibly shocked and responded, "It's important to me to not censor myself in such a homophobic way. Please don't ask me to stop. Maybe there are some places I could agree not to touch you, but I can't just agree that we'll only be partners when no one is around."*
>
> *Fran grew more and more anxious as the conversation went on. She was sure they wouldn't agree on where to come out and where not to. They hadn't really confronted this before, when they spent almost all of their time alone.*

Conclusion

In the second stage of the lesbian family life cycle, couples move into an ongoing but still unguaranteed relational commitment. Still unprepared to consider anything permanent, these women invite each other into a shared daily life. In the process they gather crucial experience together, learning about each other's personality, defensive style, future dreams, and early life. The partners tolerate new feelings of ambivalence as conflicts, differences, and episodes of relational distancing break the infatuation that characterized the first life cycle stage. In addition, they learn to balance their emerging interdependence with each one's need to maintain her separate life and identity. The couple's social relationships change as well, as they reenter the larger social world and grapple with how to incorporate their new status as an ongoing couple.

Through these challenges the couple relationship can deepen, offering each partner increased security, fuller intimacy, and a sober and realistic view of the ongoing stresses they both will face. No longer the tentative, unfamiliar pair they were in stage one, women who have navigated the challenges of stage two together enjoy the fruits of their labor. The partners' work results in a solid foundation beneath them, providing more relational security and sense of belonging than can possibly be accomplished through the limerence of early love.

8

Stage Three:
The Middle Years

OVER TIME, MANY COUPLES WHO HAVE ACHIEVED ONGOING STATUS want more. The limited nature of their relational commitment keeps them from charting long-range futures together, and it makes pursuing certain major family life goals impossible. The third stage of the lesbian family life cycle, characterized by the couple's movement into permanent or long-range commitment, invites the partners to solidify their sense of family membership, providing them with the anchoring and sense of security many couples seek.

For couples making the transition into their middle years, the long-range future is their focus. Framed as permanence by some and as a less specified long-term commitment by others, the couple nonetheless extends the definition of their commitment. This shift, however, represents a qualitative change in the partners' relational status and raises the stakes for the relationship, conjuring up strong emotional responses that include both great joy and powerful anxiety.

Unlike the first two family life cycle stages, the third stage continues for a substantial (although varying) period of years. Because this spans a wider range of experience both in the partners' individual adult development and in their unfolding life together, the timing of major developments is not completely predictable. Clearly couples do not spend all of their middle years working on their relationship, nor do they need to do so. This prolonged stage allows for much time to enjoy what the partners have already created, with neither partner

173

feeling an urgent desire to create major change. The continued deepening typical of these years sustains the partners for long periods of time as they rest in the developing intimacy of daily life.

At some point within this stage, though, most lesbian couples confront anxieties associated with extending their commitment. This period frequently exerts a very destabilizing influence, and it forces the couple into serious relational work.

For some couples, the struggles and fears that commonly accompany this transition arise as soon as the partners contemplate extending their commitment. Only later—assuming they persevere—do these couples experience the unprecedented security that deepened commitment has to offer.

> *The evening before their commitment ceremony, the couple invited their inner circle of friends and family to a private dinner at their home. "We weren't always sure we'd be standing here before you tonight," Becca began. "The last year and a half have been the hardest of our relationship, as we tried to decide about making this commitment. But we've exhausted every imaginable way of acting out our fear and lack of faith. We are ready to stop running, and tomorrow we will demonstrate our decision to deepen our relationship and continue on together. Finally we are ready to choose our relationship over all of life's other possibilities. We've come through a great storm, and we are ready to promise our futures."*

For other couples, the excitement and newfound security associated with extending their commitment surfaces first, delaying or obscuring their anxieties until later. The growing practice of lesbian commitment ceremonies may help this to be the case. Weddings and associated rituals whisk heterosexual couples through the complexities of making permanent commitments through their outpouring of ceremonial support from friends and families and the bestowing of legal and social recognition upon the couple's entry into married life.[1] Anxiety often is attributed not to the marriage but to the preparation for the wedding, further connoting the experience in celebratory terms. Lesbians performing commitment ceremonies at this juncture may enjoy a similar steering of their emotional responses to this crucial family life cycle transition.

A permanent commitment makes possible for the partners a kind of relational security and intimacy that cannot be achieved in new or uncommitted relationships. At the same time, fully choosing one relationship precludes choosing others, guaranteeing the partners that there will be unexplored possibilities, and potentials left undeveloped, in each of their lives.

Because the partners now place so much on the line, both the joys and difficulties of this stage are often pronounced. There is no substitute for the quality of connectedness this extended commitment offers, just as there are few anxieties as insistent as the partners' fears that they will lose crucial aspects of their separate selves. The themes raised through the couple's movement into long-term commitment lead many to seek therapy. Sadly, many couples who appear to have passed successfully through earlier stages do not survive the trials of this family life cycle stage.

The Joys of Long-Range Commitment

There is no shortcut to achieving the gradual intimacy that can develop between partners over time. The partners discover a qualitatively different emotional connection as they repeat their personally designed patterns of daily life and see each other in ways not possible when their relationship was new. They reap the stabilizing power of rituals repeated over time, as they can now claim "We do this every year" and "We always spend holidays in this way" and picture similar occasions yet to come. The couple's closeness is less dependent now on an endless stream of new experiences together; the partners' subtle idiosyncrasies, strengths, and insecurities supply their own foundation for intimate connection.

> *Greta came downstairs in her most faded and torn old jeans, and a favorite sweater that Tess had seen her wear hundreds of times before. Tess knew exactly why Greta had fished out these old favorites today, and she smiled as she imagined the day of resting on the couch and tending to her cold that Greta apparently had in mind. She knew how seldom Greta allowed herself a day of rest, and how she used these old clothes to help her settle down into the comfortable, sleepy mood she had trouble reaching on her own. They didn't exchange a word; Tess knew that she needed to stay quiet now. She enjoyed this glimpse of her lover in silence and gave Greta the room she needed.*

Entering into long-term commitment invites the partners to sculpt a joint future, complete with goals and wishes not seriously possible in earlier stages. No longer simply fantasizing, the partners invest themselves in their relationship's capacity to sustain them not simply for the immediate future but for a long time to come.

> *The couple's friends descended on their apartment with a congratulatory cake and bottle of champagne. When Jane and Louise saw them coming, they felt the excitement of today's house closing all over again. "Congratulations!" one woman exclaimed. "It's not every day you buy a cottage on the lake." "Actually," another friend interjected, "the cake's for us. We were all sick of hearing you two obsess about whether you should buy it or not."*
>
> *"Very funny, Donna," a third replied. "Come on, let's make a toast to Christa and Sue. You two worked overtime shifts for three years to make this down payment. You always seemed to know this day would come, and your faith in that has made it so. Congratulations, you guys. We're all really happy for you."*

Long-range plans, though, are not limited to economically privileged couples. They can be of any description, and the priorities they reflect may be shaped by the partners' religious, racial, or ethnic identity, class background, personal wishes, or other considerations. Regardless of its content, this shared scheme generates cohesion, an infusion of new passion, and a context for investing in life beyond the day to day. No new relationship can realistically offer the partners this expansive assumption of continued togetherness.

Even the couple's approach to their relationship's difficulties can contain the special rewards that accompany extended commitment. Earlier in the relationship, each partner may have held on to defenses that she considered essential within a still-impermanent relationship. Because this attitude limits many partners' willingness to change ingrained personal patterns, most couples in the early years of their relationship reach areas of stalemate, where particular conflicts remain unresolved. Within a long-range commitment, however, the partners gradually deepen their trust and become more willing to let go of these individual patterns. In the process, the partners reinforce their belief in their partnership's capacity to grow and change over time.

For years, the partners had fought over their weekend time. Gayle got furious whenever Vicky tried to make separate plans with her friends. Gradually the partners had submerged the fight, with Vicky asking infrequently and Gayle trying to swallow how mad these occasions made her. Earlier this year Vicky had made friends with someone who really meant a lot to her, and she couldn't abide by their covert stalemate anymore. Six months ago she had come home and said she was spending all day with Rebecca (her friend) no matter how Gayle felt about it. They fought like crazy, and had been in a cold war ever since. Vicky accused Gayle of not being sufficiently available to their relationship. Vicky retorted that she would not be controlled by Gayle any longer. On they went, weekend after weekend, looking for all the world like a couple about to break up.

Under this heightened pressure, though, Gayle began to look deeper into her resistance to Vicky's request. Remembering a previous experience with a lover in which an outside friendship had led to a full-fledged affair, she realized that she had transferred her fears to Vicky. While on some level Gayle had always known of this connection, she was now able to admit vulnerably to Gayle how it was still affecting her, and she agreed to work harder to separate the past from the present.

For her part, Vicky saw how insensitive she became in these fights. Ignoring Gayle's pain, she felt compelled to persevere, afraid she would be suffocated if she agreed to Gayle's objections. While not relinquishing her need to see friends on weekends, she softened her approach with Gayle, finally supplying the reassurance that allowed the parameters of the relationship to expand as she needed. Over the next several months, the couple implemented their new dynamic, enjoying new levels of sensitivity and individual freedom between them.

There is reason for great joy in the middle years, as couples discover that they are able and willing to adapt their relationship to support each woman's continued growth. These shifts and changes as the partners fine-tune patterns (instead of setting them for the first time) reveal the increased flexibility and level of commitment that come from years of deepened devotion. The opportunity for the partners to witness and encourage each other's personal evolution over the years brings an added dimension to both personal and relational milestones during this period of years, distinguishing this period from the more tentative relational conditions of the first two family life cycle stages. This shared knowledge and experience is a reward all its own; it can also bolster the partners against the powerful challenges that accompany this period of years.

Fears of the Middle Years

For all of the joys that come with rooted and solid coupled life, long-term commitment has another face as well. In promising to stay with their relationship, the partners agree to take on more permanently the limitations inherent both in each other and in the nature of committed life itself. In the process, many of the same relational elements that provide the couple's greatest rewards also confront them with their deepest fears.

No matter how successfully couples achieve the accommodations required earlier in their relationship, areas of enduring difference remain. The partners have by now discovered repeatedly disappointing aspects of each other and have implored each other to change. As each woman becomes newly fearful of the more permanent ramifications of her partner's imperfections, however, the middle years make it harder to take no for an answer, as one or both partners imagine stilted personal growth or insufficient vitality between them.

The heightened awareness of loss that emerges during these years can be frustratingly amorphous. Partners reckoning with life's inescapable compromises seek a more concrete battleground, and they may find the couple relationship an obvious target. Fueled by fear, the partners scrutinize previously tolerable sacrifices. While making compromises is not new to couples in their middle years, the indefinite extension of these sacrifices escalates the associated anxiety for the partners.

Specifically, the anxiety associated with extended commitment causes the partners to fear that life could become deadening, even with a beloved partner.[2] As she grapples again with her partner's limitations, a woman may now worry that those disappointments will forever narrow her own opportunity to develop herself fully, creating a kind of death within herself that she attributes to the couple relationship. There is often some truth to these fears. The mortality feared at this juncture is specifically a *relational* mortality, in which the partners fear that the liveliness of the partnership will die and the relationship will become stagnant. (This is distinguished from the more literal, physical mortality addressed in the discussion of the next family life cycle stage.)

While newness abounds in earlier stages of the family life cycle, in the middle years neither the relationship's passion nor its dailiness seem new. Aware that their union continues to require the energy of new experience, the partners must take particularly active roles in generating elements of surprise and novelty.[3] The settled quality life frequently takes on during the middle years can drain this needed excitement, however, leaving the couple vulnerable to potentially dangerous periods of predictability and relational fatigue. In extreme cases, the partners may see their hard-earned stability degenerate into relational stagnation. These twin searches—for newness in a no-longer-new relationship, and for stability that does not degenerate into stagnation—constitute the primary tasks of the couple's middle years.[4]

The Influence of Midlife

Partners in their own chronological midlife may experience the above concerns with additional intensity. Newly aware of their own personal mortality, many adults in midlife feel a greater motivation to seize life's opportunities. Frequently depicted as a period of significant personal awakening, midlife has been described as a challenge to re-embrace one's "shadow side"—previously de-emphasized aspects of the self that now vie for a more central position in a person's life.[5] This desire to develop the undeveloped within oneself sets the stage for the popularized "midlife crisis" that wreaks havoc on well-established patterns of daily living.

When midlife does stimulate one or both partners to embrace major change, their couple relationship—chosen long ago—may be in for a rough ride. The combined influence of midlife and the middle-years stage of the family life cycle can heighten partners' fears of personal and relational stagnation and lead them to equate deeper commitment with greater restriction. The partners may associate long-term commitment with a promise to stay the same just when they most want change. Many couples are affected by this interplay, since both midlife and the middle-years stage span a number of years and are therefore likely to overlap.

Inevitably, the partners will fail to achieve some of the changes they want. All couple relationships include incompatibilities that prove impervious to change, yet lesbian couples may have little access to this perspective. Without sufficient support or information about the normal experiences of other lesbian couples—including the knowledge that this family life cycle stage typically contains both intense closeness and also great struggle—partners may more quickly conclude that their differences mark a doomed relationship. If armed instead with the awareness that these contrasting responses are to be expected, more couples could retain their sense of basic security in the midst of what can often be a protracted period of struggle.

Disrupting the Relationship

Some partners accept the more permanent nature of their choices relatively calmly. Never losing sight of their relationship's rewards, these couples maintain their confidence in its capacity to contain their conflicted emotions. Influenced by personality factors, the partners' ages, and their previous life experiences, these couples treasure the unique intimacy possible in their middle years and proceed when necessary to the work that accompanies this deepened connection. While even these partners experience conflict, they nonetheless more readily acknowledge the bargains of their lives.

Not everyone, however, arrives right away at such sanguine acceptance of the costs of long-term commitment. Resistance to negotiating these substantial compromises comes in various forms, not all of which will be depicted in the following discussion. Generally, some couples act out their reactions, whereas other partners actively attempt to submerge their own and each other's commitment-related fears. While either strategy exacts a toll on couple relationships, neither spares the partners from ultimately confronting directly the trade-offs of long-standing or permanent commitment.

Formation of an Actual Triangle

In the film *Moonstruck*, the character played by Olympia Dukakis struggles to make meaning of her husband's extramarital affair. Speaking to a friend, she inquires, "Why would a man need more than one woman?" Verifying her own personal theory, her friend answers, "I think it's because they fear death." Returning home, she informs her husband, "Cosmo, I just want you to know that no matter what you do, you're going to die just like everyone else." "Thank you, Rose," he replies. "You're welcome," she responds.

There are many kinds of death. In the middle years, some partners lose faith that their couple relationship can stay truly alive over time. The ramifications of the couple's movement into long-term commitment can expose the genuine, often submerged terror that vital aspects of the self are being rendered obsolete within the couple relationship. Seeking rejuvenation, some partners enlist an outsider (in the form of a timely sexual attraction) to provide respite from their emerging and powerful fears. This new woman offers immediate newness and imagined protection from stagnation at exactly the moment the primary relationship appears unable to supply these reassurances. Persuaded both that the ongoing relationship cannot generate new passion and that the recruited substitute can rescue disappearing parts of her identity, the panicked partner (whom I will call the "outside-involved partner") is strongly induced to deepen her outside involvement. Her fear reflects the exaggeration that comes with unconscious panic, distorting both the supposedly deadening long-term relationship and the apparently enlivening outside flirtation.

As the crisis escalates, the partner's misperceptions seem verified as contact with the woman to whom she is attracted seems exciting and supportive, and her returns home lead to turmoil and increasing confrontation. Attributing unrealistic significance to this exaggerated contrast, her perceptions of the two relationships frequently continue to split, creating a triangle that supports tenacious, if oversimplified impressions of both relationships.[6]

For the outside-involved partner, this period is often excruciating. Frequently unable to account for the seemingly sudden change in her feelings, she feels pressured to make tremendously important choices, with seemingly intolerable trade-offs attached to each option. How, she may wonder, did the life that so fulfilled her come to also feel deeply frightening and constricted? While this dilemma is not unique to lesbians, female couples often particularly emphasize their anchored, ritualized home life as a way to secure and nourish the partners. For them to sense this precious and hard-earned stability at risk of becoming stagnant leaves both women feeling an enormous loss.

> *Sandy was increasingly sure she had lost her mind. What was she doing, flirting outrageously with Nan at work—sending out constant signals that she was available to pursue the heat they felt when they were together? She loved Carol without question and wasn't at all considering ending their longtime relationship. And yet she hadn't felt like this in years, consumed by an excitement that increasingly intruded on her thoughts and dreams. It was like she was single again. She felt out of control, as if someone else was directing her actions. Watching herself suggest a drink after work, Sandy's alarm was overshadowed by the thrill of Nan's saying yes. Careening toward disaster, Sandy could only hope she would catch herself, promising herself this would be the last time, vowing not to take this any farther.*

Meanwhile, the second partner in the primary relationship may be operating from oversimplifications of her own. Terrified by the sudden threat to the relationship, she may have difficulty identifying with her partner's quest for new vitality, instead working to restabilize the relationship by becoming the spokesperson for secure, committed life. Her response to the outside attraction therefore may appear restrictive rather than protective. Further highlighting the triangle, each partner is reduced to a caricature of her true self, as one holds the couple's quest for new passion and the other appears solely focused on the boundaries of committed life.

> *"What do you mean you can't stop seeing her?" Kim screamed at the top of her lungs. "You just admit to me that you are practically sleeping with this woman, and you think you're going to go on seeing her? Do I look like some kind of fool to you?"*
>
> *"I could lie to you and tell you what you want to hear, but I just can't stop seeing her. I don't know what's happening to me," Meredith cried. "I know I have to stop seeing her. I just don't know how I'm going to*

*make myself do it! I'm so confused. I don't know what's happening to me.
I just can't make this go away."*

*"Do you realize what you're risking? We've got our whole life together
on the line, and all you can say is that you're confused?" Crying also
now, Kim's voice became more pleading. "Things between us have been
good for so long now. I love our life together. So, Okay, we're not new and
exciting anymore, but we have something different. You've always valued it as much as I do. How can that all have changed all of a sudden?"*

*"I can't get to that feeling now for some reason. I think of home and
all I can feel is, well . . . I don't know."*

"No, tell me. I have to hear this."

*"Well . . . I feel kind of trapped, like some parts of me are just gone
forever. Like parts of me just don't belong here. It didn't bother me for a
long time. But, well, Denise brings them out in me, if you really want to
know. I feel like if I stop seeing her, I'm going to have to go back to not
seeing those parts of me. I don't know why that's so important all of a
sudden, but I feel like I'm going to lose myself somehow."*

*Pounding her fist on the table, Kim erupted at hearing these words.
"So now being with me means losing yourself? You think just running off
with someone new will suddenly mean you find yourself again? Have you
completely lost track of who I am? I am your lover, not your prison war-
den! When did our life together become such a drag to you?"*

At least temporarily, affairs stack the deck in favor of the brand-
new coupling. The furtive, occasional nature of the new relationship
invites both the long-term partner and "the other woman" to see
themselves and each other in their best light, as the built-in distance
keeps intimacy fears at bay and easily fires the passion that is so difficult to generate in the long-term relationship. In addition, the emotional distance inherent in a new relationship allows the partners to
spin particularly positive and exaggerated projections about themselves and each other, while achieving these fantasies remains more
difficult within the close proximity of the committed relationship.

The partners have split what needs to be an integrated challenge—
to create both security and continuing newness within the same relationship. Because the stress of this situation is so extreme, and the
central struggles so difficult, the couple can each remain stuck within
their positions for some time. Many couples do not survive this sce-

nario. An outside-attracted woman may become sufficiently persuaded by the contrast in her two lovers' images that she leaves the established relationship. The other partner may leave as well, acutely aware of her desire to share ongoing commitment and less aware of her own fears of its attendant personal sacrifices.

Nonetheless, some couples do choose to weather the storm, recognizing a bit at a time that the themes contained in their triangle are inherent in life's unfolding, not unique inadequacies of their own personalities or relationship. These couples may regain their capacity to question their own overgeneralizations. The outside-involved partner has probably not lost her capacity to sustain committed partnership, regardless of her present struggle. Likewise, her primary partner has probably not lost her interest in newness and excitement despite her present campaign in favor of continued commitment. In the interim, however, the partners' reactions to confronting the inherent trade-offs of long-term commitment wreak havoc on the suddenly challenged primary relationship. The resulting relational crisis confronts the partners with the work of the middle-years stage, now with the additional challenge of disengaging from the overly symbolic representations contained within the triad.

The Formation of an Imagined Triangle

Even without an outside attraction developing for either partner, the couple can confront strong fears within themselves related to the extension of their commitment. As a result, one or both partners may become particularly preoccupied with the other's apparent shortcomings. This increased anger or disappointment is linked to the woman's perhaps-unconscious terror that her own future will be diminished if she accepts her partner's limitations. Seeking a reprieve from these now-inflamed sacrifices, affected partners conjure up an image of an improved version of their real-life partner. This image serves as a rival to the actual partner, directing the affected partner's demands and returning the partners to areas of familiar conflict with new and panicked urgency.

"I am sick and tired of hearing that our future hangs on my making changes!" Elizabeth told Sherry. "You have known who I am for years

now, and I've already told you I don't want to change in the way you want. I like who I already am, and I'm not going to let you decide for me what I should do differently in my life! We haven't fought about this in a long time. What's going on for you all of a sudden that you bring us back to this?"

"I don't want it to be this way for the rest of my life! How can you just sit there and say it will never *change, as if that's all there is to it? What, I just deal with it the way it is* forever, *with no possibility of anything getting better?*

"Sherry, you act like this is a life-and-death battle between us! We've lived with this difference between us all along. Okay, neither of us like it much, but it doesn't wreck what we have. Why are you going overboard all of a sudden, like it's this huge problem that will make or break us?"

The truth is, Sherry wasn't sure why. Elizabeth was right: they'd dealt with this well enough up until now, so why did it suddenly feel so upsetting? "Maybe I'd always thought she would relent over time," Sherry thought. The thought of it never changing felt so different than living with this disappointment at earlier stages in their relationship.

The partners can experience this period as especially painful and damaging to their bond. Resolving specific disputes will bring only temporary relief, because the underlying source of the conflict pertains to the partners' free-floating fears—although they may be partially or wholly unaware of the central role this anxiety plays in their ensuing relational dynamic. The real challenge is for both partners to accept truly limiting aspects of each other and of their partnership, yet choose to remain together nonetheless.

If the partners do not recognize how much their conflict revolves around their reactions to extended commitment, they can be left feeling deeply criticized. The triangle constructed between the two actual partners and the imagined improvement of the targeted partner creates feelings that are difficult to tolerate, especially after the partners have tasted the rewards and joys associated with this stage. If their struggle escalates sufficiently, the partners may be persuaded that their relationship has come to an end—sometimes over differences that had previously appeared manageable.

Using the couple relationship as a forum for grappling with inevitable compromises may be especially likely at some point during the middle-years stage. Couples who emerge strengthened from this period learn to take deepened responsibility for their choice to remain together, and they more clearly delineate the line between attainable and impossible change within the relationship. At the same time, not all couples survive this upheaval. Perhaps isolated couples are in the most danger; without others' assistance in identifying their underlying struggle, these couples may attribute exaggerated importance to the literal content of a particular area of disappointment. Repeated often enough, these painful exchanges may persuade the partners that they no longer choose each other or their relationship. In fact, distinguishing manageable from unacceptable disappointments within a now long-term relationship is difficult for all couples, lesbians and nonlesbians alike.

Avoidance of Disruption

Some couples commit themselves to avoiding the disruptions this stage can elicit. Believing that their relationship cannot tolerate intensified conflict or mutual disappointment, these couples ward off both triangulations and sustained struggle, fearing that their relationship will falter in the face of the resulting challenge. Mistaking their avoidance for stability, these couples submerge feelings they consider dangerous to their relationship, keeping the peace at all costs.

Lesbian couples have particular reason to defend against disruptive relational influences, given the multiple stresses they must absorb. Depending on their relationship to supply continual certainty and reassurance, these partners may see periods of disappointment, doubt, or outside attraction as especially destabilizing. The gradual and not-always-conscious decision to suppress fears associated with commitment is often an attempt by these women to protect their relationship, though it rarely has that effect in the long run.

If chronic, the partners' censorship of stressful feelings can lead to a stagnant interpersonal dynamic. While clearly there are couples who spend their entire relationships suppressing negative emotions, the themes raised by entering into long-term commitment provide increased impetus for some couples to adopt these patterns. Actually bypassing the challenge of this stage, these couples persuade themselves that they are taking good care of their relationship. Over time, however, avoiding conflict creates an increasingly constricted relationship.

Such couples will discover increasing evidence that their relational development has stalled. The partners' sexuality often dwindles. Their range of conversation decreases, and the partners' willingness to expose needs and vulnerable feelings often diminishes. Producing a false sense of tranquility, these resistances to conflict or disappointment can become well entrenched before the partners recognize them as indicative of problems. Because the couple has already moved through the challenges and conflicts of the earlier family life cycle stages, they may convince themselves that the bulk of their work is behind them and that they have easily and fully made the transition into long-term commitment.

As their escalating avoidance costs the partners valued aspects of their relationship, some couples seek the counsel of friends or therapists. Rather than resigning themselves to live within the newly drawn boundaries of their relationship, these partners' challenge frequently is to recognize that their avoidance patterns pose a greater threat to their relationship than the content of their underlying feelings.

After delivering an excruciatingly careful preamble, Sarah finally told the therapist that she and Jane couldn't seem to make love together anymore. Continually restating their great devotion to each other, the partners told the therapist of the ceremony two years earlier in which they had permanently committed themselves to their relationship. Bewildered about the decline in sexual connection since that time, the partners were profoundly careful with each other, as though a thoughtlessly chosen word could damage their fragile stability.

"I really have no doubts about my commitment to Sarah," Jane professed emphatically. "I wouldn't change a thing about our lives. I just want us to be closer again." Probing carefully, the therapist offered, "You know, I don't know any couples who have no doubts at all. I wonder if the two of you have somehow gravitated into dismissing those doubts, as though they present some kind of risk that you'd just as soon avoid. It wouldn't mean you were any less committed to each other to have doubts. Doubts or disappointments don't have to mean your relationship is in any real jeopardy."

Made anxious by the therapist's remarks, the partners extremely gently reaffirmed their perception that they simply had no substantial disappointments. The therapist expressed appreciation for their disagreeing with her—which they immediately reframed as not a disagreement at all. A plan for the therapy began to emerge, as the partners were clearly afraid that ambivalence was a dire threat to their connection. The therapist's task would be to strengthen the couple's confidence in their capacity to endure their own and each other's feelings. Within the sessions, the couple could discover that their devotion to each other could survive periodic feelings of disappointment. Normalizing this aspect of their passage into permanent commitment, the partners could free themselves up to resume sexual intimacy and recapture the spontaneity between them that had come to represent a frightening loss of control.

Ironically, as noted above, avoiding the struggles associated with making a long-term commitment to the relationship may rival or surpass the dangers posed by constructing real or imagined triangles. Because these patterns develop gradually—often outside the partners' complete awareness—the level of constriction reached before they seek help can be considerable. One or both women may come to view their dynamic as an unchangeable pattern with grave future implications. Yet, the presently inhibited interaction between the partners may not at all demonstrate their actual capacity to relate to each other more fully. Although they may frequently require assistance, the partners can come to recognize that the true source of their relationship's stability is in the spontaneous and honest exchange of a wide range of feelings. Clearly, the partners' fears that revealing their ambivalence about long-term commitment will in some way seriously disrupt the relationship may be partially correct. Couples often discover, however, that voicing their feelings allows their ambivalence to resume its place as a manageable aspect of their journey together and that their relationship is, in fact, strong enough to survive these commitment-related fears.

Accomplishments of the Middle Years

For a baby to be born, the precious and carefully guarded stability of the womb must first be totally disrupted. A genuine crisis, this life-giving chaos nevertheless ushers in profound new life for all concerned. Similarly, new vitality in a relationship in its middle years can also come on the heels of disruptive crisis. By puncturing the stasis between them, partners can steer their relationship through the heightened struggle toward new accomplishment.

The trade-offs inherent in the middle years of a partnership appear deceptively rational. Many adults recognize that they cannot have it all, and in principle, many would understand that some of their personal potential will remain unexplored no matter which path they choose. Emotionally, however, many partners do not surrender so immediately. While couples who go more willingly into the compromises of fully committed life may arrive with less turmoil, they may be in the minority, as the limitations of living life only once lead many people to at least a brief period of passionate resistance. Yet the various forms of opposition to these losses—only some of which have been addressed in the present discussion—not only compound the obstacles the couple face but also can magnify the meaning of their ultimate achievement.

Given this frequent prelude to achieving the work of this stage, the resulting personal and relational maturation constitute a substantial reward. Sorting through complicated realities, the partners come to recognize several truths. First, the partners succeed in transcending some of the limitations within the relationship to date. In struggling with middle-years dilemmas, couple relationships are expanded, as the bond is challenged to hold more than before and to replenish its sources of newness and lively stability. The battle yields growth, as the relationship now meets the more exacting standards of a partnership worthy of a long-standing, frequently monogamous vow.

At the same time, some of the limitations contained within the relationship will not yield to the partners' attempts at expansion. The relationship is and will remain imperfect, as some of the constrictions the partners fear will indeed be proven true. The particular pairing of these two women will, in fact, limit the expression of some aspects of each one and will contain relatively unchanging areas of disappointment.

Couples who opt to remain together conclude that these compromises are justifiable in light of the overall offerings of the partnership. Changing both the partners and their relationship in the process, this reckoning calls on the women to own more fully their decision to stay a couple—a decision that now incorporates a great deal of firsthand experience with the joys and costs that result from it.

> *Annette often flirted with other women, while Nina could think of nothing that made her feel insecure faster than watching Annette come on to other people. They had fought about it for years, each one resolute and uncompromising. Annette insisted she had never touched another woman while being Nina's partner, and she felt Nina's objections seriously invaded her own personal style of interacting. Nina had grown weary over the years, as Annette refused to empathize with her pain. She knew Annette felt threatened whenever anything even seemed to intrude on her own control over her life. Nina had settled for an ironclad agreement that their relationship would remain completely monogamous. Lately she had grown more at peace with this arrangement, knowing she really was Annette's one true love, and seeing the flirtation more in terms of Annette's insecurity than any real ambivalence about being with Nina. It was a long way from perfect, but Nina knew clearly why she stayed with Annette, and together the partners had found a way to live with this heated difference between them.*

The reckoning couples reach during their middle years develops the relationship's resilience, generating confidence in the partners' abilities to weather storms and offering them a greater understanding of their relationship's strengths, vulnerabilities, conflicts, and sources of intimacy. Partners who remain together come to choose their permanently flawed yet sustaining partnership, recognizing how some relational experiences will fade over time while others develop further—some rewards become more possible, while others move out of reach.

In addition to integrating these awareness into the life of the couple, the partners may also discover that not all of their struggle pertains to the relationship itself. Wrestling with the fact that there will be roads not traveled changes one's approach in all areas of existence. Throughout adulthood—and at the midlife period particularly—people face life's inherently limited nature. As life becomes more finite, choices become more serious; as those choices cost more, they are more closely examined and perhaps more highly prized.

As couples discover that the compromises they face are not unique to their relationship, partners can achieve a different understanding of the nature of compromise itself. Accepting limitation more willingly through the work of this stage, partners can come to see the balance of gratification and frustration of their desires as a natural part of the evolution of adult life. After all, unpartnered adults face these unavoidable sacrifices as well. While the couple relationship is one very appropriate locale for these struggles, by itself it provides too narrow a context for lessons that apply across the board. Likewise, the relational accomplishments of partners in their middle years both pertain to and also supersede the now fully committed life of the couple.

Social Relationships in the Middle Years

The trials of a relationship's middle years emphasize that not even a beloved partner can meet all of a person's needs. Because of this, the partners' relationships with friends and family may take on special importance in their lives. For couples who mark their entry into extended commitment with a ceremony or other celebration, friends and relatives may be involved in the couple's arrival at this stage from its very beginning. In addition, the life changes that accompany long-term commitment are often especially visible, although some couples continue to closet their relationship through this and subsequent family life cycle stages. For those who can risk some social exposure, partners may demonstrate their increased commitment by becoming parents, buying a home together, or choosing rings. These and other events may catch the attention of people around the couple, signaling the relationship to people who did not previously see it or triggering new responses (supportive or otherwise) from those who already knew of it.

During the more difficult moments of this stage, the partners' availability to family and friends may change considerably, as the women often find themselves especially engrossed in the developments within their relationship. While families of origin may offer the couple valuable support during this period, more homophobic families may use the moment to voice their disapproval or lack of faith in the partners' bond. Many lesbian couples avoid telling their families when they experience trouble, feeling that they must present their relationship in ever-positive terms if they hope to elicit the family's respect or approval. In these situations, the partners may limit their contact with their families of origin until their relationship becomes more stable.

As the partners come to terms with the challenges of the middle years, they sort through which intimacies they will reserve for themselves and how they will develop nonthreatening "other loves" outside of the couple relationship. More than simply casual friendships, these separate social relationships may play a central and permanent role in the partners' lives, providing areas of interest and connection not available between the partners themselves. The capacity to welcome this development on the heels of their relational disruption is essential to the couple's continued growth, and it constitutes a central accomplishment of the middle-years stage.

For couples who created an actual triangle during this stage supporting such outside loves can be extremely difficult. As they have recently experienced how "other loves" can directly rival the couple relationship, these women may face particular difficulty in encouraging each partner to venture out again. Because lesbian couples are so singularly dependent on each other to secure their relational boundaries, outside attractions feel like particular betrayals, leaving the partners especially wary of further separate intimacy.

"I am sick and tired of being controlled by you all the time!" Fran shouted. "I am not going to play the bad-partner role for you anymore, Marlena. I can't undo the fact that I had an affair. I regret it, and it won't happen again. But it was a year ago now, and I'm sick of being supervised by you like some little child. I am going out with Janie and Celeste Thursday night whether you like it or not."

"Don't act like I'm this crazed control freak, Fran," Marlena shouted back. "I never paid the slightest attention to what you and your friends were doing until you blew our relationship sky-high with Trina. How do you think it feels to have to sit with all this insecurity? I didn't come to these reactions out of nowhere, you know."

"When are you going to decide to let go, Marlena? I can't possibly show you that you can trust me again until you let me go about my life without you watching over my shoulder. How am I ever going to convince you that you don't have to worry anymore?"

"I want you to be free to go wherever you want. I'm your lover, not

your mother," Marlena relented. "I just want us to be safe again. I don't want to have to worry every time you and your friends decide to go to the club for a night."

"Let me show you, Marlena. Just lighten up, and let me show you I'm with you because I want to be. It's the only way we're going to get through this. I promise you won't be sorry."

No matter how understandable the tendency to close ranks may be, the partners simply cannot rest there. In order to keep growing, they must incorporate their accumulated self-knowledge, which includes recognizing the unique contributions made by people outside the couple relationship. Couples who refuse this challenge risk the very stagnation that instigated the upheaval in their relationship in the first place.

In conclusion, the accomplishments of a couple's middle years result from a diligent reworking of the rewards and disappointments, limits and liberations contained within the now-extended relational commitment. The relationship has absorbed much of the partners' focus during this period of reckoning, especially for couples who form a triangle at some point during this stage. As the partners struggle through essential and ultimately inescapable trade-offs, their commitment to their relationship can deepen substantially, as it is now based on a more complex understanding of themselves, each other, and their particular pairing. As the work of the stage progresses, the couple's primarily inward focus becomes less necessary and gives way to a different equation of private and social involvement. Now enjoying the calm after the storm, the partners chart paths with a deepened awareness of both the preciousness and the limited nature of any couple relationship. Over time, the relevance of these lessons to the partners' individual lives becomes similarly apparent as the women address their growing awareness of a more literal mortality. In the process, the partners arrive at the transition into the next family life cycle stage.

9

Stage Four: Generativity

RELATIONSHIPS IN TURMOIL LEND THEMSELVES TO VIVID DESCRIP-
tion. Life is dramatic, if painful; challenging, if fraught with risk. The
couple often reaches the generativity stage following a genuine crisis
whose gripping emotionality masked the partners' fear that settled,
stable family life constitutes a kind of relational and personal deaden
ing. Couples who navigate their way through their middle years often
have brought themselves back from a self-imposed precipice, constructing a life filled with neither peril nor ongoing drama.

Couples do not spend their entire lives building the foundations of
their relationships. The tasks of the first three stages contain a
preparatory quality as the partners build and refine their relationship,
encountering the fundamental strains within lesbian family life and
considering the level of commitment they can realistically promise to
each other. The partners' choice of each other is powerfully tested,
and their ways of living together become flexible enough to shift with
their continued growth.

With successful passage through the middle years the couple relationship has not only survived but deepened. The reworking of the
fundamental elements of the partners' commitment infuses the relationship with much security, creating a surplus of relational energy.
Lesbian couples at this point may spend a considerable period of time
enjoying the unprecedented maturity of their relationship, honing

195

their now long-term commitment and further developing their separate identities as well.

As the partners integrate their achievements, though, a new developmental challenge inevitably surfaces. With much of the work of creating a family behind them, the partners more fully recognize their capacity to steer the direction of their family life. Signaling the beginning of the work of this stage, the partners often wonder, "What now?" At the same time, an evolving awareness of their own physical mortality leads the partners to recognize that changing or replacing the couple relationship will not win their release from the inevitability of compromise and of time running out. Instead, the partners search for a deeper sense of purpose that will nourish and engage them for years to come. By creating avenues of expression for their deepest values and heartfelt dedications,[1] the partners link themselves to a larger network of others and develop an arena in which to identify an enduring and unique sense of their particular family's identity. The partners ponder what their family truly stands for and what they want their own signature as a family to convey.

While the couple's responses frequently reflect a genuine desire to better the world in some way, their motive is not simple altruism. The couple's awareness that time and other choices are going by exposes with new urgency their underlying fears that their lives will be invisible or inconsequential in their own or others' eyes.[2] By linking themselves to enduring devotions (or "collaborations," as described by Clunis and Green[3]) the partners seek to quell these pressing personal anxieties.

Partners in the stage of generativity long to associate themselves with something that will bear their name—in other words, to provide a sense of identity that will endure beyond their own finite existence. Toward that end, couples in this stage work to create what has been termed a "personal legacy"[4] investing their energies into projects with concrete outcomes. In the process, the partners create a focus for their coupled life that is expanded beyond their earlier focus on their own relationship itself.

"This neighborhood is a pit!" Abigail had exclaimed to Georgia that first spring. The partners had gone to every neighbor they knew and announced that they were organizing a committee to oversee periodic

cleanup days in the neighborhood. Their main target was the schoolyard down the street: "We can't let the kids play in such a depressing, empty area. We have to do something about it." Now, five years later, the partners had received funding from the city for their efforts, which had expanded to offering adult supervision for various recreational events for the children. Abigail and Georgia wanted people to associate them with this project—to remember that it was their idea, and to see it as their special contribution to the kids who lived nearby.

Not every couple broadens their context of personal and family identity to take on the challenges of the generativity stage. Clearly, Some people spend not a stage but a lifetime immersed in a narrow self-absorption that precludes achieving true recognition of human interdependence. These couples run the risk of seeing their family life growing stale as they rely too heavily on immediate gratifications to provide a sense of life's direction. For couples meeting the challenge, however, committing themselves to separate and shared generative activities can infuse them and their relationship with sufficient richness to sustain them through the remaining decades of their lives.

Tasks of the Generativity Stage

The themes of generativity can seem amorphous and difficult to articulate, even when the partners are fully willing to share their inner thoughts and feelings. The challenges of earlier stages were often ushered into the couple's relationship through easily recognizable conflicts in which the need and direction for dialogue were readily apparent. Because the generativity stage is not similarly marked by relational disruption, the metamorphosis occurring within the couple relationship is easy to underestimate or miss altogether. For couples who do not recognize the underlying sources of their motivation to expand the relationship, the actual activities of the stage appear to be all that is taking place.

Left unidentified, important opportunities for intimate connection are lost between the partners, as are chances to fully understand themselves and each other. Therefore, while not all couples accomplish this task, the partners are nonetheless challenged to articulate and share not only their new behavioral expressions of generativity but their inner emotions and thought process. In so doing, the symbolic significance of the events unfolding between the partners comes to life, greatly increasing the chances that the partners' generativity activities will successfully express the real experience behind the apparently simple acts.

"Why do you think we're really here on this earth?" Victoria mused aloud to Beth. "We haven't talked about this in a long time, but I'm finding myself thinking about it a lot these days. Do you ever wonder how well we're really doing at whatever our task in this life is? It's clear to me that we're intended to both enjoy what life has given us and also pass it on in some way—use it, you know—make some kind of a difference in the world. I wonder if we're doing that—making a difference, I mean."

Lost in her reverie, she continued almost immediately. "Why do you think we've made it when so many of our friends have broken up? Not just how did we do it, but why? Don't you think there's some kind of purpose to it? Maybe something we're supposed to be able to teach somebody . . . or, I don't know, open our home to somebody, maybe or write about our journey. I think about my deathbed scene more now, too. I wonder if I'll have any major regrets, or if I'll feel like I've really left my mark. Would you say we're leaving any mark so far, or do you think we're just going through our days like some really average couple, not really doing much of anything in the world?"

Beth could feel how serious her partner was and didn't want to interrupt till she was sure Victoria was finished. The truth was, Beth had been thinking along these lines herself. They had come so far that it seemed crazy to be wondering if they were living up to their real potential, and yet there did seem to be more to do somehow. She thought back to their early days together, when they often talked until late into the night. Beth hoped they could go that deeply now; these moments of new life between them eased her fear that there was nothing new to learn.

The pressure the partners now feel to broaden the relationship's sense of purpose indicates that they are moving forward, not losing ground. Couples can actually take comfort in discovering that they have not exhausted their opportunities to enrich their relationship. At this and so many other moments in the lesbian family life cycle, couples can be powerfully supported by recognizing the stages of their family's development. With this perspective, couples can distinguish the anxiety and temporary disequilibrium that always accompany productive change from signs that they are in real trouble.

Clearly, not all couples will engage in explicitly introspective discussions of generative concerns. While as a group, lesbian partners often do approach their lives with particular self-consciousness, a variety of factors (including personality, the partners' degree of interest in this level of discourse, and their life circumstances) will determine how deliberately any particular couple contemplates the underlying meanings of their moves toward generativity. While couples are well served by identifying the movement occurring within their relationships, some couples will rely more solely on the shifts in actual activity accompanying this stage. Even when not articulated, generative activities play a central role in fostering the growth of all couples during this fourth life cycle stage.

Separate Generativity Activities

Lesbian couples who feel they must hide their relationship are severely compromised in their efforts to achieve the *family* legacy and link to the future that is the focus of the generativity stage. Unable to seek a witness to the family's shared character and accomplishments, separate generative projects may be the partners' only access to social recognition. The partners forgo the inaccessible feedback of "You are a good family" for the more limited individual acknowledgement that "you did a good thing."[5] These separate pursuits disguise as much as they illuminate, though, creating an observable individual legacy but furthering the invisibility of the couple relationship.

> *It took months for Shelly and Norma to dare to ask the older women about their relationship. Finally, in the privacy of the younger couple's living room, Shelly gently asked how long the pair had been together. After initially anxious reactions, in unnecessary whispers left over from years of automatic silence, the partners haltingly recounted the basic facts of their coupled life. They had met forty-two years ago and had promised themselves to each other soon after. It took years for them to live together, as neither dared raise suspicions beyond their already-odd unmarried status. The couple had created intricate webs of secrecy, pro-*

tecting their family life by learning to make it invisible. Norma gingerly asked them about the pain of never being clearly seen by anyone around them: "Who will know of your real lives after you die?" "We'll know," they jointly replied, without another word about the profound burden of having to make that be enough.

Due to homophobia, many lesbian couples experience the danger of being forgotten or invisible not only after death but throughout their lives as well. For these families, the generativity stage escalates an already-present stress. Couples who do not feel able to come out may be especially frustrated in their efforts to construct a recognized family legacy. Forced to collude in having their achievements misunderstood, these partners may overinvolve themselves in separate outside commitments, as though accomplishing more as a supposedly single individual will somehow transfer over to affirming their family identity.

"Don't be mad, but the coalition is meeting three nights next week," Molly sheepishly admitted. "I'm on all three committees, and so I have to go to the meetings. I don't like it any better than you do, but the work is so important, how can I pull back now?" Meredith barely heard her, as she was already bothered by something else. "I saw the newspaper article about you tonight. There must have been two whole columns on who you are and about the work you're doing. It was great coverage, and you really deserve the praise. But doesn't it make you crazy that you come across as this single person who lives with her two cats and works her head off on political work? I know we've been all through this, and I agree we have to do things this way, but God, I felt so invisible! Our entire life gets just wiped off the map all the time. When you die, people are going to think you leave no family at all."

Individual generative activities serve constructive functions for many or most lesbian couples. Through the work of the middle-years stage, each partner has renewed her agreement to develop individually the components of herself not shared by her partner. Separate generative projects offer each partner a forum in which to cultivate her unique characteristics without expecting (or perhaps wanting) the other partner to participate in the endeavor. In supporting individual generative dedications, the couple use their capacity to invite the partners to expend significant time, love, and identity apart from the couple relationship. Expanding the parameters of the relationship, the partners often utilize strengths developed during the conflicts of the previous life cycle stage.

"We could never have done this five years ago," Jan said, chuckling. "I'd have been sure you were just finding an exotic way to leave me. I'd have been so insecure I couldn't have stood it."

"We would have fought like crazy," Stacie agreed, "and our phone bills would have been more than my tuition. It's not that I won't miss you terribly—I really will. You are the center of my life, and nothing will feel the same while I'm away from you."

"I know, honey, I feel the same way. I hate that we're going to be apart for this whole year, and I know I'll be really lonely. But aren't you incredibly proud of us, too? How many couples could support a partner's lifelong goal of spending a year in seminary halfway across the country?"

"I need to do this. I know my path is to do spiritual work now, and that calling just won't wait any more. There's so much I want to give— that's why I'm going, not to get way from my partner."

"I know. I trust you, and I believe in the work you're preparing to do. We'll get through this just fine. I have total faith in us after all these years."

For each partner, grappling with generativity themes contains an inherently private contemplation. The partners have not lived identical lives and are not devoted to identical other loves. For example, a devoted Jewish partner may direct herself toward projects at her synagogue. An artist may join an "Art Against AIDS" project in conjunction with other local talent, while a survivor of some particular traumatic event may work to protect potential future victims. Thriving couples can support these separate generative passions, with each partner understanding the contribution's central place in the other's unique identity.

Joint Generative Involvements

Couples who pursue only separate generative commitments, however, are making a serious mistake. Partnerships need shared central involvements to thrive. Without shared avenues for expressing generativity, the partners' relationship may stagnate or become reduced to a resting place separate from the center of their life's activity. To remain vital, the couple relationship must demonstrate to both partners that it can continue to deepen and to address the central challenges in their lives.

Perhaps because lesbians as a group have demonstrated particular assertiveness and creativity in charting their life courses, there is a range of ways in which they express generativity. Because women are overrepresented in the service professions, many lesbians may choose their work settings as the focus of their generative projects. In addition, a disproportionate number of lesbians devote their energies to political and other social change efforts. Many lesbians work for gay rights causes not only on their own behalf but also in support of future generations of lesbians, blending caring about themselves and about others into their commitments. When shared by partners, these dedications can infuse the family unit with a shared sense of generative purpose and a link to improving the future for others.

> *The cars were parked all up and down the street. The house was packed with gay men and lesbians who had contributed to the youth project this year. Anne and Jan looked nervous but proud as they hosted the year's thank-you party, given for the top seventy-five contributors to the fund drive. The couple had clearly worked hard on this party, creating an atmosphere of success, pride, and anticipation of the services this money would buy for gay and lesbian youths. After the guests left, the couple marveled at how far they had come with their beautiful home, their solid relationship, and now this shared sense of political purpose. They felt powerful today, sure they were making a difference in the world, influencing the lives of others like themselves.*

Not all generative projects are overtly political in nature. Many activities lend themselves to generative purposes, including teaching, parenting, creating things, or protecting or improving some treasured aspect of life for future generations.[6] In addition, couples may add a generative component to endeavors that have long provided them with a sense of identity or simple pleasure. The meaning of such events broadens to serve a central function within the couple relationship. In the process, the partners both offer a generative contribution and achieve a fuller context for their individual and family identity.

Jane and Claire had played in the lesbian softball league for the past seven summers. Both loved to play and to compete with their friends on other teams. This summer, however, they decided to give it up, as it conflicted with the scheduling of the little girls' softball league games on Saturday mornings. "We're going to coach the little ones this year," Claire explained. "I think it's great that these kids are out there slugging that ball. We never got that chance at their ages. Somehow, I want to help them out."

Parenting

When young adults become parents, they are not usually focused primarily on generativity. Motivated by a desire to be in the midst of children's energy, to make their family larger, or love someone who will boost their still-developing sense of personal identity, these parents are not especially focused on life's limitations. Early in their adulthood, mortality remains a distant knowledge for most people, and they see no need to concern themselves with time or capacity running out.

Twenty years later, however, these same individuals may turn to their roles as parents both to secure their link to the next generation and also to claim their personal legacy. Likewise, midlife lesbians may become parents for the first time. For them, parenting's relevance to the challenges of the generativity stage is especially direct. After all, a child offers a direct link to the next generation, embodying the couple's own values, lifestyle, and perhaps even physical likeness. Children invite parents to revisit vicariously the time when life felt abundant, when the future was much greater than the past, and most everything was still ahead. To parents in the generativity stage, this glimpse of an earlier time may soothe the mortality fears that now lie closer to the surface.

As was discussed in Chapter 5, however, the problem for parenting lesbian couples is that their joint creation will frequently be misidentified as the product of a single parent and her "roommate." Far from securing a visible mark to last beyond the partners' deaths, this denial of the family unit escalates the very anxiety generativity attempts to ease. In this as in other family life cycle stages, the family themselves must often provide the bulk of their own recognition, a burden that severely compromises their ability to achieve the external visibility desired in this stage. Despite this lifelong stress imposed on parenting lesbian couples, children offer these couples a precious outcome of their relationship whose presence rebuts the depiction of lesbian family life as unproductive and stagnant by nature. Parenting midlife lesbians may be especially compelled by the daily opportunities to express their generative caring to their own child.

The Unique Experience of Lesbian Couples

Lesbian couples reach the generativity stage with special preparation for addressing its central tasks. Because this culture imposes particular losses and precludes opportunities for all nonheterosexual people, many gay and lesbian young adults face pressures that can build maturity. Learning early of the rich rewards and sobering costs associated with their life path, many lesbian partners know before the generativity stage that their lives must be consciously contemplated and their choices more clearly articulated, at least to themselves. The weight of these trade-offs falls heavily on most new lesbians, often creating precocious self-awareness as they confront the implications of lesbian identity. No matter how thrilled a woman is to discover her true sexual identity, loss becomes an inescapable component of her path from that point on, dramatizing the fact that traditional roads may not be traveled. While one hopes that lesbians are passionately convinced that the rewards of their lives outweigh the costs, coming out to oneself powerfully illustrates the limitations inherent in life. As a result, lesbians are especially likely to reach the generativity stage with a good deal of experience at evaluating the long-range implications of their life choices.

For all the stress oppression imposes on lesbian couples, the coping mechanisms a couple develops early in their relationship may provide good preparation for the work of this stage. With few models to follow and constant social challenges to their decision to live as lesbians, these women tend to be especially active agents in their lives, assertively charting missing paths and basing more of their choices on what works best for them. The spirit of "Just do it" or "Make it happen" typically ascribed to midlife emerges earlier for lesbian partners.

They have faced the trade-off of personal identity versus social compliance and have overcome their internalized prohibitions against social disobedience. Through the process of claiming their sexual identity, lesbians make it less likely that they will live unconsciously throughout their young adulthoods. Identified by Reinhold as the gift of those who follow socially unaccepted paths,[7] this lifelong introspection may help protect lesbian partners from a sudden midlife realization that life is passing them by.

In addition, oppression often demonstrates how the treatment received by one group member has personal relevance for the rest of the group.[8] The need for collective action may weave together the tasks of taking care of oneself and one's relationship with those of caring for the group and the next generation as well. By identifying with similar others, lesbian partners have the opportunity to recognize their personal investment in the conditions of other group members' lives and to foster generative awareness in the process. This awareness is likely to be in place long before the couple reaches the generativity stage—perhaps most of all for lesbian couples of color or partners from other oppressed communities of affiliation, who have learned of this interdependence on multiple levels. These couples may be well on their way to carving out chosen arenas for achieving the expanded sense of family identity and social interdependence called for in the work of the generativity stage.

> *Thanks to the name tags, Susan became aware of who she was standing next to at the party. "Oh, you're the couple who put both your pictures in the paper announcing your commitment ceremony! I see you've even hyphenated your last names. I want to really thank you for making such a brave move. You support every one of us when you take such bold action. What you've done makes my struggle a little bit easier."*

In addition to identifying with other lesbian couples and perhaps also with lesbians as a group, many lesbians have learned to identify with groups whose social positions and vulnerability are similar to their own. For example, many lesbians have come to identify with gay men through the AIDS crisis, knowing that society's extremely slow and ambivalent response to this disease would be the same if gay women instead of gay men had been its earliest victims. This expanded sense of identification and personal investment in the welfare of gay men has become a generative focus for many lesbians in recent years.

Finally, while not all lesbian couples identify with the group as a whole, those who do may be aided in experiencing their linkage to the past, present, and future. Present conditions have grown out of a history that has great personal relevance for individual couples, and hope is contained in people's collective work toward progress in the future. This sense of being part of a long-term movement helps many lesbian couples to restore their lost sense of membership in an ongoing, multigenerational chain.

While the ramifications of their sexual identity and other factors heighten many lesbians' awareness of generative concerns throughout their adulthood, events both in the partners' relationship and in their individual development determine the timing of this life cycle stage. As previously stated, the couple's arrival at this juncture results from the freeing up of much of the partners' energy and focus following the work of their middle years together. The couple must be ready to relinquish their intense focus on their own relationship before they can devote themselves fully to the tasks of this far more socially oriented stage.

At the same time, midlife exerts a particular influence on many or most adults that dovetails precisely with the themes of the generativity stage. Because the midlife years are most often defined broadly, a large number of lesbian couples will experience an overlap between their relationship's generativity stage and their personal midlife periods. This combination ups the ante for the partners, highlighting generativity further and increasing the partners' focus on mortality and interdependence.

The Impact of Midlife

The folklore on midlife goes something like this: at some point in their forties, a powerful awakening overtakes people, jolting them out of the notion that they have plenty of time left on this earth. Following this epiphany, these individuals finally grab hold of their destinies, living life to its fullest and actively—if not frantically—appreciating what they barely noticed before. Many apparently realize they have been passively conforming to society's steering of their life decisions and they find new resolve to chart their own course. "Who am I?" becomes a question with new meaning as forty-somethings begin an extensive and postponed evaluation of how they are living their lives.

While lesbian identity may mitigate the suddenness of these realizations, lesbians are not immune from the changes brought on by midlife. Specifically, three areas of midlife change encourage the partners to further attend to generativity themes: midlife physical changes (many of which are related to menopause), the likely transitions within both past and future generations of the partners' families, and age-related changes in the partners' perspectives on life. These changes strengthen the partners' awareness of the passage of time, as meaningful physical cycles stop and seemingly permanent capacities and relationships change or come to an end. For many people, the preview of their own eventual demise brought by the deaths of significant others changes their approach to this stage of their existence. As they recognize the limits on their time and ability, people in midlife are faced with serious choices that require a deepened recognition of life's inherent trade-offs.[9]

The physical changes attendant to midlife signify both new vulnerability and new resiliency for many women. Compelling new health concerns arise, including the risk of menopause-related hormonal imbalances, increased risk of osteoporosis and certain cancers, and elevated incidence of heart disease. Inexorably linked to the aging process, these greater susceptibilities dramatize one's arrival at midlife. While earlier stages also included physical and social indicators of life's progression, by midlife these changes also commonly signify a sense of limitation, as there is now less time ahead than already lived, and people more realistically envision the limited duration of their most productive years.

Menopause brings the most powerful evidence for many women that whole stages of adulthood are permanently over. While the physical experience of this passage and its associated symbolic meanings vary tremendously from one woman to the next, the cessation of one's reproductive cycle is a major departure from all earlier stages in a woman's adulthood. Linked explicitly to getting older, the arrival of menopause frames a key ending and a new beginning, inspiring a particular focus on generativity in many women. Regardless of their previous choices pertaining to parenthood, these women are challenged to find a figurative translation for their previously literal capacity to create new life.

Because both partners experience menopause, this milestone may occupy a central place in midlife lesbian couples' lives, providing considerable encouragement to supplement their generative focus. The homophobia-related obstacles to lesbians' opportunities to have children, however, may make negotiating this passage additionally complex. Lesbian partners who reach menopause feeling that they were prevented from bearing children based on their lesbian identity (through no access to donor insemination, adoption options, etc.) may experience additional responses to reaching the end of their physical capacity to give birth. These circumstances may compound their association between menopause and significant loss, and between their experience of menopause and the specifics of their subsequent selections of generativity commitments.

The deaths of similarly aged peers also contribute to midlife lesbians' awareness of their physical vulnerabilities. While one can lose peers to death in any life cycle stage, beginning in midlife, these deaths differently raise fears about one's own mortality. No longer dismissed as a fluke, the deaths of midlife peers trigger a deeper identification with the now-ended life of their friend, as the mourner accurately personalizes the possibility of herself or her partner suffering a similarly premature death. Equally mourned losses in earlier life cycle stages hold less of this personal identification for the individual partners and the family unit.

In addition, many midlife lesbian partners will experience their parents' deaths during this stage. With the passing of the previous generation of their families, many lesbians in midlife reach a deepened awareness of their own mortality and a qualitatively different sense of their own ultimate aloneness, regardless of their primary partnerships. For many people, losing one's parents creates new motivation to secure their own position in the multigenerational chain—a task that is frequently complicated for lesbian families.

Childless lesbian couples may particularly dedicate themselves to replacing lost generative links, as there is now no generation either ahead of them or following them within their own families. This frequently midlife-timed loss can increase the partners' urgency to make their own time count, and they may feel special motivation to create joint generative commitments in order to underscore their family connection. Lesbian partners who are estranged from their parents may experience similar urgency, as they also feel especially disconnected from the multigenerational chain.

For parenting lesbian couples, their children are likely to reach young adulthood at some point during the partners' midlife stage. As the children relinquish their full dependence on the partners, the couple is left to find or rediscover pathways apart from parenting. Like the death of their parents, launching their children disrupts the partners' position in the multigenerational family chain and adds midlife-related impetus for the couple to devote themselves to generative connections.

Midlife, however, brings not only increased vulnerability but also new resiliency. Older, wiser, and equipped with a much deeper sense of their personal identity, many people find that midlife heralds greater personal freedom to speak their own truth and to choose actively what to pursue and what to pass by in life. Women speak of a "coming into my own" that eluded them in earlier life stages, based on their accumulating life's lessons, surviving disappointments, and articulating their own personal dreams.[10] Even their unfolding understanding of life's limitations can mobilize rather than devastate, and provide the call to action that constitutes the generativity stage.

> The 25-year-old consciousness of the relationship between self, choice, power, and society is not the 45-year-old consciousness. I now think that I have a much more limited, accurate, and in some important ways more energizing and empowering sense of my own powers and limitations.[11]

Speaking directly of lesbians' experience of reaching midlife, Loulan describes the challenge to seize one's life and make the most of it: "Midlife is the time in our lives when many of us come to believe the idea that our life is not a dress rehearsal and if we don't get on with it, one day it may be too late."[12] Crux adds, "I no longer count my life from the year of my birth, but rather count forward to when I will die."[13]

In conclusion, the years of the generativity stage can offer lesbian couples special richness and contemplation. The interplay between each partner's individual development and the location of the couple in the family life cycle is especially influential in the work of this stage, adding complexity and urgency to their attempts to secure an identity and social linkage that transcends earlier relational developments. Sustaining the couple through the frequently long years of this stage, the achievements that result from this expanded life perspective prepare the partners to confront the changes attendant to the next and final family life cycle stage.

10

Stage Five:
Lesbian Couples over Sixty-Five

Nina and her lover, Ellen, went to visit their neighbor, Jan, who had recently been widowed. "You two are so lucky," Jan told the couple. "You may still have each other for years to come. God, I wish Mark hadn't died! I hate the thought of spending the rest of my life alone."

The irony of the conversation struck Nina at that moment. Her mother had been so afraid that without a husband Nina would grow old alone. Now, here was this heterosexual friend envying Nina's greater chance of being partnered through the rest of her life.

Statistically speaking, couples composed solely of women are most likely to enjoy shared old age. While this stage is promised to no one, women as a group live an average of seven years longer than men.[1] Many all-female couples therefore face widowhood later, allowing them to rely on the relationship until many years after retirement.

Generalizations about the nature and focus of the couple's experience of this final family life cycle stage are complicated by several factors. First, elderly lesbians typically maintain a particular commitment to hiding their relationships, making it difficult for others to accurately depict their experience. Key historical events—including the Great Depression, World War II, McCarthyism, and the socially conformist 1950s—have combined to impress upon these lesbians that their survival and safety are tenuous. The civil rights movements of recent decades (including those for women and homosexuals) have not sufficiently persuaded these women to come out publicly, and many have experienced the increased openness of younger lesbians as only minimally related to their own life circumstances.[2]

Second, this stage spans twenty or more years for many lesbian couples. Couples' challenges, goals, and daily lives change radically over this time as the physical, emotional, social, and financial effects of aging unfold. Life at sixty-five varies greatly from life at eighty-five.

Finally, no standard markers signifying the family's entry into this stage exist. Society's general message to women remains disempowering, as their aging is equated with diminished power, attractiveness, and social worth. Advertisers boldly assert that "forty isn't fatal," and the starring celebrity behaves as if she has proclaimed a radical idea. Oil of Olay warns women that "it is never too soon to get started" and hires a teenage tennis star to deliver the message for its purported anti-aging products. Women are pressured to appear younger than they are and to conceal the shame of being over thirty. While the extent and circumstances of delivery of these messages may vary among racial, ethnic, and class communities, few women escape the internalized effects of this ageism. As a result, entering into this life cycle stage carries neither accompanying celebratory rituals nor social recognition of the wisdom and life experience accumulated by older women.

Lesbian couples therefore once again negotiate a major passage with no social acknowledgment. Some lesbians may choose a particular birthday (age sixty-five, for example) or becoming a grandmother to symbolize this life cycle transition. Retirement, however, offers a particularly meaningful and commonly experienced milestone that can designate the couple's movement into this stage. Due to the social rejection lesbians experience in many other settings, the work environment constitutes a central link to the mainstream community and may have afforded an otherwise elusive opportunity to elicit social membership and personal validation.

Work as the Key to Autonomy

Few women could have successfully supported themselves on their own before World War II.[3] Even then, while incomes were typically meager, lesbian couples for the first time could earn enough money to live alone together. More likely than married women to work throughout their adult lives, these lesbians—and other women not financially relying on men—knew clearly that their jobs signified their precarious opportunity to live independent lives. Statistics continue to indicate that lesbians, as a group, dedicate themselves to preserving this opportunity and typically achieve both greater educational credentials and higher job status relative to heterosexual women.[4] More likely to earn advanced degrees and to be overrepresented in white-collar positions, lesbian partners frequently agree to demanding work lives in exchange for the benefits afforded by their jobs. Frequently symbolizing their ticket to sustained autonomy, lesbians' work lives hold special meanings directly related to the circumstances of the couple's oppression. Relinquishing these positions contains particular meanings for many lesbians as well.

The symbolic losses associated with this life cycle transition also hold particular, if conflicted, meanings for lesbians. The work environment sometimes offers at least a partial sense of being part of a larger group and allows some lesbians to demonstrate their talents to an otherwise critical or ignoring mainstream community. While many retirees face the daunting task of replacing this context for social membership and personal recognition, lesbians often contend with fewer available alternatives for meeting these crucial needs.

At the same time, the work world has imposed terrible obligations on many lesbians associated with the ongoing danger of being fired if their sexual identity is discovered. Financially dependent on homophobic organizations, many lesbians feel compelled to keep their personal and work lives separate, sharing little of their individual and family identities with coworkers and supervisors. The greater the dichotomy between a lesbian's work and home identities, the more she may experience both loss and relief at reaching retirement. Because many lesbians compartmentalize these contradictory feelings during their work years, this difficult social position is likely to influence their responses to reaching retirement.[5]

Timing of Retirement

Like other senior citizens, many lesbian partners may wish to retire at or before age sixty-five. For economically secure couples an early or timely retirement holds much appeal, as the anticipated freedom and increased independence offers a striking contrast to the discipline and personal constraint required during the partners' years of employment. Not all lesbians, however, enjoy equal access to timely retirement.

Lesbians appear to retire later than their heterosexual female peers. Simon's sample of never-married women worked past the age of sixty-five at a rate seven times higher than the national average. Much of the explanation for this discrepancy is based on financial necessity, as lesbian couples are particularly affected by the persistent reality of women earning less than men.[6] Despite evidence that lesbians appear to hold professional or white-collar jobs more frequently than heterosexual women, even these women report earning depressed salaries.[7]

Despite these frequent financial difficulties, lesbian elders report more extensive planning for their postretirement years than their heterosexual peers.[8] Forewarned that they will have only themselves and their partners to rely on, these women anticipate their need to secure their old age and have often budgeted these savings into their lifestyle for many years prior to leaving their jobs. In addition, some lesbians cannot retire all at once, needing instead to generate income for as long as they are physically able. Among working-class lesbians, "retirement" may involve a gradual diminishing of work until health concerns force a complete end. These women's movement into retirement may remain especially unmarked and unritualized.

Women of color are especially likely to be forced to choose between working past age sixty-five or living on extremely limited resources. The median income for African-American women after widowhood, for example, remains slightly over half the meager income earned by white widows.[9] However, women of color face the additional challenge of greater health problems as a result of racism and poverty.[10] Such women may decide to retire based on health problems, not because they choose to or because they have sufficient income to stop working. Therefore, the group that most needs to work after age sixty-five has the most constraints on their ability to do so. For couples composed solely of women, and particularly women of color, these obstacles will be central realities of this family life cycle stage.

Tasks for the Couple Relationship

This family life cycle stage is characterized by repeatedly imposed life changes, some occurring all at once and others emerging in progressive and gradual ways. These changes begin immediately as the partners retire and must reestablish the patterns and routines of their new daily lives. In most cases, partners base their balance of togetherness and separateness on the ongoing reality of their full-time jobs. Without that structure, the partners' commitments to shared and individual involvements in projects, friendships, and other activities must be reworked, as the automatic separations created by their work lives give way to increased togetherness, interdependence and available free time.

While the partners have addressed these themes at numerous earlier points (most notably during the second life cycle stage, where they became an ongoing couple), this juncture marks the first time that their work lives will exert no constraints on their time. Without built-in limits, the partners are likely to confront differences between themselves in how much each wants to supplement their togetherness and how much to increase their commitment to built-in separations. The partners' reactions to these discussions will be influenced by their capacities to articulate their needs for intimacy and separate identity, with many couples finding one or the other of these communications difficult.

> *Margaret called to suggest going to a concert tonight, Annette told Sandra vaguely. She was aware she hadn't said who exactly Margaret invited, but she couldn't get herself to admit she didn't want Sandra to come. The couple had been together every day this week, and Annette very much wanted to do something apart. "Oh, that sounds good," Sandra responded. "Did she mean the three of us, or what?" Hating herself for floundering, Annette heard herself say, "Oh, you can join us if you want to." Inside her heart sank as she now lost out on an evening alone with her friend, and she had to admit she had done it to herself. Every day presented these situations now, since both women had recently retired.*

Many couples rely on their work lives to demonstrate central distinctions between the partners' capacities, interests and routines. For some lesbians, their jobs offer a sense of personal identity either through the actual work performed or through the concrete rewards of earning a certain income or reaching a particular job title. For others, the primary rewards of employment are embedded within personal work relationships or the daily schedule and social roles carried out apart from the couple relationship. Retiring partners must assess whether these sources of identity must now be replaced with other activities, or whether the partners have sufficiently internalized these views of themselves that abandoning the daily exercise of their work lives can be done without undue disequilibrium to either partner's personal identity.

Retirement can also affect lesbian couples' sexual relationships. On the one hand, the increased interdependence of this stage can stimulate the partners' fears that they are losing autonomy, making sexual intimacy more threatening. These women may need to reestablish areas of distinct identity and separate involvements before sex can resume its place in their lives. On the other hand, many of the primary stressors in lesbians' lives are associated with their dependence on the mainstream community, frequently in regard to their need to keep their jobs. With this burden lifted after retirement, the partners may feel freer (at least privately) to express their full lesbian identities. These couples may discover that sex is actually easier now, as their social contacts are now more voluntary than at earlier points in the family life cycle.

Research on sex for women over the age of sixty-five suggests that aging lesbian couples may enjoy an advantage in their efforts to sustain sexual intimacy.[11] Aging lesbians in two large-scale studies reported continued sexual activity and identified sexuality as a still-integral aspect of their couple relationships.[12] Although they reported decreased frequency, these lesbian couples depicted their relationships as nonetheless sexually active and satisfying, providing a valued avenue for continuing intimacy.

More Available Time

Areas of distinct and shared identity emerge repeatedly throughout this stage. At first the partners may feel especially freed up, finally enjoying plenty of time for a variety of involvements and interests.

Their relative independence may result in less conflict between the partners, as time with friends or in other separate pursuits does not deplete the relationship of the time and energy it needs. For partners with children, the children's reaching adulthood may combine with the parents' retirements to create tremendous change in the day-to-day lives of the partners. Likewise, women who have devoted massive amounts of energy to their work lives (out of either choice or necessity) may face a greater adjustment. A study of African-American women, for example, found that retirement marked the first time the respondents experienced "leisure time" in their lives, which constituted a positive yet substantial additional adjustment.[13]

Because lesbians have often particularly cultivated their capacities for self-reliance across the life cycle, though giving up their work lives and full-time incomes may be difficult to accept. Because self-sufficiency serves for many lesbians as both an important source of personal identity and a buffer against oppression, retiring partners may feel newly vulnerable. At the same time, the role of friendship as a central tenet of many lesbian relationships often eases the transition into retirement.

Changes in Family Roles

With life more centered on the home environment, lesbian couples redesign their relational roles not only to accomplish the needed tasks for daily life but to provide the partners with self-esteem and decision-making power as well. Despite the flexibility with which lesbian couples frequently construct their roles, the adjustments needed following retirement can be complex.

"You won't believe all the things I did for us while you were hiking today," Eve announced proudly. Joan could already feel herself getting mad, as she had worried today that she'd come home to this yet again. Ever since Eve and Joan retired, Joan felt Eve had been horning in on things that Joan had always done for the two of them. When Eve said she had called their best friends and arranged the plans for their summer vacation together, Joan finally hit the ceiling. "I do that every year," Joan screamed, "and it's important to me to plan those trips! You find

your own things to do. Don't think you're going to just take over things I've always done, now that you're home more. I'm not giving up what's important to me to help you adjust to retirement. You have to find your own projects, and leave mine alone."

"Those are our friends, not yours," Eve shot back. "You did it all these years because you've always had more free time, not because you own this project! I have more time now, and I'm going to do more of the things I never got a chance to before. You're going to find that 'your' projects don't belong just to you."

Retirement will represent widely varying losses for different people. One partner's work may have provided particular financial security for the couple, allowing them to have children or to maintain a chosen lifestyle. Another's job may have helped shape the couple's generative commitments, if the work lent itself to this task. One woman's demanding work life may also have helped the couple maintain needed separations or infused the relationship with the rejuvenating energy of repeated reunions after business trips.

As each partner works to secure some power and a unique identity for herself within the relationship, postretirement shifts in their roles are laden with needs not fully expected of the couple relationship at earlier points. While retirees may address these themes to varying extents, many lesbians may have limited access to alternate social arenas. Lesbian partners' efforts to recreate their roles may be complicated by this additional function of the partners' previous work lives.

Clearly, decisions about roles within the relationship reflect and determine the power balance between the partners. As disparate tasks and emotional roles hold different prestige and relative importance within the relationship—and typically hold social connotation as either masculine (and more highly valued) or feminine (and devalued)—the partners may have difficulty approaching their negotiations apart from this sexist overlay. Given that what limited social recognition lesbians have been able to access has usually come from their roles as workers, giving up this arena to return more fully to the socially unrecognized arena of a lesbian home constitutes an important loss. The resulting needs to recoup some sense of personal recognition and power enter into the partners' discussions about their postretirement roles, often on a subconscious level.

Financial Interdependency

As women, lesbian couples are at high risk for having insufficient income after retirement. Women's median incomes are lower than men's throughout the life cycle, including after retirement, with women of color receiving even lower wages than white women.[14] Many female-dominated jobs supply little or no pension income, leaving those who hold them to depend on savings, social security, and their presumed marital link to a male breadwinner.[15] For women who do receive pension benefits upon retirement, their partners are rarely eligible to continue receiving this support after the employee's death. Lesbians similarly are not awarded a portion of their partner's social security benefits upon her death, as heterosexual husbands and wives are.

Without male breadwinners to rely on, though, lesbians know in advance that they must support themselves throughout retirement. Many lesbians take this responsibility into account in choosing areas of employment which may help explain their overrepresentation in white-collar positions that provide pension income upon retirement. In some ways, therefore, lesbians often do manage to offset sexism's diminishing influence on their incomes through particularly vigilant planning for their retirement.[16]

In addition to the specific amounts of retirement income, lesbian couples are also affected by changes in the balance of financial security between the partners. If the women retire at different times, they may experience a period in which the income of the still-working partner differs considerably from that of the retired partner. For couples who have a long history of shared financial resources, these changes may be managed fairly easily. The impact of these financial shifts, however, will be greatly influenced by the symbolic significance a particular couple attaches to their financial arrangements. Partners facing a significant contrast in their postretirement incomes may return to questions about each one's contributions to the relationship, and to choices about autonomy and interdependence at this late date in the relationship.

The women had always maintained separate bank accounts, with a portion of their incomes reserved for their private use. Evelyn, who had worked for a corporation for years, knew she would receive a substantial pension upon retirement. Janice had been in business for herself, reaping considerable profits some years and having to live more frugally at other times. She had managed to save well for retirement, but she couldn't possibly make her income match Evelyn's.

Six months into their retirement, the strain of their suddenly unbalanced financial resources caused the couple to fight repeatedly. "Don't you know how insensitive it is to keep suggesting plans you know I can't afford to do?" Janice exploded. "You make me feel bad every time, because I don't want to say no and hold you back, but I can't keep spending money I don't have." "I don't mind paying for you," Evelyn countered.

"I'd much rather pay your way than have to stay home just because you can't afford something."

"But I'm not used to having to take help from you with money, and I hate it," Janice said. "I want to feel like I can pay my full share and not feel like I can't carry my own weight." There was usually silence at this point in the argument, as neither had an easy solution to this dilemma. For the first time in many years, their policy of each one paying her own way just wasn't working anymore.

Unlike in earlier stages, the partners now approach their financial situation with many years of family life behind them. Because of their greater trust, the partners may find confronting interdependence in this stage to be easier than they did when they first became an ongoing couple. In addition, the deepened relational commitment between the partners may make their choices more self-evident than was true in earlier negotiations.

"We're going to join all of our money, and that's all there is to it," Betty announced to Martha over breakfast. "I've watched you suffer over paying your bills each month for the last time." "I don't want us to do that, because it's so unfair to you," Martha said. "You shouldn't have to use your money to pay for me. We've never done things like that." "Do you really think I'm going to stand by and watch you worry like this and barely get by, just because I want some extra spending money?" replied Betty. "There's no more discussion about it. We've been partners for thirty-seven years, and what happens to you happens to us both. We'll change our bank accounts today and never have to talk about it again."

Physical Interdependence

While not everyone enjoys good health in earlier life cycle stages, this final stage is the first time where failing health is predictable and normal. Precipitating perhaps the most concrete form of interdependence between the partners, serious health problems can gradually or suddenly change their lives. The compromised health of one or both women can greatly curtail the range of realistic options open to the couple at this juncture, frequently requiring yet more renegotiation of the interdependence and autonomy of the partners. They may need to welcome increasingly fluid physical boundaries and establish a possibly unfamiliar balance of dependence and caregiving into their roles. Surrendering previous self-reliance may constitute a particular loss for many lesbians.

Health emergencies frequently exert powerful influence on other aspects of the couple's life, including their financial security, their living situation, their availability for social connection, and their dependence on family and social institutions. The nature of the couple's emotional and physical intimacy may likewise be affected as they enter a stage of life containing difficult compromises and likely personal losses. As with other aging partners, challenges to lesbian couples' continued independence tend to multiply over time as changing circumstances in one arena of their lives spill over into other areas of decision making and autonomy.

When one partner's health problems are significantly more restrictive than the other partner's, the more infirm partner may grapple with feelings of envy, as well as guilt and depression resulting from the losses her physical condition imposes. At the same time, the healthier partner may wrestle with conflicting emotional responses herself. Worried for her partner and for their future together, the healthy partner may also experience resentment or depression at the limitations to her own lifestyle her partner's condition imposes. The partners may be unprepared for these particular relational strains and find them difficult to discuss, especially if the partners have enjoyed relatively unrestricted physical capacity until now. Frequently without sufficient support, the partners may find themselves either fighting or submerging their emotional responses at this juncture, adding stress to the already-taxed couple relationship.

At the same time, many lesbian couples' lifelong emphasis on friendship between the partners may offer a supportive advantage in handling the health crises typical at the end of life—not sparing them from the transitions of the stage, but providing crucial comfort along the way. Health emergencies often force each partner to reckon with a personal and relational mortality far more literal and impending than those confronted in previous stages. The resulting awareness of the partners' interdependence and their appreciation for their now-precarious access to each other may genuinely mitigate the complicated reactions to the crisis that would otherwise predominate for each partner.

Lesbian Widowhood

Sooner or later, the partners will be separated by death. While this final family life cycle stage is the expected timing for the death of one of the partners, clearly some lesbians face widowhood much earlier. Without the many years of shared memories to ease their pain, young lesbian widows may also lack access to the camaraderie of a peer group contending with a similar crisis. Robbed of the sense of life unfolding in an expected and desired pattern, these lesbians face the need to rebuild their lives in the middle of the life cycle and to do so from outside many of the social contexts that support young heterosexual widows through a similar tragedy.

Lesbians widowed in old age probably take some solace in the fact that the death was not premature. Research has indicated that when widows (or widowers) perceive that the timing of the death was "natural," their grieving proceeds more normally, with older widows showing fewer adverse affects than those seen in younger ones.[17]

Following this usually massive loss, the surviving partner is likely to experience a need to share her pain—to find a witness willing to feel the true anguish she is experiencing.[18] Through various burial rituals, grieving heterosexual spouses are offered recognition by a wide variety of people who knew of the couple's relationship. The simple knowledge that their pain is known and understood by others assists heterosexual widows in moving through the grieving process. Confident that she will be visited and cared for, particularly in the early stages of her grief, a widow finds the strength to face her loss and to slowly reconstruct her forever-changed life.

Lesbian elders facing the death of their partners frequently must do without most or all of the public component of the healing process. Funeral rituals, newspaper and other public announcements of the partner's death, and the public naming of the deceased person's next of kin are critical acknowledgements that aid in the grieving process when available, and add to the mourner's suffering when these simple acts are withheld.[19] Many closeted lesbian widows may be forced to serve as the only witness to the now-lost relationship. Cut off from full social connection, these women must tolerate or even collude in the severe invalidation of being seen as a mere family friend.

> The obituary read, "Joan Reynolds is survived by two sisters, Helen Jenkins, and Rhona Stewart, her brother John Reynolds, and one nephew." My eyes searched in vain for mention of her partner of 36 years.[20]

Social and family involvements serve as important sources of replenishment of meaning and self-definition for grieving people.[21] Typically, new heterosexual widows turn to their children in the early stages following the death of their husbands.[22] While some lesbians have grown children or other primary supports, many have difficulty accessing sufficient interpersonal connection and become vulnerable to depression as a result. In the absence of meaningful social connection, people instead commonly turn toward reminiscing and story-telling to secure their connection to and memory of their deceased partner.[23] Craving an attentive listener, the mourner wants help safeguarding her memories, preserving her sense of connection to her dead partner in one of the only ways still within her control. Couples' lifelong commitment to partial or total secrecy, however, may clash with widows' needs to share the knowledge of the magnitude and true nature of their loss.

> *"He would want you to have this," my grandmother had told me many times. "Take this scrapbook and learn about your grandfather's relatives and the important times in his life. Did I ever tell you about the time your uncle Ray was born right here in this house?" Of course she had told me many times. Her stories had an urgency, an anxiety to them; she knew she had little remaining time in which to convince her children and grandchildren to be the bearers of her memories after she*

224 The Lesbian Family Life Cycle

> *too was gone. As she told me some of her favorite stories again, my mind wandered to the hidden lesbian couples of her generation. What do you do when you can't tell your stories? Death must feel so powerful for couples who have kept their family lives a secret all these years.*

Particular physical and social vulnerabilities often accompany widowhood for lesbians. Lesbian widows are frequently seen simply as women alone, as if they had never created families at all. In the case of lesbians who once were married to men, their status as widows will relate to their long-ago-ended heterosexual marriages, not their longtime lesbian partnerships. In addition, the aloneness that often accompanies widowhood has particular implications for lesbians, as they face a still-homophobic world without their lifelong partners. The obstacles to lesbians achieving financial security and being able to remain living in their own homes increase considerably following the deaths of their partners. Widowhood, living alone, having few or no children, and surpassing the age of seventy-five top the list of factors found most influential in predicting an elder's likely need for nursing home care.[24] The death of a lesbian partner immediately increases some or all of these risk factors for the surviving widow. Indeed, Simon found never-married women (including lesbians) to be overrepresented in nursing home populations by four times the rate for the general population.[25]

Taken alone, these statistics paint a grim picture of lesbian widows unable to solicit the tools of recovery and instantly made more vulnerable to critical losses of independence. The lifelong strengths of these widows, though, may offset some of their stress.

> Trained in independence, often without family support in their youth, these lesbians have learned to make their own way, to buck the system, to make the necessary compromises with society, out of necessity, to plan for retirement.[26]

Both uniquely burdened and uniquely prepared, lesbian widows face their situations in necessarily unconventional ways. Relying on the strengths gathered across a lifetime, lesbians—like other widows—move through their grief and their changing life circumstances and continue on with their lives. While the widow's years of intimacy with their partner will follow them into everything that subsequently occurs, lesbian widows now face life on their own, finding life changed not only inside themselves but in their relationships with the world around them as well.

Relationships with Social Institutions

Early in this stage, lesbian couples fortunate enough to be in good health and basic financial security can enjoy unprecedented independence from the mainstream community. Newly free to withdraw from obligatory social contacts related to work, the retiring partners can now more fully shield themselves from many of the invalidating social connections in their lives. At the same time, their newly increased free time and energy allow the partners to devote themselves further to the meaningful connections and activities previously constrained by the demands of work. Later, as their physical capacities and general health decline, the partners face the other side of the coin. Gradually or suddenly losing their previous hiatus from full social interdependence, they may find themselves in particular need of community services. For many, the years between age sixty-five and death contain this evolving contrast between relative social independence followed by increasing reliance on others.

Social Changes Following Retirement

Because financial constraints have required many lesbian couples to work long and hard throughout their adult lives, the sudden emancipation retirement brings can be exciting, indeed.

"We're just going to get in our trailer and take off!" Jennifer said. I can't believe I don't have to go to work anymore, and that we really are free to do whatever we want with whomever we choose. I feel drunk, I'm so excited about it! We've never had more than a week off at a time, and even then I knew I had to go back. Don't get me wrong, I loved my work—but I just feel like this huge burden has been lifted off both our shoulders. It's just us, now, and we're going to do whatever we want."

While basking in their newfound independence may hold particular meaning for this oppressed group, relinquishing such a major tie to the surrounding social community elicits other reactions as well.

For most lesbian couples, social membership is as desirable and needed as it is complicated. Their work lives are likely to have both met crucial needs and imposed serious stresses on the partners. Their withdrawal from this world can thus seem like a double-edged sword as the partners may now be more independent and safe, but also more socially cut off and vulnerable.

Losses to Personal and Social Identity

In the absence of social recognition for their personal and family lives, retiring lesbians relinquish a great deal when they end their work lives. Having internalized the powerful social disapproval of a homosexual identity, many older lesbians imbue their work roles with compensatory significance in their self-image. As Kehoe, one of the most well-known lesbian researchers older than sixty-five admits:

> Now I am extremely out of the closet, but, even so, with mixed feelings. Like so many lesbians of my generation, I am not comfortable with such a label. It does not describe my identity, which is still best delineated by the term "academic"[27]

Kehoe's example is especially powerful not because of the active closeting it demonstrates, but because it shows how even women who have publicly identified themselves as lesbians still prefer to rely on their work titles for their primary social identity. Such a situation suggests that for many women, retirement constitutes a stunning social loss and raises difficult questions about how they will replace their previous work identity.

Other Social Relationships

Relying now on other links to the surrounding community, retiring lesbian couples must replenish needed social connections. Many couples' lives can be greatly enriched through involvement with communities of affiliation, their families of origin, and (although less likely for *presently* elderly lesbian couples in the 1990s) the lesbian community. These vital ties protect the partners from increased social isolation as they move through the changing circumstances within this final family life cycle stage.

While life on the social periphery is hardly new to many retiring lesbian couples, their previous experience with limited social connection may ameliorate the stress of this transition.[28] Lesbian partners' coping strategies are well developed by the time the couple reaches the last years of their lives.[29] While the couple probably is aided by this past experience, it is clear that lifelong experience with social isolation overall is hardly an asset for lesbians or for any other couples.[30]

The Social Needs of Elderly Lesbian Couples

As the partners reach old age, social institutions frequently become more needed without becoming more safe. While social connections earlier in the stage were primarily based on mutual interest and social needs, now many partners' dependence on outsiders for basic assistance increases. This transition is far more gradual for some than for others, and it may be hardly experienced by partners whose deaths come suddenly and without previous health problems. For many lesbian couples, however, the contrast between their earlier independence and their social dependence in their final years will be clearly felt.

As the partners lose their ability to care independently for themselves and each other, they face critical decisions. Less likely to have support from their families of origin to prolong their independence from mainstream services, lesbian couples may more frequently be forced to consider some form of home health care or group residential care in their final years. Because their home has provided needed and elusive privacy for many elderly lesbian couples, this loss of independence may cost the partners their sole setting for uninhibited expression of their couple relationship. Couples may realistically fear that they will not be recognized as an intact family unit by the health care workers. Entry into a nursing home of some kind may constitute an even more total loss to the partners' expression of intimacy.

Increasing dependence on the mainstream community leads some lesbian partners to reconsider lifelong decisions to keep their relationship a secret. Partners dismissed as friends or roommates may find they have little voice when their loved one cannot speak on her own behalf. The equation of safety and stress associated with their previous decisions to hide may change significantly during a health crisis.

Miriam and Vivian often marveled at their satisfaction with their lives. They had reached their late seventies and felt grateful for their shared forty-seven years. Then, unexpectedly, Miriam suffered a stroke. Vivian insisted on riding in the ambulance, but once at the hospital, Miriam was whisked off immediately. The ICU nurse told Vivian she was not immediate family and barely included her in what was going on. Relegated to the waiting room, Vivian stood dumbfounded, caught between telling this woman the secret they had never shared with a stranger or leaving Miriam totally alone. She really began to worry about what lay ahead.

Limited legal safeguards are becoming more available to lesbian couples in these situations. In some states, lesbian partners can authorize each other to employ power-of-attorney rights in times of crisis. Sometimes a lesbian can name her partner her "health care proxy" or decision maker, effectively identifying her as next of kin. Likewise, certain protections are available to provide for one's partner financially in the event of death, and partners who will their assets to each other gain both legal protection and tax advantages in many situations. Closeted lesbian couples in their final years may find approaching a lawyer, bank, or hospital staff to assert their rights as a couple to be especially difficult. The common problems associated with aging, however, provide a specific impetus to reconsider the very concrete risks associated with maintaining secrecy about the couple's relationship.

As the less-closeted next generation of lesbians and gay men plan for their retirement and old age, options available to lesbian couples are likely to increase. Two researchers each found that gay people presently approaching this life cycle stage are expressing interest in gay and lesbian retirement housing.[31] Offering many social and practical advantages, these options can provide assistance in a range of circumstances, from social connections to concrete advocacy and protection in times of emergency.

With or without the advantage of gay retirement housing, other social connections may serve as important alternatives to full dependence on the mainstream community. Families of origin—particularly the partners' adult daughters and sons—may extend the couple's period of independence greatly by providing support. Families can provide crucial social connection to aging members, as well as argue for their interests in their dealings with mainstream services.

While the norms in white families vary concerning the degree of care members provide to elders, African-American, Hispanic, and Asian-American families typically place high value on caring for older members of their extended kinship networks.[32] These families typically view community nursing care as an undesirable last resort. Female members shoulder most of the burden of providing care, working hard to protect aging relatives from dependence on the mainstream community. Particularly when these families' networks reside within a reasonably small geographical area, they are frequently successful in caring for senior family members throughout the remainder of their lives.[33]

While many white families also care for their own seniors, families of color frequently ascribe particular value to the role of their oldest members. For Hispanic families, elders are viewed as "wise, knowledgeable, and deserving of respect."[34] Within the African-American community, the central role played by grandmothers especially elevates aging women's status within the family.[35] Asian-American families also promote a strong sense of intergenerational obligation.[36] For immigrant families, elders connect younger family members with their original culture and traditions, in ways not typical within white families.[37]

It is not clear how much of this intrafamilial support is extended to recognizably lesbian family elders or to a closeted elder whose "friend" may or may not be accepted as a member of the family. These groups tend to define family broadly, however, and more readily invite chosen "kin" into the family unit. This tradition may ease the way for lesbian couples to avoid unwanted dependence on the mainstream community, although how clearly the relatives understand the nature of the partners' relationship varies in each situation.

Communities of affiliation may also supply some lesbian couples with vital connections and services in the partners' final years. Often active as contributing members of these groups throughout their lives, aging lesbians who now need primarily to *receive* services may challenge these communities to extend themselves to the lesbian members of their group. Potentially providing rich networks of connection, these communities of affiliation can provide both membership and validation to lesbian couples—depending, of course, on whether the partners are recognized as lesbians and as a family unit.

In addition, couples' participation in meaningful events and activities can balance the time the partners would otherwise spend alone together. For couples in which only one member belongs to a given community of affiliation, the resulting separations can replace prior arenas for individuation and separate activity.

While elderly lesbian couples at present rarely participate in lesbian communities, services are slowly being developed that may encourage future generations of elders to become more involved. Led by organizations pioneered in New York City and San Francisco, several service organizations presently provide services to elderly lesbians and gay men as their primary mission. Offering social programs, assistance with shopping, meal preparation, and advocacy with mainstream community services, these service providers are being used as prototypes for similar organizations in other areas of the country. The next generation of lesbian elders may enjoy significantly more support from the lesbian and gay communities and may reconsider their reluctance to participate in these communities of affiliation.

As younger lesbians enjoy the social and economic gains achieved through the women's movement, the increased visibility and pockets of social support achieved through the efforts of the gay rights movement, and the potential for meaningful social participation offered through lesbian communities, lesbians experience of old age may change significantly. Finally able to create their own multigenerational families, aging lesbian couples can enjoy the fruits of this labor as they claim their own linkage to the larger social world during this and other critical family life cycle stages.

The stresses associated with being female, lesbian, and elderly are likely to continue as central features of life for aging lesbian couples. Lesbians of color will experience racism throughout the foreseeable future as well. Despite these enduring obstacles, elderly lesbian couples negotiating these final years of life frequently achieve the serenity and acceptance of life's trade-offs that have been centerpieces of lesbian existence throughout the family life cycle. Perhaps their passage may be eased by knowing that their lives have contributed to the social changes awaiting younger lesbians. The quiet strength and unacknowledged suffering of these women continue to pave the way as younger voices speak more loudly, and achievements unimagined by earlier generations come to real fruition.

Conclusion

To find unity, a group must name its common ground. Often looking to elders for these clear and needed connections, many groups offer their next generation an understanding of the group's unique identity, encouraging the new members to emulate cherished traditions and welcoming them into full group membership.

As a group, lesbian couples have little basis for shared identity. Coming from particularly diverse backgrounds, their most obvious commonality lies in who they are *not*, as achieving lesbian identity requires a dangerous social disobedience in the refusal of a heterosexual identity. As for who lesbian partners actually *are*, few other groups are composed of individuals who take such active roles in choosing their own personal identities. This process does not lead all couples to the same place, nor does it make simple the task of generalizing about their lives.

Lesbian couples' most meaningful commonality may come from their looking inward for direction as they chart their futures. Following paths illuminated by their own personal calling, lesbian partners dare to redefine the very concept of family and to design especially personalized approaches to their own family lives.[1] Eschewing predetermined mores, these partners are as inspired as they are stressed by the lack of models for their relationships. Starting from scratch, they look to themselves and each other to construct their partnerships, devoting tremendous energy to imagining and experimenting with possible ways to proceed.

Writing about their creations is a delicate and dangerous task. The very specialness of lesbian family life lies in its creative originality, as the partners hone their capacity to trust their own inner wisdom, turning to themselves and each other to lovingly craft their particular family's life. Ultimately, the freedom and special character of lesbian family life spring from developing this inner confidence, and from the partners' transcendence of many mainstream social pressures.

By generalizing about lesbians' family lives, we run the risk of flattening the very creativity we so highly value. While the stages outlined in this book are not intended as prescriptions for the one "healthy" course for lesbian couples' relationships, those couples who are anxious enough for assistance could eschew their own approaches in favor of emulating the proposed depictions of their life stages. At times, though, such couples may be better supported by being encouraged to clear a space for their own unique directions to emerge.

Yet so much wisdom is lost when lesbians cannot speak freely with each other. Separated from mentors and peers, couples remain alone, ill equipped to distinguish growing pains from serious family problems. With inadequate markers for reaching crucial milestones and no conception of the stages of family life, each generation is left to begin again, needlessly unprotected and open to homophobic influence.

So together lesbians carefully continue to articulate what general truths exist about our family lives, guarding against the inhibiting influence that overgeneralization can produce. Gathering our wisdoms together, we hear each others' stories, mindful of those still absent from this simple, essential exchange. In the process, all of us are expanded, and not one but many paths are cleared for lesbian families' lives.

Notes

Chapter 1. Lesbian Families

1. Many authors writing on lesbian experience have contributed to making this point, including, but not limited to, the following sources: Berzon, B. (1988), *Permanent partners* (New York: Penguin); Brown, L. (1989), "New voices, new visions: Toward a lesbian/gay paradigm for psychology," *Psychology of Women Quarterly*, 13:445–458; Weston, K. (1991), *Families we choose* (New York: Columbia University Press); Laird, J. (1993), "Gay and lesbian families," in F. Walsh (ed.), *Normal family processes* (New York: Guilford), pp. 282–328.
2. Berzon, B. & Leighton, R. (1979), *Positively gay* (Millbrae, CA: Celestial Arts); Crawford, S. (1987), "Lesbian families: Psychosocial stress and the family-building process," in Boston Lesbian Psychologies Collective (eds.), *Lesbian psychologies* (Chicago: University of Illinois Press), pp. 195–214; Weston (1991).
3. Laird, J. (1989), "Women and stories: Restorying women's self-constructions," in M. McGoldrick, C. Anderson, & F. Walsh (Eds.), *Women in families: A framework for family therapy*, (New York: Norton), pp. 427–450.
4. Slater, S., & Mencher, J. (1991), "The lesbian family life cycle: A contextual approach," *American Journal of Orthopsychiatry*, 61(3): 372–382.
5. Ibid.
6. Clunis, D., & Green, G. (1988), *Lesbian couples* (Seattle, WA: Seal).
7. Carter, B., & McGoldrick, M., eds. (1989), *The changing family life cycle: A framework for family therapy* (Boston: Allyn & Bacon).

233

234   *Notes*

. The following references are only a partial listing of the authors making this point: DuVall, E. (1988), "Family development's first forty years," *Family Relations*, 37:127–134; Hare-Mustin, R. (1988), "Family change and gender differences: Implications for theory and practice," *Family Relations*, 37:36–41; Leupnitz, D. (1988), *The family interpreted: Feminist theory in clinical practice* (New York: Basic Books); Walters, M., Carter, B., Papp, P., & Silverstein, O. (1988), *The invisible web: Gender patterns in family relationships* (New York: Guilford); Candib, L. (1989), "Point and counterpoint: Family life cycle theory—a feminist critique," *Family Systems Medicine*, 7(4):473–487. Carter, B., & McGoldrick, M. (1989); Laird (1989).

9. Laird (1989), p. 438.

10. Candib (1989).

11. The following references are only a partial listing of the authors making this point: McGoldrick, M., Pearce, J., & Giordano, J., eds. (1984), *Ethnicity and family therapy* (New York: Guilford); Keefe, S. (1984), "Real and ideal extended familism among Mexican Americans and Anglo Americans: On the meaning of 'close' family ties," *Human Organization*, 43(1):65–70; Boyd-Franklin, N. (1987), "Group therapy for black women: A therapeutic support model," *American Journal of Orthopsychiatry*, 57(3):394–401; Boyd-Franklin, N. (1989), *Black families in therapy: A multisystems approach* (New York: Guilford); Chow, E. (1987), "The development of feminist consciousness among Asian American women," *Gender and Society*, 1(3):284–299; Bryant, Z., & Coleman, M. (1988), "The black family as portrayed in introductory marriage and family textbooks," *Family Relations*, 37:255–259; Yee, B. (1990), "Gender and family issues in minority groups," *Generations*, 14(3):39–42.

12. Candib (1989); Hartman, A., & Laird, J. (1983), *Family-centered social work practice* (New York: Free Press).

13. Clunis & Green (1988).

14. Walters, Carter, Papp, & Silverstein (1988), p. 2.

15. Imber-Black, E. (1988), "Rituals of stabilization and change in women's lives," in McGoldrick, Anderson, & Walsh (1989), pp. 451–469.

16. Roth, S. (1985), "Psychotherapy with lesbian couples: Individual issues, female socialization, and the social context," *Journal of Marital and Family Therapy*, 11(3):273–286.

17. Ibid.; Crawford (1987).
18. DuVall, E. (1977), *Marriage and family development* (Philadelphia: Lippincott); Carter, E., & McGoldrick, M., eds. (1980), *The family life cycle: A framework for family therapy* (New York: Gardner).
19. Carter & McGoldrick (1989), p. 255.
20. Slater & Mencher (1991).
21. Carter & McGoldrick (1989), p. 4.
22. Slater & Mencher (1991), p. 375.
23. Roth, S. & Murphy, B.C. (1986), "Therapeutic work with lesbian clients: A systemic therapy view," in J. Hansen & M. Ault-Riché (eds.), *Women and family therapy* (Rockville, MD: Aspen Press), pp. 78–89; Weston (1991).
24. Brown (1989).

Chapter 2. A Model of the Lesbian Family Life Cycle

1. Slater, S. & Mencher, J. (1991), "The lesbian family life cycle: A contextual approach," *American Journal of Orthopsychiatry*, 61(3): 372–382.
2. Duvall, E. (1977), *Marriage and family development* (Philadelphia: Lippincott); Carter, B., & McGoldrick, M., eds. (1980), *The family life cycle: A framework for family therapy* (New York: Gardner).
3. Carter, B., & McGoldrick, M., eds. (1989), *The changing family life cycle: A framework for family therapy* (Boston: Allyn & Bacon).
4. Slater & Mencher (1991).
5. Ibid.
6. Berzon, B. (1988), *Permanent partners* (New York: Penguin).
7. Schafer, S. (1976), "Sexual and social problems of lesbians," *Journal of Sex Research*, 12(1):50–69; Riddle, D., & Morrin, S. (1977, November), "Removing the stigma: A status report," *APA Monitor*, pp. 16, 28; Bell, A., & Weinberg, M. (1978), *Homosexualities: A study of diversity among men and women* (New York: Simon & Schuster); Vetere, V. (1982), "The role of friendship in the development and maintanence of lesbian love relationships," *Journal of Homosexuality, 8*(2):51–65.
8. Spaulding, E. (1982), "The formation of lesbian identity during the 'coming out' process," *Dissertation Abstracts International*, 43:2106A; Faderman, L. (1984–1985), "The new 'gay' lesbians," *Journal of Homosexuality*, 10(3–4):85–95; Sophie, J. (1985), "A critical examina-

tion of stage theories of lesbian identity development," *Journal of Homosexuality, 12*(2):39–51.

9. Sophie (1985); Faderman (1984–1985); Burch, B. (1993); *On different terms: The psychology of difference in lesbian relationships* (Chicago: University of Illinois Press).

10. Ponse, B. (1978), *Identities in the lesbian world* (Westport, CT: Greenwood); Golden, C. (1987), "Diversity and variability in women's sexual identities," in Boston Lesbian Psychologies Collective (Eds.), *Lesbian psychologies* (Chicago: University of Illinois Press), pp. 18–34; Burch (1993).

11. Ponse (1978); Golden (1987).

12. Ponse (1978); Golden (1987); Charbonneau, C. & Lander, P. (1991), "Redefining sexuality: Women becoming lesbian in midlife," in B. Sang, J. Warshow, & A. Smith (eds.), *Lesbians at midlife: The creative transition* (San Francisco: Spinsters), pp. 35–43; Falco, K. (1991), "Lesbian identity formation," in K. Falco (Ed.), *Psychotherapy with lesbian clients: Theory into practice* (New York: Brunner/Mazel), pp. 80–105; Burch (1993).

13. Faderman (1984); Sophie, J. (1987), "Internalized homophobia and lesbian identity," *Journal of Homosexuality*, 14(1–2):53–65; Charbonneau & Lander (1991).

14. Sophie (1985).

15. Faderman (1984); Sophie (1985).

16. Cass, V. (1979), "Homosexual identity formation: A theoretical model," *Journal of Homosexuality*, 4:219–235; Faderman (1984); Lewis, L. (1984), "The coming out process for lesbians: Integrating a stable identity," *Social Work*, 29(5):464–469; Sophie (1985); Charbonneau & Lander (1991); Kahn, M. (1991), "Factors affecting the coming out process for lesbians," *Journal of Homosexuality*, 21(3): 47–70.

17. Chapman, B., & Brannock, J. (1987), "Proposed model of lesbian identity development: An empirical examination," *Journal of Homosexuality*, 14(3–4):69–80; Charbonneau & Lander (1991).

18. Gramick, J. (1984), "Developing a lesbian identity," in T. Darty & S. Potter (eds.), *Women-identified women* (Palo Alto, CA: Mayfield); Groves, P. (1985), "Coming out: Issues for the therapist working with women in the process of lesbian identity formation," *Women and Therapy*, 4(2):17–22; Sophie (1985); Roth (1985); Chapman & Brannock (1987); Charbonneau & Lander (1991).

19. Cass (1979); Coleman, E. (1982), "Developmental stages of the coming out process," *Journal of Homosexuality*, 7(2–3):31–43.
20. Lewis (1984).
21. Mencher, J. (1992), "Beyond 'meet and marry': Expanding possibilities for lesbian couple formation," Families in Focus Sixth Annual Speakers Series, Cambridge, MA.
22. Cass (1978); Coleman (1982); Sophie (1985); Troiden, R. (1989), "The formation of homosexual identities," *Journal of Homosexuality*, 17(1–2):43–73.
23. Groves, P., & Ventura, L. (1983), "The lesbian coming out process: Therapeutic considerations," *Personnel and Guidance Journal*, 62(3):146–149; Gramick (1984).
24. Roth, S. (1985), "Psychotherapy with lesbian clients: Individual issues, female socialization, and the social context," *Journal of Marital and Family Therapy*, 11(3):298.
25. Ibid.
26. Nichols, M. (1988), "Bisexuality in women: Myths, realities, and implications for therapy," *Women and Therapy*, pp. 235–252; Zipkin, D. (1992), "Why bi?" in E. Weise (ed.), *Closer to home: Bisexuality and feminism* (Seattle, WA: Seal).
27. Weise, E., ed., (1992), *Closer to home: Bisexuality and feminism* (Seattle, WA: Seal).
28. Ibid.
29. Zipkin (1992).
30. McKeon, E. (1992), "To be bisexual and underclass," in E. Weise (ed.), *Closer to home: Bisexuality and feminism* (Seattle, WA: Seal), pp. 27–34.
31. Lorde, A. (1984), *Sister outsider* (Trumansburg, NY: Crossing), p. 120.
32. Espin, O. (1987), "Issues of identity in the psychology of Latina lesbians," in Boston Lesbian Psychologies Collective (eds.), *Lesbian psychologies* (Chicago: University of Illinois Press), pp. 35–55.
33. Slater & Mencher (1991).
34. Ibid.
35. Ibid.
36. Murphy, B. C. (1989), "Lesbian couples and their parents: The effects of perceived parental attitudes on the couple," *Journal of Counseling and Development*, 68:46–51.

37. Laird, J. (1993), "Gay and lesbian families," in F. Walsh (ed.), *Normal family processes* (New York: Guilford).

Chapter 3. Persistent Stressors in Lesbian Couples' Lives

1. Roth, S. (1985), "Psychotherapy with lesbian clients: Individual issues, female socialization, and the social context," *Journal of Marital and Family Therapy*, 11(3):273–286; Slater, S., & Mencher, J. (1991), "The lesbian family life cycle: A contextual approach," *American Journal of Orthopsychiatry*, 61(3):372–382.
2. Slater & Mencher (1991).
3. Weinberg, G. (1972), *Society and the healthy homosexual* (New York: St. Martin's).
4. Krestan, J., & Bepko, C. (1980), "The problem of fusion in the lesbian relationship," *Family Process*, 19:277–289; Roth (1985).
5. Neison, J. (1990), "Heterosexism: Redefining homophobia for the 1990's," *Journal of Gay and Lesbian Psychotherapy*, 1(3):21–35.
6. Saghir, M., & Robins, E. (1973), *Male and female homosexuality: A comprehensive investigation* (Baltimore, MD: Williams and Wilkins); Bell, A., & Weinberg, M. (1978), *Homosexualities: A study of diversity among men and women* (New York: Simon & Schuster); Jay, K., & Young, A. (1979), *The gay report: Lesbians and gay men speak out about sexual experiences and lifestyles* (New York: Simon & Schuster).
7. Lewis, C., Saghir, M., & Robins, E. (1982), "Drinking patterns in homosexual and heterosexual women," *Journal of Clinical Psychiatry*, 43(7):277–279; Swallow, J. (1983), *Out from under: Sober dykes and our friends* (San Francisco: Spinsters); Anderson, S., & Henderson, D. (1985), "Working with lesbian alcoholics," *Social Work*, 30(6):518–525; Nicoloff, L., & Stiglitz, E. (1987), "Lesbian alcoholism: Etiology, treatment, and recovery," in Boston Lesbian Psychologies Collective (eds.), *Lesbian psychologies* (Chicago: University of Illinois Press), pp. 283–293.
8. The following references are only a partial list of the authors making this point: Krestan & Bepko (1980); Burch, B. (1982), "Psychological merger in lesbian couples: A joint ego and systems approach," *Family Therapy*, 59(3):201–208; Decker, B. (1983), "Counseling gay and lesbian couples," *Journal of Social Work and Human Sexuality*, 2(2–3):39–52; Roth (1985); Crawford, S. (1987), "Lesbian families:

Psychosocial stress and the family-building process," in Boston Lesbian Psychologies Collective (eds.), *Lesbian psychologies* (Chicago: University of Illinois Press), pp. 195–214.

9. Roth (1985); Slater & Mencher (1991).
10. Crawford (1987), p. 202.
11. Krestan & Bepko (1980), Roth (1985).
12. Gartrell, N. (1984), "Combatting homophobia in the psychotherapy of lesbians," *Women and Therapy*, 3(1):24.
13. Crawford (1987), p. 202.
14. While not specifically addressing lesbians, the following source emphasizes the crucial relationship between families and their social environments: Hartman, A., & Laird, J. (1983), *Family-centered social work practice* (New York: Free Press).
15. Blumstein, P., & Schwartz, P. (1983), *American couples* (New York: Morrow).
16. Krestan & Bepko (1980); Burch (1982); Nichols, M. (1982), "The treatment of inhibited sexual desire (ISD) in lesbian couples," *Women and Therapy*, 1(4):49–66; Decker (1983); Kaufman, P., Harrison, E., & Hyde, M. (1984), "Distancing for intimacy in lesbian relationships," *American Journal of Psychiatry*, 141(4):530–533; Roth (1985); Crawford (1987); Pearlman, S. (1988), "Distancing and connectedness: Impact on couple formation in lesbian relationships," *Women and Therapy*, 8(1–2):77–88; Mencher, J. (1990), "Intimacy in lesbian relationships: A critical re-examination of fusion," Stone Center Working Papers Series, Wellesley, MA.
17. Mencher (1990).
18. Roth (1985); Krestan & Bepko (1980).
19. Roth (1985).
20. Vetere, V. (1982), "The role of friendship in the development and maintenance of lesbian love relationships," *Journal of Homosexuality*, 8(2):51–65.
21. Crawford (1987).
22. Slater & Mencher (1991).
23. Krestan & Bepko (1980); Decker (1983).
24. Krestan & Bepko (1980); Roth (1985).
25. Decker (1983), p. 47.
26. Chow, E. (1987), "The development of feminist consciousness among Asian American women," *Gender and Society*, 1(3):284–299; Yee, B.

(1990), "Gender and family issues in minority groups," *Generations*, 14(3):39–42.

27. Turner, C. (1984), "Psychosocial barriers to black women's career development," Stone Center Working Papers Series, Wellesley, MA; Pinderhughes, E. (1986), "Minority women: A nodal position in the functioning of the social system," in J. Hansen & M. Ault-Riché (eds.), *Women and family therapy* (Rockville, MD: Aspen), pp. 51–63; Boyd-Franklin, N. (1989), *Black families in therapy: A multisystems approach* (New York: Guilford).

28. Decker (1983); Slater & Mencher (1991).

29. Blumstein & Schwartz (1983).

30. Ibid.; Decker (1983); Roth (1985); Rothberg, B., & Ubell, V. (1985), "The co-existence of systems theory and feminism in working with heterosexual and lesbian couples," *Women and Therapy*, 4(1):19–36; Lynch, J., & Reilly, M. (1986), "Role relationships: Lesbian perspectives," *Journal of Homosexuality*, 12(2):53–69.

31. Blumstein & Schwartz (1983).

32. Ibid.

33. Crawford (1987); Muzio, C. (1993, June), "Lesbian co-parenting: On being/being with the invisible (m)other," *Smith College Studies in Social Work*, pp. 215–229.

34. Loulan, J. (1986), "Psychotherapy with lesbian mothers," in T. Stein & C. Cohen (eds.), *Contemporary perspectives on psychotherapy with lesbians and gay men* (New York: Plenum), pp. 181–208; Crawford (1987); Muzio (1993).

35. Lynch & Reilly (1986).

36. Lindenbaum, J. (1985), "The shattering of an illusion: The problem of competition in lesbian relationships," *Feminist Studies*, 11(1):85–103. Rothberg & Ubell (1985).

37. Nichols (1982); Blumstein & Schwartz (1983).

38. Blumstein & Schwartz (1983).

39. Ibid.

40. Lynch & Reilly (1986).

41. Blumstein & Schwartz (1983), p. 130.

42. Ibid., p. 53.

43. Miller, J., Jacobsen, R., & Bigner, J. (1981), "The child's home environment for lesbian vs. heterosexual mothers: A neglected area of research," *Journal of Homosexuality*, 7(1):49–56.

44. Turner, P., Scadden, L., & Harris, M. (1990), "Parenting in gay and lesbian families," *Journal of Gay and Lesbian Psychotherapy*, 1(3):55–66.
45. Blumstein & Schwartz (1983).
46. Ibid.; Lynch & Reilly (1986); Loulan, J. (1988), "Research on the sex practices of 1,566 lesbians and the clinical applications," *Women and Therapy*, 7(2–3):221–234.
47. Blumstein & Schwartz (1983); Loulan (1988); Rothblum, E., & Brehony, K. (1991), "The Boston marriage today: Romantic but asexual relationships among lesbians," in C. Silverstein (ed.), *Gays, lesbians and their therapists* (New York: Norton), pp. 210–226.
48. Blumstein & Schwartz (1983); Roth (1985); Brown, L. (1986), "Confronting internalized oppression in sex therapy with lesbians," *Journal of Homosexuality*, 12(3–4):99–107; Nichols, M. (1987), "Lesbian sexuality: Issues and developing theory," in Boston Lesbian Psychologies Collective (eds.), *Lesbian psychologies* (Chicago: University of Illinois Press), pp. 97–125; Loulan (1988).
49. Clunis, D. & Green, G. (1988), *Lesbian couples* (Seattle: Seal); Loulan (1988); Mencher (1990).
50. Benjamin, J. (1988), *The bonds of love: Psychoanalysis, feminism, and the problem of domination* (New York: Pantheon).
51. Rosen, W. (1993), "On the integration of sexuality: Lesbians and their mothers," Stone Center Working Papers Series, Wellesley, MA.
52. Loulan (1988), p. 216.
53. Ibid.; Rosen (1993).
54. Nichols (1982); Roth (1985); Clunis & Green (1988); Loulan (1988).
55. Roth (1985), p. 277.
56. Berzon (1988); Loulan (1988).
57. Russell, C. (1987), "Ageing as a feminist issue," *Women's Studies International Forum*, 10(2):125–132; Loulan (1988).
58. Friedan, B. (1963), *The feminine mystique* (New York: Norton); Millett, K. (1969), *Sexual politics* (New York: Simon & Schuster); Morgan, R. (1970), *Sisterhood is powerful* (New York: Vintage); Steinem, G. (1983), *Outrageous acts and everyday rebellions* (New York: Holt, Rinehart, & Winston); Faludi, S. (1991), *Backlash: The undeclared war on American women* (New York: Doubleday).
59. Freud, S. (1925), "Some psychical consequences of the anatomical dis-

tinctions between the sexes," in J. Strachey (ed.), *The standard edition of the complete psychological works of Sigmund Freud* (London: Hogarth).

60. Greene, B. (1986), "When the therapist is white and the patient is black: Considerations for psychotherapy in the feminist heterosexual and lesbian communities," *Women and Therapy*, 5(2–3):41–65.

61. Perez, E. (1991), "Gulf dreams," in C. Trujillo (ed.), *Chicana lesbians: The girls our mothers warned us about* (Berkeley, CA: Third Woman), p. 99.

62. Keefe, S. (1984), "Real and ideal extended familism among Mexican Americans and Anglo Americans: On the meaning of 'close' family ties," *Human Organization*, 43(1):65–70; Chow, E. (1987); Clunis & Green (1988); Yee (1990); Cole, C. G. (1992), "Cultural diversity: Implications for theory and practice," Stone Center Working Papers Series, Wellesley, MA.

63. Perez (1991); Trujillo, C., ed. (1991), *Chicana lesbians: The girls our mothers warned us about* (Berkeley, CA: Third Woman Press).

64. Barrera, M. (1991), "Cafe con leche," in C. Trujillo (Ed.), *Chicana lesbians: The girls our mothers warned us about* (Berkeley, CA: Third Woman Press), p. 83.

Chapter 4. Lesbian Couples' Strengths and Coping Mechanisms

1. Karpel, M. (1976), "From fusion to dialogue," *Family Process*, 15(1):65–82; Peplau, L., Cochran, S., Rook, K., & Pedasky, C. (1978); "Loving women: Attachment and autonomy in lesbian relationships," *Journal of Social Sciences*, 34(3):7–27; Krestan, J., & Bepko, C. (1980), "The problem of fusion in the lesbian relationship," *Family Process*, 19:277–289; Burch, B. (1982), "Psychological merger in lesbian couples: A joint ego and systems approach," *Family Therapy*, 59(3):201–208; Decker, B. (1983), "Counseling gay and lesbian couples," *Journal of Social Work and Human Sexuality*, 2(2–3):39–52; and many other works since these references.

2. Krestan & Bepko (1980).

3. Ibid.; Mencher, J. (1990), "Intimacy in lesbian relationships: A critical re-examination of fusion," Stone Center Working Papers Series, Wellesley, MA.

4. Elise, D. (1986), "Lesbian couples: The implications of sex differences in separation-individuation," *Psychotherapy*, 23(2):305–310.

5. Krestan & Bepko (1980); Burch (1982); Decker (1983); Roth, S. (1985), "Psychotherapy with lesbian couples: Individual issues, female socialization, and the social context," *Journal of Marital and Family Therapy*, 11(3):273–286; Elise (1986); Eldridge, N. (1987), "Gender issues in counseling same-sex couples," *Professional Psychology Research and Practice*, 18(6):567–572; Pearlman, S. (1988), "Distancing and connectedness: Impact on couple formation in lesbian relationships," *Women and Therapy*, 8(1–2):77–88; Mencher (1990).

6. Miller, J. B. (1976), *Toward a new psychology of women* (Boston: Beacon); Chodorow, N. (1978), *The reproduction of mothering: Psychoanalysis and the sociology of gender* (Berkeley: University of California Press); Gilligan, C. (1982), *In a different voice* (Cambridge, MA: Harvard University Press); Kaplan, A. (1984), "The 'self-in-relation': Implications for depression in women," Stone Center Working Papers Series, Wellesley, MA; Miller, J. B. (1984), "The development of women's sense of self," Stone Center Working Papers Series, Wellesley, MA; Stiver, I. (1984), "The meaning of 'dependency' in female-male relationships," Stone Center Working Papers Series, Wellesley, MA; Jordan, J. (1984), "Empathy and self-boundaries," Stone Center Working Papers Series, Wellesley, MA; Surrey, J. (1985), "Self in relation: A theory of women's development," Stone Center Working Papers Series, Wellesley, MA. The subsequent work of these authors offers much additional elaboration of these concepts.

7. Chodorow (1978); Benjamin, J. (1988), *The bonds of love: Psychoanalysis, feminism, and the problem of domination* (New York: Pantheon).

8. Chodorow (1978).

9. Burch (1982); Pearlman (1988).

10. Mencher (1990).

11. Moses, A. (1978), *Identity management in lesbian women* (New York: Praeger); McCandlish, B. (1982), "Therapeutic issues with lesbian couples," *Journal of Homosexuality*, 7(2–3):71–78; Peplau, L., Padesky, C., & Hamilton, M. (1982), "Satisfaction in lesbian relationships," *Journal of Homosexuality*, 8(2):23–35; Vetere, V. (1982), "The role of friendship in the development and maintenance of lesbian love relationships," *Journal of Homosexuality*, 8(2):51–65; Blumstein, P., & Schwartz, P. (1983), *American couples* (New York: Morrow); Eldridge (1987); Mencher (1990).

12. Mencher (1990), p. 4.

13. Burch (1982); Nichols, M. (1982), "The treatment of inhibited sexual desire (ISD) in lesbian couples," *Women and Therapy*, 1(4):49–66; Brown, L. (1986), "Confronting internalized oppression in sex therapy with lesbians," *Journal of Homosexuality*, 12(3–4):99–107.

14. Krestan & Bepko (1980); Burch (1982); Decker (1983); Roth (1985); Elise (1986); Crawford, S. (1987), "Lesbian families: Psychosocial stress and the family-building process," in Boston Lesbian Psychologies Collective (eds.), *Lesbian psychologies* (Chicago: University of Illinois Press), pp. 195–214; Pearlman, (1988).

15. Burch, B. (1987), "Barriers to intimacy: Conflicts over power, dependency, and nurturing in lesbian relationships," in Boston Lesbian Psychologies Collective p. 140.

16. Pearlman (1988); Mencher (1990).

17. Carter, E., & McGoldrick, M. (1980), *The family life cycle: A framework for family therapy* (New York: Gardner); Carter, B., & McGoldrick, M. (1989), *The changing family life cycle: A framework for family therapy* (Boston: Allyn & Bacon); Wolin, S., & Bennett, L. (1984), "Family rituals," *Family Process*, 23(3):401–420; Imber-Black, E. (1988), "Celebrating the uncelebrated," *Family Therapy Networker*, 12(1):60–66; Laird, J. (1988), "Women and stories," in E. Imber-Black, J. Roberts, & Whiting R. *Rituals in families and family therapy* (New York: Norton); Roberts, J. (1988), "Setting the frame: Definition of rituals, functions, and typology," in E. Imber-Black, J. Roberts, & R. Whiting (eds.), *Rituals in families and family therapy* (New York: Norton).

18. Slater & Mencher (1991), p. 373.

19. Ibid.

20. Ibid.

21. Carter & McGoldrick (1980); Wolin & Bennett (1984); Imber-Black (1988); Roberts (1988); Carter & McGoldrick (1989).

22. Slater & Mencher (1991).

23. Carter & McGoldrick (1980); Wolin & Bennett (1984); Imber-Black (1988); Roberts (1988); Carter & McGoldrick (1989).

24. Imber-Black, E., Roberts, J., & Whiting, R. (1988), *Rituals in families and family therapy* (New York: Norton); Wolin & Bennett (1984).

25. Wolin & Bennett (1984).

26. Imber-Black (1988).

27. Slater & Mencher (1991).

28. Wolin & Bennett (1984); Slater & Mencher (1991).

29. Laird, J. (1989), "Women and stories: Restoring women's self-constructions," in M. McGoldrick, C. Anderson, & F. Walsh (eds.), *Women in families: A framework for family therapy* (New York: Norton), pp. 427–450.
30. Imber-Black (1988).
31. Slater & Mencher (1991), p. 374.
32. Imber-Black (1988).
33. Slater & Mencher (1991).
34. Butler, B. (1990), *Ceremonies of the heart: Celebrating lesbian unions.* (Seattle, WA: Seal); Sullivan, E. (1991), Lesbian commitment ceremonies: A contextual understanding," unpublished master's thesis, Smith College School for Social Work, Northampton, MA.
35. Butler (1990), p. 49.
36. Sullivan (1991), p. 7.
37. Butler (1990).
38. Slater & Mencher (1991).
39. Ibid.
40. Ibid., p. 380.
41. Ibid.
42. Ibid.
43. Kreiger, S. (1983), *The mirror dance: Identity in a women's community* (Philadelphia: Temple University Press); Pearlman, S. (1987), "The saga of continuing clash in lesbian community, or will an army of ex-lovers fail?" in Boston Lesbian Psychologies Collective (eds.), *Lesbian psychologies* (Chicago: University of Illinois Press), pp. 313–326; Weston, K. (1991), *Families we choose* (New York: Columbia University Press).
44. Pearlman (1987), p. 318–319.
45. Ibid.
46. Lourde, A. (1984). *Sister outsider* (Trumansburg, NY: Crossing); Greene, B. (1986), "When the therapist is white and the patient is black: Considerations for psychotherapy in the feminist heterosexual and lesbian communities," *Women and Therapy*, 5(2–3):41–65.
47. Weston (1991), p. 134.
48. Greene (1986), p. 62.
49. Lockard, D. (1986), "The lesbian community: An anthropological approach," *Journal of Homosexuality*, 11(3–4):83–95.
50. Laird, J. (1993), "Gay and lesbian families," in F. Walsh (ed.), *Normal family processes* (New York: Guilford), pp. 282–327.

Chapter 5. Lesbian Families with Children

1. Benkov, L. (1994), *Reinventing the family: The emerging story of lesbian and gay parents* (New York: Crown).
2. Polikoff, N. (1987), "Lesbians choosing children: the personal is political," in S. Pollack & J. Vaughn (eds.), *Politics of the heart: A feminist anthology* (Ithaca, NY: Freebrand), p. 49.
3. Benkov (1994).
4. Ibid.
5. Ibid.
6. Green, R. (1978), "Sexual identity of 37 children raised by homosexual or transexual parents," *American Journal of Psychiatry*, 135(6):692–697; Hoeffer, B. (1981), "Children's acquisition of sex-role behavior in lesbian-mother families," *American Journal of Orthopsychiatry*, 51(3):536–544; Kirkpatrick, M., Smith, C., & Roy, R. (1981), "Lesbian mothers and their children: A comparative study," *American Journal of Orthopsychiatry*, 51(3):545–551; Kweskin, S., & Cook, A. (1982), "Heterosexual and homosexual mothers self-described sex-role behavior and ideal sex-role behavior in children," *Sex Roles*, 8(9):967–975; Golomok, S., Spencer, A., & Rutter, M. (1983), "Children in lesbian and single-parent households: Psychosexual and psychiatric appraisal," *Journal of Child Psychology and Psychiatry*, 24(4):551–572; Harris, M., & Turner, P. (1985–1986), "Gay and lesbian parents," *Journal of Homosexuality*, 12(2):101–113. Kirkpatrick, M. (1987), "Clinical implications of lesbian mother studies," *Journal of Homosexuality*, 14(1–2):201–211; Gibbs, E. (1988), "Psychosocial development of children raised by lesbian mothers: A review of research," *Women and Therapy*, 8(1–2):65–75; Turner, P., Scadden, L., & Harris, M. (1990), "Parenting in gay and lesbian families," *Journal of Gay and Lesbian Psychotherapy*, 1(3):55–66.
7. Polikoff, N. (1986), "Lesbian mothers, lesbian families: Legal obstacles, legal challenges," *Review of Law and Social Change*, 14:907–914.
8. Ibid., p. 908.
9. Blumstein, P., & Schwartz, P. (1983), *American couples* (New York: Morrow).
10. Stiglitz, E. (1990), "Caught between two worlds: The import of a child

on a lesbian couple's relationship," in J. Knowles & E. Cole (eds.), *Woman-defined motherhood* (New York: Harrington Park) p. 112.
11. Benkov (1994).
12. Muzio, C. (1993, June), "Lesbian co-parenting: On being/being with the invisible (m)other," *Smith College Studies in Social Work*, pp. 215–229.
13. Ibid.
14. Lewin, E. (1993), *Lesbian mothers* (Ithaca, NY: Cornell University Press).
15. Muzio (1993).
16. Tortorilla, T. (1987), "On a creative edge," in S. Pollack & J. Vaughn (eds.), *Politics of the heart: A lesbian parenting anthology* (Ithaca, NY: Firebrand), pp. 168–174.
17. Crawford, S. (1987), "Lesbian families: Psychosocial stress and the family-building process," in Boston Lesbian Psychologies Collective (eds.), *Lesbian psychologies* (Chicago: University of Illinois Press), p. 205.
18. Erlichman, K. (1988), "Lesbian mothers: Ethical issues in social work practice," *Women and Therapy*, 8(1–2):207–224.
19. McCandlish, B. (1982), "Therapeutic issues with lesbian couples," *Journal of Homosexuality*, 7(2–3).71–78; Rohrbaugh, J. (1989), "Choosing children: Psychological issues in lesbian parenting," *Women and Therapy*, 8(1–2):51–64.
20. Rohrbaugh (1989), p. 61.
21. Pagelow, M. (1980), "Heterosexual and lesbian single mothers: A comparison of problems, coping, and solutions," *Journal of Homosexuality*, 5(3):189–204; Kirkpatrick, Smith, & Roy (1981).
22. Gibbs (1988); Baptiste, D. (1987), "The gay and lesbian step-parent family," in F. Bozett, *Gay and lesbian parenting* (New York: Praeger), pp. 112–137.
23. Kirkpatrick, Smith, & Roy (1981), p. 550.
24. Pagelow (1980).
25. Lewin (1993), p. 128.
26. Arbeitman, L. (1993), "Joint adoptions by unmarried cohabitants," *Family Law Section News*, 11(1):113–115; Benkov (1994).
27. Hunter, N., & Polikoff, N. (1976), "Custody rights of lesbian mothers: Legal theory and litigation strategy," *Buffalo Law Review*, 25:705–711.

28. Lewin (1993).
29. Steinhorn, A. (1982), "Lesbian mothers—the invisible minority: Role of the mental health worker," *Women and Therapy*, 1(4):35–48.
30. Erlichman (1988).
31. Benkov (1994).
32. Ibid.
33. Crawford (1987).
34. Polikoff (1986).
35. Crawford (1987).
36. Benkov (1994).
37. Ibid., p. 191.
38. Clausen, J. (1987), "To live outside the law you must be honest: A flommy looks at lesbian parenting," in S. Pollack & J. Vaughn (eds.), *Politics of the heart: A lesbian parenting anthology* (Ithaca, NY: Firebrand), p. 336.
39. Crawford (1987).
40. Muzio (1993).
41. Lewin (1993).
42. Laird, J. (1993), "Gay and lesbian families," in F. Walsh (ed.), *Normal family processes* (New York: Guilford), pp. 282–328.
43. Loulan, J. (1986), "Psychotherapy with lesbian mothers," In T. Stein & C. Cohen (eds.), *Contemporary perspectives on psychotherapy with lesbians and gay men* (New York: Plenum), pp. 181–208; Kirkpatrick (1987); Levy, E. (1989), "Lesbian motherhood: Identity and social support," *Affilia*, 4(4):40–53. Lott-Whitehead, L., & Tully, C. (1993, June), "The family lives of lesbian mothers," *Smith College Studies in Social Work*, pp. 265–280.
44. Crawford (1987); Muzio (1993).
45. Weston, K. (1991), *Families we choose* (New York: Columbia University Press).
46. Snitow, A. (1992), "Motherhood: Reclaiming the demon texts," in I. Reti (ed.), *Childless by choice: A feminist anthology* (Santa Cruz, CA: Herbooks), pp. 5–11.
47. Felman, J. (1992), "Meditation for my sisters: On choosing not to have children," in I. Reti (ed.), *Childless by choice: A feminist anthology* (Santa Cruz, CA: Herbooks), p. 79.

Chapter 6. Stage One: Formation of the Couple

1. Flaubert, G. (1858), *Madame Bovary: Moeurs de Provence* (Paris: Miche Levy-Freres).
2. Tennov, D. (1979), *Love and limerence: The experience of being in love* (Chelsea, MI: Scarborough House).
3. Ibid.
4. Berzon, B. (1988), *Permanent partners: Building gay and lesbian relationships that last* (New York: Penguin); Clunis, D., & Green, G. (1988), *Lesbian couples* (Seattle, WA: Seal); Loulan, J. (1988), "Research on the sex practices of 1,566 lesbians and the clinical applications," *Women and Therapy*, 7(2–3):221–234; Pearlman, S. (1988), "Distancing and connectedness: Impact on couple formation in lesbian relationships," *Women and Therapy*, 8(1–2):77–88; Slater, S., & Mencher, J. (1991), "The lesbian family life cycle: A contextual approach," *American Journal of Orthopsychiatry*, 61(3):372–382. Mencher, J. (1992), "Beyond 'meet and marry': Expanding possibilities for lesbian couple formation," Families in Focus Sixth Annual Speaker Series, Cambridge, MA.
5. Slater & Mencher (1991).
6. See note 6 for Chapter 4 for a listing of authors offering primary contributions to contemporary conceptions of women's developmental pathways.
7. Mencher (1992).
8. Ibid.
9. Benjamin, J. (1988), *The bonds of love: Psychoanalysis, feminism, and the problem of domination* (New York: Pantheon).
10. Rosen, W. (1991), "Gender construction in lesbian sexuality," unpublished paper.
11. Mencher (1992).
12. Ibid.
13. Clunis & Green (1988); Roth, S. (1985), "Psychotherapy with lesbian couples: Individual issues, female socialization, and the social context," *Journal of Marital and Family Therapy*, 11(3):273–286.
14. Mencher (1992), pp. 10–11.
15. Pearlman (1988).
16. Mencher (1992).

17. Slater, S., & Mencher, J. (1990, October), "The lesbian family life cycle," unpublished paper presented at the annual meeting of the American Association of Marriage and Family Therapy, Washington, DC.
18. Ibid.
19. Ibid.
20. Ibid.
21. Clunis & Green (1988).
22. Mencher (1992).
23. Mencher (1992).
24. Groves, P., & Ventura, L. (1983, November), "The lesbian coming out process: Therapeutic considerations," *Personnel and Guidance Journal*, 62(3):146–149.

Chapter 7. Stage Two: Ongoing Couplehood

1. Slater, S., & Mencher, J. (1991), "The lesbian family life cycle: A contextual approach," *American Journal of Orthopsychiatry*, 61(3):372–382.
2. Blumstein, P., & Schwartz, P. (1983), *American couples* (New York: Morrow); Loulan, J. (1988), "Research on the sex practices of 1,566 lesbians and the clinical applications," *Women and Therapy*, 7(2–3):221–234.
3. Blumstein & Schwartz (1983); Mencher, J. (1990), "Intimacy in lesbian relationships: A critical re-examination of fusion," Stone Center Working Papers Series, Wellesley, MA.
4. Blumstein & Schwartz (1983).
5. Lindenbaum, J. (1985), "The shattering of an illusion: The problem of competition in lesbian relationships," *Feminist Studies*, 11(1): 85–103.
6. Slater & Mencher (1991).
7. Clunis, D., & Green, G. (1988), *Lesbian couples* (Seattle, WA: Seal); Kurdek, L. (1989), "Relationship quality in gay and lesbian cohabiting couples: A one-year follow-up study," *Journal of Social and Personal Relationships*, 6(1):39–59; Pearlman, S. (1988), "Distancing and connectedness: Impact on couple formation in lesbian relationships," *Women and Therapy*, 8(1–2):77–88.
8. Clunis & Green (1988).

9. McWhirter, D., & Mattison, A. (1984), *The male couple: How relationships develop* (Englewood Cliffs, NJ: Prentice-Hall).
10. Clunis & Green (1988).

Chapter 8. Stage Three: The Middle Years

1. Sullivan, E. (1991), "Lesbian commitment ceremonies: A contextual understanding," unpublished master's thesis, Smith College School for Social Work, Northampton, MA.
2. Slater, S., & Mencher, J. (1990, October), "The lesbian family life cycle," paper presented at the annual meeting of the American Association of Marriage and Family Therapy, Washington, DC.
3. Slater, S., & Mencher, J. (1991), "The lesbian family life cycle: A contextual approach," *American Journal of Orthopsychiatry*, 61(3):372–382.
4. Slater & Mencher (1990); Slater, S. (1994), "Approaching and avoiding the work of the middle years: Affairs in committed lesbian relationships," *Women and Therapy*, 15(2):19–34.
5. Gerzon, M. (1992), *Coming into our own: Understanding the adult metamorphosis* (New York: Delacorte).
6. Slater (1994).

Chapter 9. Stage Four: Generativity

1. Erikson, E. (1963), *Childhood and society* (New York: Norton).
2. Ibid.
3. Clunis, D., & Green, G. (1988), *Lesbian couples* (Seattle, WA: Seal).
4. Erikson (1963).
5. Slater, S., & Mencher, J. (1991), "The lesbian family life cycle: A contextual approach," *American Journal of Orthopsychiatry*, 61(3):372–382.
6. Erikson (1983).
7. Barbara Reinhold, personal communication, 1994.
8. Ritter, K., & O'Neill, C. (1989), "Moving through loss: The spiritual journey of gay men and lesbian women," *Journal of Counseling and Development*, 68:9–15.
9. Adin Delacour, personal communication, 1994.

10. Carter Heyward, personal communication, 1993.
11. Stewart, A., & Gold-Steinberg, S. (1990), "Midlife women's political consciousness: Case studies of psychosocial development and political commitment," *Psychology of Women Quarterly*, 14:543–566.
12. Loulan, J. (1991), "'Now when I was your age': One perspective on how lesbian culture has influenced our sexuality," in B. Sang & A. Smith (eds.), *Lesbians at midlife: The creative transition* (San Francisco: Spinsters), pp. 10–18.
13. Crux, L. (1991), "The ripening of our bodies, the deepening of our spirits," in B. Sang & A. Smith (eds.), *Lesbians at midlife: The creative transition* (San Francisco: Spinsters), pp. 22–28.

Chapter 10. Stage Five: Lesbian Couples over Sixty-Five

1. U.S. Bureau of the Census (1991), *Statistical abstract of the United States* (Washington, DC: Government Printing Office).
2. Almvig, C. (1982), "The invisible minority: Aging and lesbianism," unpublished master's thesis, Utica College of Syracuse, Utica, NY; Kehoe, M. (1989), *Lesbians over 60 speak for themselves* (New York: Haworth).
3. Simon, B. (1987), *Never married women* (Philadelphia: Temple University Press); Kehoe (1989).
4. Almvig (1982); Essex, M., & Nam, S. (1987), "Marital status and loneliness among older women: The differential importance of close family and friends," *Journal of Marriage and the Family*, 49:93–106; Simon (1987); Kehoe (1989).
5. Julie Mencher, personal communication, 1992.
6. Kehoe, M. (1986), "Lesbians over 65: A triply invisible minority," *Psychology of Women Quarterly*, 12(3–4):139–152.
7. Kehoe (1989).
8. Simon (1987); Kehoe (1989).
9. U.S. Bureau of the Census (1991).
10. Allen, K., & Chin-Sang, V. (1990), "A lifetime of work: The context and meanings of leisure for aging black women," *Gerontologist*, 30(6):734–740.
11. Nadelson, C. (1984), "Geriatric sex problems," *Journal of Geriatric Psychiatry*, 17(2):139–148.

12. Bell, A., & Weinberg, M. (1978), *Homosexualities: A study of diversity among men and women* (New York: Simon & Schuster); Kehoe (1986).
13. Allen & Chin-Sang (1990).
14. U.S. Bureau of the Census (1991).
15. Simon (1987).
16. Kehoe (1989).
17. Hansson, R., & Remondet, J. (1988), "Old age and widowhood: Issues of personal control and independence," *Journal of Social Issues*, 44(3):159–174.
18. Martin, A. (1991), "Power of empathic relationships: Bereavement therapy with a lesbian widow," in C. Silverstein (ed.), *Gays, lesbians, and their therapists* (New York: Norton), pp. 172–186.
19. Slater, S., & Mencher, J. (1991), "The lesbian family life cycle: A contextual approach," *American Journal of Orthopsychiatry*, 61(3):372–382.
20. Ibid., p. 376.
21. Rosenblatt, P. (1988), "Grief: The social context of private feelings," *Journal of Social Issues*, 44(3):76–78.
22. Bumagin, V., & Hirn, K. (1982), "Observations on changing relationships for older married women," *American Journal of Psychoanalysis*, 42(2):133–142.
23. Rosenblatt (1988).
24. Lucco, A. (1987), "Planned retirement housing preferences for older homosexuals," *Journal of Homosexuality*, 14(3–4):35–56.
25. Simon (1987).
26. Kehoe, M. (1986), "A portrait of the older lesbian," *Psychology of Women Quarterly*, 12(3–4):159–172.
27. Ibid., p. 163.
28. Friend, R. (1980), "GAYging: Adjustment and the older gay male," *Alternative Lifestyles*, 3:231–248.
29. Kimmel, D. (1974), *Adulthood and aging: An interdisciplinary, developmental view* (New York: Wiley).
30. Lee, J. (1991), "Foreword: Special issue on gay midlife and maturity," *Journal of Homosexuality*, 20:xiii–xix.
31. Almvig (1982); Berger, R. (1984), "Realities of gay and lesbian aging," *Social Work*, 29(1):57–62; Kehoe (1989).

32. Keefe, S. (1984), "Real and ideal extended familism among Mexican Americans and Anglo Americans: On the meaning of 'close' family ties," *Human Organization*, 43(1):65–70; Boyd-Franklin, N. (1989), *Black families in therapy: A multisystems approach* (New York: Guilford); Carter, B., & McGoldrick, M. (1989), *The changing family life cycle: A framework for family therapy* (Boston: Allyn & Bacon); Yee, B. (1990), "Gender and family issues in minority groups," *Generations*, 14(3):39–42.
33. Stack, C. (1984). *All our kin: Strategies for survival in a black community* (New York: Harper & Row); Keefe (1984); Sotomayer, M. (1989), "The Hispanic elderly and the intergenerational family," *Journal of Children in Contemporary Society*, 20(3–4):55–65.
34. Yee (1990).
35. Ibid.
36. Ibid.
37. Sotomayer (1989).

Acknowledgments

First and foremost, I thank the generations of lesbian women who came before me, charting new paths as they went and transmitting the courage and independence so often seen in lesbians' lives today. In addition, I thank my clients and friends for sharing intimate details of their most private relationships with me, transforming my own life in the process and guiding my thinking throughout this project. This book is full of your teaching.

Many authors and researchers have previously investigated topics related to this book. While I have tried to note their specific contributions where relevant, I want also to thank them for their often groundbreaking efforts to illuminate lesbians' lives.

A number of people offered me specific assistance in the writing of this book. I am indebted to the women who read or discussed various chapters with me and to those who shared special insights. My work is enriched greatly by their input. Debra Marshall, Maria Zavala, Natalie Eldridge, Wendy Rosen, Judy Dixon, Adin Delacour, Barbara Reinhold, and Carter Heyward are among those who supported me in this way. I appreciate Jeane Anastas for her similar availability. I thank Jean Baker Miller and also my research assistant, Erika Noebl, whose dedicated efforts went beyond the call of duty. Her competence and encouragement greatly reduced the stress I carried through this work.

I am grateful also to my agent, Charlotte Sheedy, for guiding me through a world I knew absolutely nothing about and for her confidence in me long before she had a finished product to read. Likewise, my editor, Susan Arellano, was truly a help to me, offering both guidance and time extensions in a balance that greatly facilitated this process. I also thank Chris Kelly for his helpful editing of this manuscript.

I thank Kath for sustaining me through my long working hours and periods of preoccupation in the earlier stages of writing this book. Her belief in my work buoyed me time and time again.

My parents, brothers, sister, and their partners have encouraged me from the beginning of the project through the surprise party they organized when I finally finished the manuscript. I love and thank them all.

To Judy go my heartfelt thanks for luring me away from my computer and grounding me in our rich and compelling home life. I'd still be revising if not for all you offer me.

Finally, this book is a direct outgrowth of my collaboration with Julie Mencher. Her input has been irreplaceable, and her feedback and editing have been of enormous importance to me. The quality of her thinking has challenged me from the day I met her, and I am greatly expanded by her influence. I cannot thank her enough for her contribution to this work.

Index

Families of origin *(cont.)*
  lesbians of color and, 59,
    60–61
  middle years and, 191–92
  old age and, 227, 228–29
Family legacy, 199–200
Family life cycle transition rituals, 74–77
Family roles, 217–18
Family traditions, 71–74, 75
Fathers, 99, 100–102
Fears, of middle years, 178–79
Felman, J., 117
Female socialization
  couple formation and, 125
  fusion and, 65–66, 67, 68–69,
    168
  power and, 49–50
Feminism
  children and, 92
  fusion and, 65
  heterosexual, 83
  lesbian identity development
    and, 24–25
  power and, 50
  relational roles and, 48
  sexuality and, 54
Friends
  couple formation between heterosexual, 140–43
  couple formation between lesbian, 138–40
  couple formation between
    lesbian/heterosexual,
    143–45
Fusion, 64–69
  couple formation and, 130
  dangers of, 67–69

distance and, 166–70
ongoing couplehood and,
  157–58, 160, 166–70

Gartrell, N., 41
Gay men
  AIDS and, 205–6
  children and, 51
  distance and, 168
  fusion and, 65, 68
  identity formation in, 24
  lesbian alliances with, 83
Gay rights causes, 202
Gender identity, 92
Gender roles, 47, 48
Generativity, 195–210
  joint involvements in, 201–3
  midlife influence in, 206–10
  separate activities in, 199–201
  tasks of, 197–99
  unique experience of lesbian
    couples in, 204–6
Grandparents, 111–14
Green, G., 167, 196
Greene, B., 85

Health care proxy, 228
Health problems, 221–22
Heterosexism, 38
Heterosexual privilege, 29
Heterosexuals, 63
  affairs and, 137
  children and, 106–9
  cohabitation and, 155, 156
  couple formation between,
    140–43
  couple formation with
    lesbian friends, 143–45

dating in, 135–36
feminism and, 83
fusion and, 68
life cycle models of, 7–8,
12–14, 19
money issues and, 50–51
opposite-sex friendships in, 138
rituals and, 76, 174
Hispanic lesbians
old age and, 229
racism and, 60
Holiday rituals, 77–80
Homophobia, 141
children and, 105, 108, 109,
110, 111
custody and, 100–102
defined, 38
in families of origin, 109, 110,
111
fusion and, 65, 160
internalized, 22, 24, 27, 35,
39, 40
lesbian communities and, 81
lesbian identity development
and, 22, 24, 26, 27
lesbians of color and, 30, 58, 60
limerence and, 123
public versus private identities
and, 44
sexuality and, 52
as a stressor, 38–40
Homosexuals: *see* Gay men

Identity confusion, 21
Identity development: see Les-
bian identity development
Identity foreclosure, 22
Imber-Black, E., 71

Individual development, 19–21
Individual legacy: see Personal
legacy
Internalized homophobia, 22,
24, 27, 35, 39, 40
Interracial lesbian relationships,
61–62
Invisibility, 200

Jews, 33, 77
Jordan, J., 65

Kaplan, A., 65
Kehoe, M., 226

Laird, J., 9
Laws, anti-homosexuality, 6
Lesbian adolescence, 25, 145
Lesbian communities, 33, 64,
80–87
children and, 114–15
couple formation and, 147–48
evolution of, 82–87
lesbians of color and, 61–62,
84–85
Lesbian identity development,
18–19, 21–31
in bisexuals, 22, 28–30
couple formation and, 124
lesbian family life cycle and,
25–27
in lesbians of color, 18–19,
30–31
ongoing couplehood and,
156–57
partners in different stages of,
27–28
pathways to, 24–25

4684